The
SCHOOLWIDE
ENRICHMENT MODEL
READING FRAMEWORK

THE SCHOOLWIDE ENRICHMENT MODEL READING FRAMEWORK

EDITED BY
SALLY M. REIS, ELIZABETH A. FOGARTY,
REBECCA D. ECKERT, & LISA M. MULLER

PRUFROCK PRESS INC.
WACO, TEXAS

Prufrock Press Inc.
P.O. Box 8813
Waco, TX 76714-8813
Phone: (800) 998-2208
Fax: (800) 240-0333
http://www.prufrock.com

Acknowledgements

We gratefully acknowledge all of the principals, teachers, students, and district personnel who have helped in our research on SEM-R over the last five years. We also are grateful to all of our colleagues and thanks to Lisa Muller, who helped coordinate all phases of our SEM-R work.

Research for this document was supported under the Javits Act Program (Grant No. S206A040094) as administered by the Office of Elementary and Secondary Education, U. S. Department of Education. Grantees undertaking such projects are encouraged to express freely their professional judgments. This manuscript does not necessarily represent positions or policies of the Government, and no official endorsement should be inferred.

Contents

CHAPTER 1

INTRODUCTION TO AN ENRICHED & DIFFERENTIATED MODEL IN READING

SALLY M. REIS & REBECCA D. ECKERT

Imagine diverse classrooms in schools all across the country with one common occurrence during reading class—young boys and girls engaged in joyful reading that is interrupted only by rapidly turning pages, chuckles of amusement, serious focus, and occasional eruptions of laughter. Imagine a group of four boisterous, active boys, reading quietly and with an intense focus for 30–40 minutes in a corner of a classroom. Imagine a classroom of students who read everyday; while their teacher circulates around the classroom having differentiated conferences with individual students of varying reading levels. During the last 4 years, in schools across the country, an alternative approach to traditional reading instruction has occurred on a daily basis, with the help of interested teachers and principals. Their suggestions enabled the Schoolwide Enrichment Model Reading Framework (SEM-R) (Reis, Eckert, Schreiber, Jacobs, Briggs, Gubbins, Coyne, & Muller, 2005), an enrichment-based approach to reading, to evolve. The theory for this approach to reading emerged from the Schoolwide Enrichment Model (SEM) (Renzulli, 1977; Renzulli & Reis, 1997), a widely used approach to providing enrichment and talent development opportunities for all students.

The SEM-R focuses on enrichment for all students through engagement in challenging, self-selected reading, accompanied by instruction in higher-order thinking and strategy skills. A second core focus of the SEM-R is differentiation of instruction and reading content, coupled with more challenging reading experiences and advanced opportunities for metacognition and self-regulated reading. In other words, the SEM-R challenges all students, from those who read at a remedial level to those who are extremely talented in reading!

1

The SEM-R encourages enjoyment of the learning process with a focus on the development of self-regulated readers, planned enrichment experiences, and differentiated instruction. In some schools, the SEM-R is integrated into regular reading instruction; in others it is implemented as an additional literacy block, or as an afterschool literacy extension. Our experiences suggest that with minimal professional development and this book, describing all aspects of this approach, teachers can learn to use the SEM-R to differentiate instruction and integrate higher-order thinking skills to challenge and engage students of all reading levels. The three phases of SEM-R expose students to good literature, encourage readers to become more self-directed and self-regulated, and allow learners to apply higher-level thinking skills to their reading while they learn to enjoy reading and to pursue their interests through books.

THEORETICAL BAKCGROUND OF THE SEM-R

The theoretical base of the SEM-R is Joseph Renzulli's Enrichment Triad Model (Renzulli, 1977) based on almost 30 years of field-testing and research (Renzulli & Reis, 1994) related to the Schoolwide Enrichment Model. The Triad Model encourages enjoyment in learning and gives students the opportunity to pursue creative work through exposure to various topics, areas of interest, and fields of study. The Enrichment Triad Model also further trains students to apply advanced content and methodological training

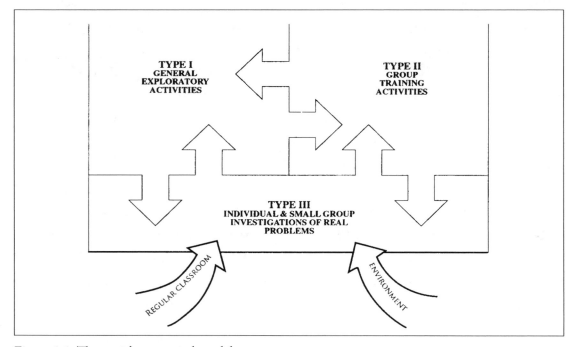

Figure 1.1. The enrichment triad model.

to self-selected areas of interest (Renzulli, 1977). Three types of enrichment are included in the Enrichment Triad Model (see Figure 1.1).

Type I enrichment is designed to expose students to a wide variety of topics, issues, and activities not ordinarily covered in the regular curriculum. In the SEM-R, Type I enrichment occurs when teachers expose their students to exciting read-alouds of parts of books and stories that teachers purposefully select to develop and stimulate student interests. Interesting and enjoyable selections of literature representing various genres (nonfiction and fiction) are read aloud to promote enjoyment in reading and listening.

Type II enrichment involves teaching methods that are designed to promote the development of thinking and feeling processes, such as creative thinking, problem solving, and communication skills. In addition to these skills, Type II training involves critical thinking, affective processes, skills needed for the appropriate use of advanced-level reference materials, and skills in written, oral, and visual communication. In SEM-R, Type II enrichment enables students to choose challenging, high-interest books with which their teachers provide higher- level questioning strategies, more advanced and complex reading strategy use, and method training (how to do certain things) using individualized instruction.

Type III enrichment enables students who become interested in particular topics to pursue self-selected areas of study for more intensive individual or small group involvement. Type III studies provide opportunities for applying interests, knowledge, creative ideas, and task commitment to a self-selected problem or area of study. These opportunities allow students to acquire advanced level understanding of the knowledge (content) and methodology (process) used within particular disciplines.

GOALS OF THE SEM-R

The SEM-R has three distinct goals: increasing enjoyment in and attitudes about reading, encouraging students to pursue independent reading at appropriately challenging levels, and improving reading fluency and comprehension. The SEM-R includes three general categories of reading instruction that are dynamic in nature and designed to enable some flexibility of implementation and content in response to both teachers' and students' needs.

In the SEM-R, each of the three general categories is referred to as a "phase" of instruction. Phase 1 of SEM-R includes listening comprehension with advanced, high-interest books and process training skills in which exposure to a variety of literature, appropriate levels of reading challenge, and interests are emphasized. The second phase of the SEM-R emphasizes the development of students' capability to engage in independent reading of self-selected books of above-level content for extended blocks of time. Finally, Phase 3 encourages students to move from teacher-directed work to self-choice reading activities in areas such as student-directed projects, enrichment using technology, literature circles, advanced questioning and thinking skills, and creativity training as applied to reading (see Figure 1.2).

SCHOOLWIDE ENRICHMENT MODEL READING FRAMEWORK

The SEM-R is an enrichment-based reading program that has resulted in increased reading fluency and achievement as well as more positive attitudes toward reading in research studies based on this enriched approach to reading (Reis & Fogarty, 2006; Reis, Gubbins, Briggs, Schreiber, Richards, Jacobs, Eckert, & Renzulli, 2004). These results were achieved through an instructional framework that employs high-interest, student self-selected books that are slightly above current reading levels to stimulate interest and joy in reading. After just a few weeks of participating in the SEM-R, we have

PHASE 1 - EXPOSURES	PHASE 2 - TRAINING & SELF-SELECTED READING	PHASE 3 - INTEREST & CHOICE COMPONENTS
• High-interest books to read aloud • Picture Books • Novels/Fiction • Non-Fiction • Poetry • High order thinking probing questions • Bookmarks for teachers with questions regarding Bloom's Taxonomy, biography, character, illustrations and other topics relevant to the study of literature	• Training and discussions on Supported Independent Reading • Supported Independent Reading • One-on-one teacher conferences on reading strategies and instruction • Bookmarks for students posing higher-order questions regarding character, plot, setting, considering the story, and other useful topics	• Introducing creative thinking • Genre studies • Library exploration • Responding to books • Investigation centers • Creative thinking • Exploring the Internet • Reading non-fiction • Focus on biographies • Buddy reading • Books on tape • Literature circles • Creative or expository writing • Type III investigation
TYPE I ACTIVITIES	TYPE II ACTIVITIES	TYPE II & III INVESTIGATIONS

Figure 1.2. Components of the schoolwide enrichment model reading framework.

found that students begin to read more challenging material on a regular basis and more importantly, demonstrate a willingness to do so. The SEM-R is not intended to constitute a complete language arts program, as it primarily focuses on reading and increasing reading comprehension and fluency, as well as self-regulation in reading. Although students are encouraged to complete a written reflection each week in their student logs, the focus of the SEM-R is as the reading component of a more comprehensive language arts program. Most teachers who have used this approach have coupled the SEM-R with instruction in vocabulary development, spelling, language mechanics, and writing. They have found the creative use of books as suggested in the SEM-R to be a welcome enhancement to a direct instruction program or a more teacher directed whole class/ group basal program. In this chapter, each phase of the SEM-R program is explained briefly as an introduction to subsequent chapters that focus on the implementation of and practical suggestions for incorporating the SEM-R into your school or classroom. Figure 1.2 shows a layout of the three phases in the SEM-R.

Phase 1: Hooking Kids on Literature With Teacher Read-Alouds

In Phase 1 of the SEM-R, teachers select diverse literature across a variety of genres to read aloud to students, interspersed with higher-order questioning, the use of specific reading strategies, and thinking skills instruction. These "Book Hook" sessions usually begin with 10–15 minutes of high-interest, challenging books designed to "hook" children on reading and gradually decrease to 5 or 10 minutes as students begin to spend more time reading independently in Phase 2.

Phase 1 of the SEM-R includes listening comprehension and process training skills within the context of exposing students to a range of literary works, authors, and genres. Through the use of challenging, high-interest books as focal points for student listening skills, teachers read aloud from high-quality, exciting literature with follow -up that includes higher-order questioning and thinking skills instruction. Each day, the teacher shares a snippet from a different book or books to "hook" students into reading books and expand learners' "reading horizons." SEM-R emphasizes enjoyment of the process of reading, and selections for these Book Hooks are made based on student engagement with content, reactions to previous Book Hook selections, and a desire to promote interest and subsequent engagement in independent reading. Moreover, teachers use "Bookmarks" with higher-order questions in Phase 1 to help differentiate instruction and pose reading strategy, literary term, and higher-order thinking skills questions with all students. A comprehensive collection of these Bookmarks is available in Appendix A.

The approximate time of this phase of SEM-R varies, but it averages between 10–25 minutes daily; the goal is to decrease the time spent on Phase 1 over a period of weeks. As the students' ability to maintain their focus longer and their self-regulation on Phase 2 supported reading increases, Phase 1 time is shortened to enable more independent reading time. Details about how to implement Phase 1 of SEM-R are included in the next chapter.

Phase 2: Supported Independent Reading and Differentiated Conferences

Phase 2 of the SEM-R is designed to increase students' engagement and self-direction in independent reading of self-selected books, supported by individualized, differentiated reading conferences with their teachers. During this Supported Independent Reading (SIR), teachers encourage students to select books that are slightly above their current reading level to promote continuous growth in reading skills and strategies. Teachers continually assess whether books are an appropriate match through weekly or biweekly conferences with students. Our experiences with SEM-R have demonstrated that initially, the majority of the students select books that were quite easy for them. They are instructed to bring these easier books home to read, because during school, it is their job to select books that were more challenging to read. Appropriately challenging books contain some words they did not know and some ideas that were new to them. In other words, teachers urge students to engage in reading in an area of personal interest that was slightly above their current independent reading level.

Phase 2 focuses on the use of differentiated instruction of reading strategies that allows students to modify their reading processes to facilitate greater fluency and comprehension in the challenging books they are reading. During individual conferences, teachers and students discuss and consider critical-thinking questions focusing on synthesis, making inferences, and determining importance. The questions give open-ended opportunities for children of all reading levels to reflect upon and discuss their books, and teachers are able to provide scaffolding as necessary to enable readers of all ability levels to think critically about text.

In prior SEM-R studies, most elementary students initially could read independently for only 5–10 minutes a day without losing concentration or focus and most displayed little self-regulation in reading. Teachers subsequently worked to add a minute or two during each day of reading time, eventually extending the time students read to 30–45 minutes daily. This extended SIR time allowed teachers to circulate around the room conducting short (4–5 minute) conferences to provide individualized support and differentiated instruction for several students each day. The types and levels of reading strategies as well as higher-order thinking skills instruction helped increase students' skills and self-regulation in reading. Suggestions on how to increase self-regulation in reading are also provided in Chapter 3.

Both informal and formal methods are used to create and identify students' interests and to encourage students to develop and pursue these interests in reading. An adapted version of an interest assessment questionnaire called the Interest-a-Lyzer (Renzulli, 1977), the Reading Interest-a-Lyzer (Appendix B), can be completed by students to assist teachers in helping identify interests in reading and with the selection of challenging and interesting books. More information is available on implementing Phase 2 of SEM-R in subsequent chapters and all forms and student and teacher logs are included in the Appendices as well.

Phase 3: Interest and Choice Activities

The ultimate goal in Phase 3 is for students to progress from teacher-directed and provided opportunities to independent, self-choice activities over the course of SEM-R implementation. The intent of these experiences is to provide opportunities for students to spend time engaging in areas of personal interest and to foster enjoyment in reading. Student-choice activities can include opportunities to explore technology and read online (e.g., eBooks, children's authors web pages); writing activities; creativity training in language arts; learning centers on topics in which students have an interest; interest-based projects; continuation of self-selected reading; reading with a friend; book chats in literature circles; or independent or small group studies, such as those in the Enrichment Triad Model. These experiences enable students to develop and explore their interests, as well as to apply creative and critical thinking skills to self-selected, literature-based explorations. Phase 3 enables students to learn to read critically, synthesize what they have read and apply it in a new context, and locate other enjoyable and stimulating reading materials, especially high-quality, challenging literature.

Teachers usually begin Phase 3 by giving students three or four different teacher-selected options for 15 minutes each day or during a weekly one-hour block of reading/language arts. Within this structure, teachers can provide the parameters and scaffolding necessary to help students develop both the cognitive and affective skills needed to become self-directed, independent learners. As students become more comfortable with independent work, Phase 3 activity choices expand to involve more student-directed opportunities while the teacher's role shifts from instructor to facilitator. Each component of the SEM-R was developed to help students enjoy reading, increase their reading skills with individual differentiated reading strategies, and apply higher order thinking and reading strategy instruction while reading books in an area of personal interest. Additional information is available on Phase 3 in subsequent chapters.

RESEARCH ON THE SEM-R

We have implemented the SEM-R in both suburban and urban schools using the highest standards of educational research by randomly assigning students to the SEM-R group or to a control group in which students continued with normal reading instruction. Teachers were also randomly assigned to teach either the treatment or control group classes. In our first year study, the SEM-R was implemented in two urban schools with a population of more than 90% culturally diverse students and with nearly the same percentage of students receiving lunch free or at reduced rates. Students in these schools participated in a direct instruction 90-minute reading block in the morning and SEM-R was implemented in an additional one-hour afternoon literacy block for 12 weeks during the second semester. Students who participated in the SEM-R had significantly higher attitudes toward reading, reading comprehension scores, and oral reading fluency scores (Reis et al., 2004). During a subsequent year of the study, the SEM-R was implemented in two other schools for 12 weeks as half of a regular 2-hour basal language arts program. One of the schools had a majority population of culturally and linguistically diverse students who spoke Spanish as their first language. Students who were in the SEM-R group had significantly higher reading fluency and comprehension, and all readers, from talented to average and below average readers, benefited from the program (Reis, et al., 2005). In another study, an afterschool reading program was implemented in an urban school using SEM-R, and after only 6 weeks and 12 two-hour sessions, most students had significant increases on reading fluency when compared to a control group (Reis & Boeve, in press). Most recently, we have studied the implementation of this approach to reading over an entire academic year in five other schools, both those with suburban students and those with high populations of students of poverty and cultural diversity. In summary, our research on this enrichment method for reading has shown that students who participate in the SEM-R have positive attitudes toward reading, increased reading fluency and comprehension scores, and increased confidence in answering higher-order thinking questions.

The positive changes that resulted from this research extend beyond the increases in test scores. We saw students who could not wait to begin reading time, students groaning when it was time to put their books down at the end of a reading period. Students, who rarely read prior to the intervention, devoured an entire book series. Teachers have consistently reported positive changes in their own teaching practices and a general excitement about reading and using higher-order thinking skills in reading instruction. Teachers described their surprise at the ability of students to have more advanced and engaging conversations about literature. As a teacher in one of our research studies explained, "My Phase 2 SEM-R conferences with kids expanded from one word answers at the beginning of the year to long, thoughtful conversations about literature and themes. I actually had to cut them off; I am completely convinced now that this was due to the SEM-R training in higher-order thinking skills." In that school, after a year of using this approach, the number of students who did not pass the state mastery test decreased by 66%.

CHAPTER 2

PHASE ONE: HOOKING KIDS ON BOOKS

ANGELA HOUSAND, ELIZABETH A. FOGARTY,
REBECCA D. ECKERT, & SALLY M. REIS

One of the goals of SEM-R is to increase student enjoyment of and interest in reading. An excellent way to achieve this goal is with a high-interest read aloud, or Book Hook, during Phase 1 of SEM-R. When discussing SEM-R with teachers, we ask them to think about a Phase 1 Book Hook as a movie trailer for a book. In the same way a movie trailer is designed to inform, engage, and entice audience members to see a particular movie, a Book Hook is designed to educate, inform, engage, and entice a student to read.

As you read aloud to students, the books you choose and the environment you create will play a key role in encouraging positive feelings and excitement about reading. Often one of the easiest ways to "hook kids on books" is to ensure the availability of and exposure to a wide range of high-quality, high-interest literature. Exposure to books, modeling reading strategies, and generating enthusiasm about reading are the primary goals of Book Hooks. In this chapter, we offer suggestions and ideas for instilling a love of reading in students during this phase of the SEM-R, while simultaneously embedding thinking skills instruction and discussion skills.

Introducing students to literature by exposing them to short segments of books during Phase 1 can open new worlds. The goal of Phase 1 is to introduce students to a wide range of literature and to read from a different book each day. In doing so, teachers purposefully expose students to a variety of genres (poetry, historical fiction, or non-fiction for example), authors, themes, interest areas, subjects, and domains. The Phase 1 Book Hook time can encourage students to develop a wide range of interests and knowledge because that students will be more engaged in reading when they select literature related to their interests. Finally, remember that a Book Hook is not just a read-aloud and that

Phase 1 is not intended to be a time in which teachers read the entire book to the students. The goal of Phase 1 is to read only a part of the book that will "hook" a student. If you are successful, be prepared for multiple students to ask to read the book from which you have just revealed an enticing section. What an exciting idea it is to consider that a list of students waiting to read a book that you have introduced during Phase 1 might develop!

BOOK HOOKS: PLANNING IN ADVANCE

Listening to good books is one of the best ways for a child to begin to love reading. Even at a young age, children begin to associate feelings of comfort and happiness with the time that they spend listening to and reading aloud with family and teachers. These feelings can eventually translate into similar feelings and attitudes toward books and a realization that books can give them comfort, knowledge, inspiration, and the opportunity to take charge of their own learning.

When teachers love to read and read aloud to their students, students benefit as they are exposed to literature they may not otherwise have learned about and read. With a little pre-planning and practice, teachers can bring stories and characters to life by sharing short, dramatic segments from children's literature. In addition, students can learn to listen carefully and reflect on literary details and devices when teachers ask carefully crafted questions. It is important for successful Book Hooks to be planned in advance.

Getting Started

As you begin to implement the SEM-R, taking small steps toward larger goals can ease your transition to what may be a different way of teaching reading. As you plan Book Hooks, you can select some of the following suggestions and then continue to incorporate the additional ideas to enhance your Book Hooks as the year progresses.

- Find an area in your classroom where every child can sit and both see the illustrations and hear you read. Introduce each book by briefly explaining the author, (and/or the illustrator), the title, and the topic. If possible, relate the book to some aspect of the children's experience (prior knowledge of the author/ illustrator, the topic, etc.).
- One of your first Book Hooks might help introduce your students to the classroom library. If your classroom library is arranged by levels or by genre, you can begin to discuss reading strategies on the first day by talking about genre and modeling book

selection criteria. This is an excellent way to coach students to identify books that interest them and provide appropriate challenge levels (a metacognitive strategy).

- Begin the read-aloud with a book chat. You might tell students what you like about the book or explain what the publication information or dedication tells the reader. (*Squids Will Be Squids* by John Scieszka and Lane Smith is one of our favorites to use to introduce publication information because, like the entire book, it is written with humor).

- Choose the book in advance of Book Hook time and take the time to select a section of the book that is interesting, entertaining, or intriguing. The idea of a Book Hook is not to read the entire book, but rather to read just enough so that students will want to know more and ask to read the book. Remember that the most inviting part of a text for your students may not be the first few pages; try a selection from the middle, on the flyleaf, or in the author's notes. Vary your selection so that you expose your students to different genres, literary elements, and styles of narration and writing.

- Select a book for a Book Hook that you enjoy in some way. It may be the illustrations, the topic, or the style of writing that you love, or you can select a book that was a childhood favorite. Whatever the reason, share it with your students. For example, you may choose one of your favorite books from your teenage years and share a fond memory associated with the book (while simultaneously modeling a text-to-self connection).

- Have fun with these Book Hooks and consider it a personal challenge to engage all of your students in the process of enjoyment as they listen to you read. Use a range of intonations, speeds, and volumes in your voice as you read to explore the range of characters in the book. Use pauses and facial expressions to add drama to your read-alouds.

- Match the book to your students' interests and exposure. If you know that a number of students in your class are interested in mummies, find a book on the topic to create additional incentives for them to read. After you have read one book on mummies, you may want to expose your students to other books on the same topic that will expand their awareness of different genres, such as non-fiction, historical fiction, or other general fiction books to explore the many different ways in which one topic can be introduced across texts. Exposure to different genres helps a broader group of students become interested in and knowledgeable about many different types of literature.

- When choosing a book for a Book Hook, consider how you might encourage the development of a wide range of interests and knowledge with your book selection. If, for example, the book is a mystery, perhaps you can encourage students with an interest in geography to understand that mysteries are set in different states, countries, and locations and that the settings are often integrated into both the plot and the eventual outcomes.

- When an author seems to be popular with your students, read selections from books written by the same author. This process not only offers students a series of books that they will enjoy, but also helps them to gain an understanding of the author's voice. Some authors write books at varying levels of complexity, and exposure to books of differing levels of depth will enable students of varying abilities to gain access to the same author.

- Do not expect all students to be interested in all of the books you introduce during Book Hooks. Some students just aren't interested in a particular book or even in a specific genre. If the book does not interest some or even many of your students, move on to another book. The primary focus of Book Hooks should be enjoyment and pleasure for most of your students.

- Consider using a good book on tape occasionally and having students listen to a part of the book read on tape by an outstanding reader. If you were to use a few minutes of one of the *Harry Potter* tapes, for example, you could expose your students to an outstanding storyteller, as well as to the enjoyment of listening to a British accent and someone with the talents to use several different voices and intonations representing different characters.

- Invite a special guest reader to do a Book Hook in your classroom. Students love listening to the principal, another teacher, the librarian, a parent, or an older student from a nearby middle or high school. This part of Phase 1 Book Hooks can be very enjoyable for students.

- Use picture books to stimulate interest in a theme or idea. Picture books are an ideal way to help older students who have turned off to reading become more interested in a topic. For example, using Barbara Cooney's beautiful picture book, *Miss Rumphius*, to stimulate students to consider beauty in the world and how each of them might contribute to making the world a more beautiful place is an outstanding use of a Book Hook. The same book can also be used as a way to introduce students to the idea of an individual's pursuit of a quest in life, a theme that is repeated in many different fiction and non-fiction books.

- Using books that tie into other aspects of a student's day is another exciting way to introduce a unit in another content area or to generate some advance enthusiasm for an upcoming project related to the regular curriculum in another content area or during Phase 3 of the SEM-R. Reading an interesting book about tornadoes, for example, would be an excellent way to explore non-fiction texts with students while at the same time introducing them to a weather unit. A math poetry book might be used to get students interested in a new mathematical concept. Whereas sharing a book as follow-up to student demonstrated interest in science or social studies might also serve as an introduction to opportunities for independent study during Phase 3 of the SEM-R. In other words, if you get an idea for a project or some type of follow-up during a Book Hook, students will have the time to pursue these emerging interests during Phases 2 and 3.

Finding the Right Book for Your Book Hooks

Thousands of children and young adult books are published annually representing all genres and a wide range of reading levels. Given the wealth of print material for young people available today, how can you help young people find the an appropriate book to challenge and interest them? The first step is to consider the books already readily available. In order to accomplish this you may:

- Peruse your classroom bookshelves to find favorite books that you have forgotten. Consider reorganizing the books on your shelf by genre, author, topic, or level of challenge and complexity. See Chapter Six for more suggestions on organizing and developing your classroom library.
- Explore the available materials in your school or local public library. Ask the librarian where the new books are featured. Examine a couple of books on the shelf from different sections of the library each week. Flip through the books and assess how they might spark your students' interests. Don't limit your explorations to the young people's portion of the library—remember talented readers may be particularly grateful for the complex ideas or information found in adult non-fiction.

Authors and Publishers on the Internet

The Internet is an excellent source of information about numerous children's writers and illustrators. Using a search engine with an author's name can result in finding a broad array of personal websites and websites maintained by publishers, fans, scholars, and readers.

Table 2.1. Author Websites.

AUTHOR WEBSITES
Judy Bloom http://www.JudyBlume.com Gary Paulsen http://www.randomhouse.com/features/garypaulsen/ Beverly Cleary http://www.beverlycleary.com/index.html J.K. Rowling http://www.jkrowling.com

Fortunately, many of these sites are designed to promote enjoyable reading experiences and encourage growth in reading. Some of our favorite authors with attractive websites encouraging students to continue to learn about them and the books that they have written are listed in Table 2.1.

Some publishers of children's literature (such as DK Publishing or Random House) also have excellent websites designed to engage kids with reading and, of course, promote their publications in the process. We encourage students and teachers to find their favorite publishers when searching for new electronic reading sources. Table 2.2 lists many popular children and young adult publishers.

Book Lists and Bibliographies

Hundreds of awards are given to outstanding books annually. Some of the most prestigious awards given to the authors and illustrators of children's and young adult fiction include:

Table 2.2. Publisher Websites.

PUBLISHER WEBSITES
Random House Publishing This is a great resource for teachers. It is organized by grade level from preschool to 12th grade featuring reading programs, classroom clubs that teachers can join, links to author sites, and even book talks searchable by title or author. http://www.randomhouse.com/teachers/
Dorling Kindersley (DK) Originally a Dutch publishing company, DK has become a leader in publishing non-fiction children's literature. Their website provides an overview of the many non-fiction titles available. http://us.dk.com/
Scholastic This website is full of great resources for SEM-R teachers. The book match tool in the Online Activities Section allows teachers or kids to search for books. http://www.scholastic.com

- Caldecott Medal: This medal was named in honor of Randolph Caldecott, a nineteenth-century English illustrator, and is awarded annually to the outstanding American picture book for children.
- Newbery Medal: Named in honor of John Newbery, a British bookseller in the eighteenth-century, and this award is given annually to the author of the year's outstanding contribution to American literature for children.
- Coretta Scott King Award: Commemorating and honoring the lives of Dr. Martin Luther King Jr. and Coretta Scott King, who fought for peace and brotherhood, the award recognizes outstanding African American authors and illustrators for noteworthy contributions to children's and young adult literature.
- Pura Belpré Award: This medal was named for Pura Belpré, the first Latina librarian at the New York Public Library, and is awarded annually to commemorate the outstanding contribution of a Latino/Latina writer or illustrator to children's literature.

A book list of the recent (at the time of this publication) winners of the prestigious literary awards mentioned in this section is provided in Appendix C. Additional book lists can be found at the SEM-R website: www.gifted.uconn.edu/semr. In addition to the SEM-R book lists on the website and book lists of award winners in Appendix C, we have included a list of other websites to assist you and your students in choosing high-quality, high-interest books at appropriately challenging levels. Table 2.3 (on the next page) lists websites offering diverse recommendations for young people.

INTEGRATING READING STRATEGIES AND SKILLS INTO BOOK HOOKS

Using Bookmarks During Phase 1 of the SEM-R

As briefly introduced earlier, we have developed reproducible Bookmarks that can be used in both Phase 1 and 2 of the SEM-R (Appendix A). The Bookmarks encourage wider student exposure to literature and help students think both analytically and creatively about literature. The Bookmarks serve several purposes during Phase 1, as they help teachers

- develop a repertoire of higher-order thinking questions that can be employed when reading aloud to the class,
- model questioning that will enable students to gain skills in focusing attention and higher-order thinking, and
- help students develop self-questioning techniques to assist in future literary analysis.

Using these questions during a Book Hook can help stimulate student thinking and provide practice applying complex comprehension strategies. To make the purpose of particular Bookmarks clear, each has been categorized with a heading indicating the literary element or genre of the questions focus on the bookmark. Our research with SEM-R has demonstrated that the Bookmarks are good tools for both teachers and students to use, resulting in the use of higher level questioning skills for students of all levels of achievement. The following suggestions have helped teachers to assist students who need additional support in thinking about their reading:

+ During the read aloud, teachers can model their own process of applying comprehension strategies by answering some of their own questions and engaging

Table 2.3. Book Lists Available on the Internet.

BOOK LISTS ON THE INTERNET

American Library Association
http://www.ala.org/ala/alsc/alsc.htm
> This list is maintained by the Association for Library Service to Children (ALSC), a division of the ALA. Click on 'Building a Home Library' for several lists.

http://www.ala.org/ala/yalsa/booklistsawards/booklistsbook.htm
> This list is maintained by the Young Adult Library Services Association (YALSA), a division of the ALA. Remember when looking through these book lists that they are slightly more advanced in content and may contain subject matter not appropriate to some readers.

http://www.ala.org/yalsa/booklists/obcb
> This list, also maintained by the Young Adult Library Services Association (YALSA), lists Outstanding Books for the College Bound. The book lists are separated by content areas including history, humanities, literature and Language Arts, science and technology, and social science.

The Bulletin of the Center for Children's Books
http://www.lis.uiuc.edu/puboff/bccb/
> This list is maintained by The Bulletin of the Center for Children's Books, a journal dedicated to reviews of children's literature.

Carol Otis Hurst
http://www.carolhurst.com
> This comprehensive site features reviews of hundreds of children's books, as well as ideas for integrating them into the curriculum.

Children's Book Council
http://www.cbcbooks.org
> This website provides links to a variety of book lists including: graphic novels and 'Not just for children anymore!', and 'Hot Off the Press' books.

---

in "thinking aloud" procedures. This enables teachers to model critical and creative thinking processes as they answer questions themselves or by coaching students in these strategies as part of an open-ended discussion in a classroom. For example, a teacher might ask, How would the problem change if the story took place elsewhere? The teacher might respond to a student struggling to answer by saying: "Let me give you one example of how I might answer that question. First I would think of a different place or setting—maybe a place in our town. Then I would think about what is different between that place and the setting in the book. (She could talk about some of these differences.) Now I would think about how these differences might change the problem."

Table 2.3. Book Lists Available on the Internet (continued).

BOOK LISTS ON THE INTERNET (CONTINUED)

Children's Literature Web Guide

http://www.ucalgary.ca/~dkbrown/

> Another great guide with many resources, this website has a conference bulletin board in which users can post messages in addition to specialized booklists, including a list for famous children's authors to name their own favorite children's books.

International Reading Association

http://www.reading.org/resources/tools/choices.html

> This site is maintained by the International Reading Association and includes many wonderful booklists and teacher resources.

National Council of Teachers of English (NCTE)

http://www.ncte.org

> The NCTE maintains this comprehensive site where teachers can search for book lists generated by teachers at either the elementary level or middle/high school level.

http://readwritethink.org

> Also powered by NCTE, the Read Write Think website has a calendar that shows literary events through the year including birthdays of famous authors, etc.

Notable Social Studies Trade Books for Young People

http://www.socialstudies.org/resources/notable

> The book lists at this site are maintained by the National Council for the Social Studies and include biographies of famous people as well as books on a wide range of societal issues including homelessness, civil rights, and women's rights.

Outstanding Science Trade Books for Children

http://www.nsta.org/ostbc

> The book lists at this site are maintained by the National Science Teachers Association and include biographies of scientists, as well as books in the various science content standards, including life science, earth and space science, and science and technology.

+ When students answer questions during the read aloud, teachers can ask them to explain what evidence from the text they considered and what thinking processes they used that led to their response. Teachers can help students to reflect on how they answered the question, thereby encouraging the strategy of metacognition.

+ Teachers can provide practice for students to use more advanced strategies by asking and answering similar types of questions on consecutive days or for multiple books.

+ When responding to Bookmark questions (whether orally or in writing), one important concept to emphasize with students is to move beyond providing a plot summary. Many students who have difficulty with critical analyses or synthesis should be encouraged to provide opinions and hypotheses, which are supported by evidence that they have collected from the book.

Using blank Bookmark templates encourages students to create their own questions about literature and can build a deeper understanding of both literary analysis and higher-order thinking. It may also serve as a way to regenerate enthusiasm when answering Bookmark questions becomes routine. A complete set of the Bookmarks and a template for blank Bookmarks are in Appendix A.

THEMED BOOK HOOKS

A themed Book Hook is another excellent way to enhance the complexity of Phase 1 as well as to explore major themes or subjects in depth. Weekly Book Hooks can be based on author studies or themes (such as the idea of struggle or power, or the notion of prejudice and its interaction with race). Teachers can introduce "big questions" with their themed Book Hooks about hatred and man's inhumanity to man, or the redemptive power of love. Teachers can also focus on historical events during Book Hooks, such as the Gold Rush, the Civil War, or even events during World War II, such as Hiroshima. Book Hooks can also be used to introduce pertinent social and emotional issues such as bullying or making courageous choices. Books can be a method for examining life and for helping students address areas of personal concern. Table 2.4 lists additional examples of themed Book Hooks.

Themed Book Hooks are based on exposing your students to a big idea or broad concept such as prejudice and presenting several books from different genres and ability levels that illustrate this big idea. In the example in Table 2.4, the themed Book Hook focuses on varying details or plots that relate to prejudice and the exploration of this big

Table 2.4. Example of a Themed Book Hook.

Theme:		
People's Harsh Treatment and Inhumanity to Others: Prejudice		
BOOK TITLES	**COMPREHENSION STRATEGY**	**STATE STANDARDS**
Martin's Big Words *I Have a Dream*	Making Connections (Text to Text) (Text to Self) (Text to World)	• Develops vocabulary by listening to, reading, and discussing both familiar and conceptually challenging selections
My Brother, Martin *The Voice that Challenged the Nation: Marian Anderson and the Struggle For Equal Rights*	Making Connections (Text to Text) Making Inferences	• The student identifies specific personal preferences relative to fiction and nonfiction reading
Maniac Magee *The Watson's Go to Birmingham* *Roll of Thunder, Hear My Cry* (author study of Mildred Taylor) *Let the Circle Be Unbroken* *Song of the Trees* *The Well* *The Land* *Witness* *The Diary of Anne Frank* *Butterfly* *Six Million Paper Clips*	Making Connections (Text to Text) Questioning Making Inferences Making Connections (Text to World) (Text to Text) Visualization Making Connections (Text to World) (Text to Text) (Text to Self) Synthesizing	• Identifies and discusses the author's purpose in text • Knows the similarities and differences of events presented within and across fourth or higher level selections • Knows that the attitudes and values that exist in a time period affect stories

idea continues for a week, targeting different books each day. The example in the table is organized to show the reading strategies and state standards that teachers could integrate when conducting Book Hooks on these texts.

A Book Hook theme can also be used to further explore an idea from another discipline. For example, while studying weather in science, you may augment this unit with literature during your Book Hooks. One day you might do your Book Hook on tornadoes and hurricanes, the next day on snow, another day on clouds, and you may conclude the week with a book about the effects of drought. The books that you use might be non-fiction, but they might also include poetry about the sky, fiction books about snow, books about snowboarding, and even historical fiction on the dust bowl. The themes and big ideas that can be used are unlimited, and some of our most creative and insightful teachers have used Book Hooksthat have engaged and excited every child about reading. The examples in Table 2.5 can help you get started.

The ideas are endless and we have found many resources for ideas about themed Book Hooks. One of our favorites is the Carol Hurst Children's Literature Site. On the Carol Hurst website, for example, there are multiple book lists organized by theme and content: www.carolhurst.com/subjects/subjects.html.

PHASE 1: INDICATIONS OF HIGH QUALITY

Each of the chapters on the 3 Phases of the SEM-R will conclude with a brief listing of the indicators of high quality. Our intention in including these is to provide teachers with goals and standards to strive toward in their implementation of the SEM-R. Some of these things are likely to be second nature because they will be similar to current teaching methods. Others of these will be more difficult. However, our research in SEM-R has demonstrated that the most successful teacher Book Hooks occur when:

- Book Chats model book selection behaviors, and book choices are effective in demonstrating the identified purpose.
- You have engaged students in a discussion of genre characteristics, including comparisons and contrasts with other texts.
- You have performed the read-alouds in such a way that your expression enhanced the listeners' connection to the text.
- Most of the students regularly demonstrate visible excitement and/or emotional involvement with the book.
- You have modeled higher-order thinking skills and encouraged students to apply them and literary concepts to frame the discussion of the read aloud.
- You frequently use open-ended questions or strategies that allow entry and challenge at multiple levels.
- Students make multiple connections (text to text, text to self, and text to world) through modeling, direct questions, and ongoing discussion.

Table 2.5. Themed Book Hooks.

Theme: Overcoming Difficulty in Life (Using the Great Depression as a Case in Point)
Books: *Out of the Dust* by Karen Hesse
        A Year Down Yonder by Richard Peck
        Bud, Not Buddy by Christopher Paul Curtis
        The Dust Bowl by David Booth & Karen Reczuch

Theme: Human Connections to Nature (Focusing on Native Americans)
Books: *Birchback House* by Louise Erdich
        The Desert is Theirs by Byrd Baylor & Peter Parnall
        Kokopelli's Flute by Will Hobbs

Theme: Overcoming Difficulty in Life (Using Weather as an Example)
Books: *The Log Cabin* by Ellen Howard
        Snow by Uri Shulevitz
        Snow Treasure by Marie McSwigan
        The Winter Room by Gary Paulsen
        Snowflake Bentley by Jacqueline B. Martin & Mary Azarian

CHAPTER 3

PHASE 2: SUPPORTED INDEPENDENT READING & DIFFERENTIATED TEACHER CONFERENCES

ELIZABETH A. FOGARTY, SALLY M. REIS, & REBECCA D. ECKERT

In previous decades, many teachers believed that creating good readers was as easy as unleashing good books on kids and giving them time to read each day. Programs with acronyms such as DEAR (Drop Everything and Read) and SSR (Sustained Silent Reading) were used to signal to students that it was time to begin reading. Currently, little scientific evidence supports the long-established belief that increases in independent reading will lead to improved reading fluency and comprehension. In fact, after a large-scale analysis of the limited research on this topic, the National Reading Panel (2000) concluded that, "there is a clear need for rigorous experimental research on the impact of programs that encourage reading on different populations of students at varying ages and reading levels ... and where the amount of independent reading is carefully monitored" (p. 3-4). Thus far, limited findings suggest that neither resources nor additional time alone are sufficient to promote reading growth in students (Anderson, Wilson & Fielding, 1988; Taylor, Frye, & Maruyama, 1990). This information continues to inform and shape SEM-R research and the development and implementation of the two key Phase 2 activities: Supported Independent Reading (SIR) and differentiated individual conferences.

One of the main differences between a traditional Sustained Silent Reading program and the Supported Independent Reading (SIR) in the SEM-R is that teachers conduct individual conferences with students and provide individual instruction on the use of reading strategies, as well as higher-order questions to challenge and engage readers. Individual student conferences in the SEM-R also provide time to assess the match between students and the books they select. The conferences emphasize student self-selection of appropriately challenging material that is personally interesting. In addition, teachers may use this time to discuss student interests and the possibility of pursuing independent work during Phase 3.

This chapter summarizes the specific strategies that successful teachers use when they implement Phase 2 of the SEM-R. Phase 2 focuses on the development of students' capability to engage in structured, independent reading time of self-selected, high-interest books. This is supported with individualized, differentiated reading conferences. Throughout Phase 2, teachers work with students to select books that are slightly above their current reading level to ensure continued development in strategy use and vocabulary knowledge for readers at all levels—including talented readers.

CREATING LIFELONG READERS

Unlike many other reading programs, the most important goal of the SEM-R is to increase students' enjoyment of reading. Typically, publishers of reading programs designate increasing student achievement as their top priority, but these decisions may put the cart or buggy before the horse.

The analogy of a horse and buggy explain students achievement. For example, that the buggy is student achievement. On its own, the buggy will not get anywhere. The student's interest is the horse in this example. The link between the two pieces, then, is motivation and hard work. If a student is interested in something, he or she will be more likely to believe that the motivation and hard work are necessary to raise his or her achievement. Therefore, when student interest (the horse) is used to motivate a student to commit time and energy (harness and reins) to a task, achievement will follow (buggy). It is impossible to expect the buggy to move when the horse and harness are not in place! However, many teachers are expected to create student achievement without student motivation and interest in place. At times, students may be willing to expend the time and energy to achieve, but without a personal interest, they are unable to sustain enough energy to increase their reading achievement. In the SEM-R, students are asked to expend time and energy to read more, but are also encouraged to read books in an interest area of choice.

Developing lifelong readers cannot be accomplished simply by giving multiple choice tests to measure students' comprehension each time they finish a book. If adult book clubs were conducted in the same manner, no one would join! Students should be given the chance to interact with literature the same way that adults do, through reading and discussion. Adults do not read to score well on a knowledge-level test of our comprehension of the elements of a story, but rather, adults read to appreciate life, to find happiness, to

---

MINI-LESSON #1: DISCUSSING PURPOSE FOR READING

Goal: To set the stage for extending Supported Independent Reading (SIR) in class

Objective: To develop students' understanding of the purpose of SIR through a teacher-facilitated class discussion

Supplies Needed: Reading materials representing a variety of genres from the school library and classroom collection

Activities: Begin by sharing a variety of reading materials with your students, such as books, manuals, handbooks, magazines, or newspapers that represent a variety of reading purposes. As you display each type of reading material to the class, emphasize the variety of reasons for reading. Some possible discussion questions include:
Why would you read this?
What might someone learn from reading this?
Where might you find this reading material?

Next, focus the discussion on students' personal reasons for reading and have them brainstorm responses to the following questions:
Why do you read?
Why do you think that being able to read is important?

Possible student responses will vary but may include the following:
To learn
For enjoyment
To find out things
To build vocabulary/language
To share thoughts/ideas with others

---

escape reality, or to better understand our place in the world. The following introductory lesson can be used during Phase 2 in the SEM-R to explore some of these ideas.

BOOK MATCH: FINDING APPROPRIATELY CHALLENGING READING MATERIAL

An essential feature of Phase 2 is student selection of books that are sufficiently challenging. SIR is based on the premise that students will benefit more from the experience of reading independently if they are challenged by complex content, ideas, and language in the text. This is especially true if the book is of personal interest to the student and he/she is motivated to read it. However, if books are too challenging, students may become frustrated and their fluency and comprehension will fail to improve. Evaluating the appropriateness of student book selections is challenging, yet it is a critical aspect of ensuring the success and effectiveness of the SIR.

Deciding whether a book is an appropriate choice for SIR will be different for each student. For example, talented readers may choose books with a word-reading level that is at or above grade level. However, the student may not be sufficiently challenged by the book's content, and because of the students' strong word-reading fluency, they should be encouraged to choose a more advanced book with more complex content.

On the other hand, struggling readers might select books with more challenging content and ideas. However, because of less-developed reading skills, students may have to expend a great deal of energy simply to decode words that they are unable to understand. These student should be supported in choosing books with equally challenging content, but with a word-reading level that they can read fluently and is matched with their reading ability.

Because students in your class will have very different reading skills and comprehension, there are no specific rules for deciding whether a book is an appropriate choice for Phase 2 SIR. We consider four factors for every student: readability, complexity, subject matter appropriateness of the text, and each student's interest.

Word-reading Level

Word-reading level refers to the readability level of the words in the text. The readability level is designated on many texts in today's classrooms to help teachers match readers with books. When trying to determine the appropriateness of texts, teachers usually expect their students to be able to read most of the words on a page with little difficulty in decoding. They also expect that students should be able to read with a moderate degree of fluency (i.e., smoothly and quickly).

Teachers have long used the 'five finger rule' to help learners determine whether or not a text will be too difficult for them. Typically, readers are asked to hold up five fingers as they read a page of text. Each time a reader sees a word that he or she cannot read, the child puts one of her fingers down. At the end of the page, the student should determine, based on the number of fingers left in the air, whether or not the book is too difficult. Most teachers tell students that if they have put all five of their fingers down when reading a page that the text is too difficult for them to read. In many cases this is true. What teachers often do not mention to students, however, is that if only one or two of their fingers are down at the end of a page of text, the book may be too easy. Moreover, students may simply assume they do not know a new word without attempting to use contextual

---

MINI-LESSON #2: MAKING APPROPRIATE BOOK CHOICES

Goal: Improve the quality and quantity of student engagement with a book

Objective: To provide students with strategies for choosing a challenging, enjoyable book to read

Supplies Needed: A collection of books representing a variety of genres and styles from the library, classroom collection, or other sources

Activities: Begin by asking students to work with a partner to brainstorm a list of strategies students can use to decide if a book is right for them (e.g., examining cover art, reading a summary, etc.). As a class, discuss student responses and compile a list of strategies on the board.

Next provide each pair of students with a book and ask them to employ some (or all) of the strategies listed on the board to make suggestions about who might be interested in this book. (You may find it helpful to model this process for your students before they begin.)

Have each group share their recommendations as well as the strategy and information gained that led to their decision. You may discover that some students may be able to make very specific suggestions (e.g., "We think Marc will like this book because we have heard him say how much he likes books written by Andrew Clements and this is his newest novel.")

Finally, discuss with students how they determine if a book is a good match for reading during SIR time with an emphasis on appropriate challenge level. You may find the following questions helpful:

- Have you ever read a book that was too hard for you to read by yourself? How did you know that it was too difficult? What advice would you give me if I had a book that I REALLY wanted to read but it was just too tough for me to read right now?
- Have you ever read a book that was too easy for you to read? How do you feel when you are reading an easy book? Why do you think I might ask you to pick a more challenging book during SIR time?
- Are there any strategies in our list that you could use to help you decide if a book is too easy or too difficult for you to read during SIR? (circle strategies) Do we have any other strategies we should add to help us decide if a book is the right challenge level?

---

clues to determine its meaning which will change the assessment of text difficulty. Our experiences in classrooms have indicated that teachers usually tell a student not to read a text that is too difficult, but rarely encourage them to read a book that is challenging.

In an appropriately challenging book, students must encounter some words that are unfamiliar and new to them. Students will learn to read new words when they are fluent with the other words in the sentences and paragraphs. Growth in reading will also occur when students are encouraged to read appropriately challenging texts in the context of a supportive environment that engages students as they learn the new words they are reading. The rule of thumb for students in the SEM-R is that if they can already read most of the words on a page, the book they have selected is likely to be too easy.

A common mistake is to assume that because a text contains more difficult words, it will be appropriate for a talented reader. Often as the word-reading level increases, the complexity and subject matter also increase. Just because a talented reader can decode difficult text does not mean that it is appropriate reading material for him or her. For instance, we have seen very young children (ages 4-5) who can accurately decode text to "read" the Wall Street Journal. We can all agree, however, that the Wall Street Journal is not appropriate reading material for a four year old. Though a young child may be able to accurately read the words, perhaps even with a great deal of fluency, he cannot understand complex ideas in the text, as the subject matter is neither appropriate nor interesting to a young child.

Complexity of Content

Complexity of content refers to students' understanding, appreciation, and critical thinking about the content matter of their reading selection. After reading any passage, students should be able to answer basic questions about the character, setting, and plot of the passage. Additionally, students should be able to interact with a text at a more complex level by making inferences, analyzing and synthesizing information, and relating content to their own experiences. The content, ideas, and language in a book should challenge the boundaries of what students can understand easily or with little effort. Books should encourage students to use and develop critical thinking skills, expand their knowledge and understanding, and think about ideas differently.

Teachers will be able to gauge whether the text is sufficiently complex for a student during each conference. If a student reads fluently and responds to questions with answers that come easily and require little thought, the text may be too easy. Teachers should ask students whether they have questions about what they have read. A text that is read without any effort and that does not leave some questions in a student's mind, will not present an opportunity for the reader to grow.

Age Appropriate Content or Subject Matter

A major concern when working with all readers, and especially talented readers, is finding material with both complexity and age-appropriate subject matter. Finding a text that is sufficiently complex may involve story lines and topics that are not appropriate for young readers. For a late primary reader or an early intermediate talented reader, for example, the options may include literature that is written for adolescents and young adults. However, themes like dating and choosing whether or not to use drugs are not necessarily topics that teachers and parents would select for younger students.

Finding books with appropriate subject matter may be the most challenging piece of the puzzle that teachers face when matching books to individual readers. Educators may feel cautious about making recommendations, especially in communities where they perceive that parents expect diligence, as teachers work to understand the families they serve. Age-appropriateness of reading material is influenced by many factors, including family beliefs and culture. It is also important to consider a student's social and intellectual levels of development, rather than just chronological development. For that reason, the appropriateness of a text becomes a decision that teachers should make with each child. The challenge for educators is twofold—knowing and understanding both individual students and the literature that children enjoy. You may find that your school media specialist or local children's librarian is a helpful resource. Teachers facing the dilemma of young talented readers often revisit beloved classic literature from authors like L.M. Montgomery, Jules Verne, and Charles Dickens with success.

Reading Interest

The final consideration faced when helping children choose books focuses on their interests. Most students have or are developing interests around which teachers can match any number of books. A helpful tool developed as part of the research surrounding SEM-R is called the Reading Interest-a-Lyzer. Included in Appendix B, it can be used to pinpoint students' reading interests. Some students will indicate their preferences for certain genres of text, while other students will indicate that they only enjoy reading about one topic. It may be more difficult to find books for these students than for other students with more diverse reading interests; however, the effort will be worth it once these students begin to enjoy the process of reading. Remember the more literature you introduce in Phase 1, the more likely students are to diversify their reading tastes. Interest identification and development is crucial because encouraging students to enjoy reading is the foundation of the SEM-R program.

Reading Conferences: Differentiating to Meet the Needs of All Readers

Most teachers in our studies faced the challenge of teaching a heterogeneous class of up to eight to ten grade levels of reading achievement and instruction in the classroom. In many of the heterogeneous third grade classrooms, students were reading from kindergarten or preschool level all the way to the eighth or ninth grade level. The prevalence of this wide range of student's of abilities in today's classrooms makes it necessary for us to use varying methods and processes to reach learners. We must also be sure that our instruction is directed toward differing levels of skills ensuring that those who enter school ahead of their peers can be sufficiently challenged and those who are behind their peers will also be challenged at an appropriate level. Using conferences in Phase 2 will help to differentiate the reading instruction and materials that students receive.

We have found that when they begin using the SEM-R, many teachers share a common concern that they will not be able to conduct conferences on books that they have not read. They worry about having to read every book that their students are reading to be able to determine students' comprehension of plot, characterization, and author's message. Of course, such expectations would be unreasonable. In fact, all of the teachers we worked with could conduct challenging, high-level conferences on books they have not read. They learned that while teaching reading without an answer key can be challenging, it also encourages thoughtful, reflective practices.

Though a conference assumes the feel of a conversation about the book, it also provides instruction for the student and specific feedback to the teacher on the student's progress. Though conferences may appear to be somewhat informal, remember that they are a crucial component of Supported Independent Reading. During this time, students should be asked to use higher-order thought processes and integrate new reading strategies into their repertoire.

Suggested Conference Format

In our experience with many teachers using the SEM-R, the most successful teachers have developed a standard format or expected routine for the conferences. Although the order of the components described below may vary, each is likely to occur during a conference. For example, when a child is struggling with fluency, you may spend more time providing strategies, modeling, and practice to help him or her develop greater fluency. In other conferences, you may spend very little time working on the fluency of a student's reading, choosing instead to spend the majority of time building comprehension strategies by asking the student to synthesize information or make connections. The format of the conference should be easily differentiated to meet the needs of the student.

- When you begin a conference, sit down with the student and ask him/her to tell you a little bit about the book.

- Ask the student to describe if he/she likes the book so far, and why.

- Ask the student to read a little bit of the book aloud to you, starting wherever they stopped when you dropped in. Have the student read about a page or for about a minute.

- If the student comes to a word he/she does not know, wait a few seconds and then tell the student the word. Allow the narrative flow to keep going, rather than interrupting with too much time spent trying to figure out the word.

- If the student is missing so many words that it is impossible for a narrative flow to occur, stop the student and suggest that maybe this is a book he/she should save to read later on, after he/she has had a little more time to practice reading. Have the student write the name and author of the book on the sheet "Books I Want to Read Later," and then help the student choose a new book.

- Pay careful attention to how the student reads the passage. Listen for the number of words that are difficult for the student, for expression, and for other indications of comprehension.

- When the student finishes reading, offer some comments that reflect praise—try to be specific (e.g., "I really liked how you used different voices for the characters!" or "I liked how you went back and corrected yourself on a word that you missed!"). Then ask the student a few follow-up questions about the reading. You may want to use one of the Bookmarks as a guide or you may want to ask some questions more specific to the passage itself.

- The questioning portion of the conference should take just about 3 minutes. The overall conference should only take about 5-7 minutes at the most.

- Try to ask questions that go beyond just recall of what happened in the text. Ask "why" questions and remind students to support answers with evidence from the book.

- Try to ask questions that are individually challenging for the student. Varying your questions will help you to differentiate your conference discussions.

- Ask the student to talk about what he/she likes or does not like about the book, but do not limit your questions to that!

- Another good source of questioning is the connections that can be made with the text. We classify connections questions as "text to text," "text to self," and "text to world." See Chapter Five for further guidance.

- The follow-up questioning time is also a good time to review words that the student might have missed. You can go back and point out some words that were a little challenging and ask the student how he/she might have tried to figure out the words. Talk about strategies for figuring out words, such as using context clues, using pictures, and looking for parts of the words that are familiar.

+ In some cases, the reading and discussion portions of the conference, together or separately, might indicate that the book is too hard to too easy for the student. If this is the case, encourage the student to try a different book. In the case of books that are too easy, talk to the student about the importance of reading challenging books while at school where someone can help. Encourage the student to read the easier book on his/her own time. In the case of books that are too hard, encourage the student to save the book for later, as noted above.

+ Initial the student's conference record on the appropriate date to show that the conference was conducted. You may want to list any major strategies that you worked on or difficulties the student might have had. Thank the student for sharing some reading time with you.

During each conference, you should use informal assessment measures to obtain information that can be used to determine the student's reading progress and their ability to use reading strategies. You will be able to measure a student's reading fluency, his or her comprehension of selected literature, and other reading experiences including enjoyment of and engagement in the book. You will read more about documenting student progress and ways to manage student conferences in Chapter Six.

Assessing and Improving Reading Fluency

The concepts of reading fluency and comprehension are closely intertwined. Readers who struggle with fluency concentrate on deciphering and identifying words rather than constructing meaning, while fluent readers have automatized word recognition enabling more cognitive resources to focus on higher-level thinking and interpreting text. Therefore, helping students increase their ability to read fluently should be an important goal for teachers of young readers. Readers should be able to read at a pace that enables them to connect phrases together contributing to meaningful comprehension of the text.

At the beginning of each conference, the teacher should have each student read a short section from his or her current book. This allows for a quick determination as to the appropriateness of the book based on what is heard in just that minute of reading. If a student can read every word with a high rate of fluency and with expression that matches the text, it becomes obvious that the readability is a good match for the student, or perhaps that the text is too easy; however, this judgment should also be combined with a comprehension check.

On the other hand, when students struggle to decode the text they are reading or cannot read with any degree of expression, the readability of the text may be too difficult for them. Again, this should be determined only after you've had a chance to gauge the student's comprehension of the text. If, for instance, you have a student who struggles with decoding the text, but accurately answers questions about the plot and seems interested enough to keep reading, you should provide the student with some strategies for increasing fluency and encourage him to keep reading. Even though he may be missing words occasionally as he reads, it has not hampered his ability to comprehend.

When conducting a conference with a student who is misreading words, it is usually better to write down the words as you hear them, rather than interrupt and correct the student each time they miscue. Once the student has read a paragraph or two, stop him and begin to talk about some of the words he missed. Ask him to go back into the text with you to examine the context of the sentence that might have helped him determine the word's meaning. Or, ask the student to chunk the word into smaller and more manageable pieces. For example, if a student has missed the word "unforgivable," ask her if she can see a part of a smaller word within. Once she has identified forgive, discuss the meaning of both the prefix and suffix. Modeling the process of self-correction shows the reader that this is what good readers do when they read. Once you have modeled self-correction, ask the student to read a bit more and try to use the new strategy if she runs into a word she doesn't know how to read.

If, however, the student reads a word and seems to hesitate or goes back to self-correct, this is the perfect opportunity to stop the student and model the behavior of self-correcting. You might ask the student how he knew that he had read the word incorrectly, or whether he noticed that it didn't make sense in the context of the rest of the text. You might also give him additional strategies to use when fluency breaks down.

Remember, the best way to increase reading fluency is for students to practice!

Using Questioning and Conversation to Assess Comprehension

Another purpose of SIR is to help students develop their ability to comprehend text. Students who understand what they read actively construct meaning as they interact with text. They have an in-depth understanding of story elements such as character, setting, and plot as well as the structure of non-fiction work. They are also able to think critically about what they are reading, know when they have problems with understanding, and how to resolve those problems as they occur. Strengthening the reading comprehension of students enables them to become better readers of both creative and expository texts and provides students with greater access to information from both the literary world as well as from the realms of content areas such as science and history.

The conversation between the teacher and the student in Phase 2 is like any conversation that two readers would have over a book. In adult conversations about books, readers might try to get a sense of the story, the author's purpose, and possible connections to their own lives. It is probable that the bulk of the conversation will focus on big ideas like these, rather than small details from the book, such as the color of shoes the character wore or the name of the cousin who attended the party. The readers will almost certainly discuss whether or not they are enjoying the book. Conferences during SIR should take on a similarly important tone and should not simply become oral recitations of multiple choice tests.

Initially, these conferences may be difficult to conduct. Ideally, the conference should involve an authentic conversation, as well as strategy instruction. However, in the beginning you may be trying to integrate several reading strategies into the conference thereby losing the authentic feel of the conversation. Conversely, some teachers become so involved in listening to a child talk about his book, that they forget to integrate strategy instruction and appropriately challenging questions into the conference. Although this occasionally happens at the beginning of SEM-R implementation, teachers quickly adapt and integrate all aspects of the conferences. The Bookmarks discussed in the previous chapter on Phase 1 have been instrumental in helping teachers integrate these higher-order questions throughout the conferences.

The Bookmarks (Appendix A) can be used to identify higher-order thinking questions that are appropriate for use in the conferences. The questions on the Bookmarks can also be used to assess students' reading strategy use. To accomplish this, you must be clear about which strategy you intend to assess. For instance, to determine whether a student was able to make connections between personal experiences and the story characters, you might ask, "During which scene of the story did you feel as if you could relate to the main character the most and why?" This question asks readers to make a direct comparison of their own feelings to those of the main character. However, if you intended to find out whether the same reader could make an inference, you might ask a slightly different question. In order to answer the Bookmark question, "In what scene do you believe that the main character feels the saddest due to the events of the story and why do you believe that?" the reader would need to infer the answer. By examining the nuances of the plot since the answer is not directly stated in the text the reader uses inferencing strategies. Such fine distinctions in questioning illustrate the importance of teachers' understanding of the reading strategies, as well as the assessments they hope to conduct during each conference.

Modeling "Think Aloud" Strategies During Conferences

When a student is unable to answer comprehension questions, teachers can provide model "think aloud" examples, see the following example for details:

> Emily's teacher sat down next to her to begin her reading conference. Emily was nearly finished with The Higher Power of Lucky by Susan Patron and Matt Phelan and told her teacher, Mrs. Dahl, that she was really enjoying the book. Mrs. Dahl asked Emily to briefly summarize what had been happening in the story. As Emily summarized, it was clear to her teacher that though Emily could provide a cohesive summary of the plot, there were overall themes that Emily might not be realizing. When Mrs. Dahl asked Emily to read a page of text Emily read fluently and with expression. Emily's teacher decided to ask Emily questions about theme and author's message to see if she could provide enough scaffolding to get Emily to think at a deeper level about why some of the events in the story occurred. She began by asking Emily why she believed that the main character, Lucky, felt worried so much of the time.
>
> Emily thought for a while. Finally she said, "I think that Lucky was sad that her mother had died."
>
> "What makes you say that?" asked Mrs. Dahl.
>
> "I'm not sure. I just know that if my mother died I would be so sad all of the time just like Lucky," Emily responded.
>
> Mrs. Dahl, who had not yet read the book, decided to probe further realizing that Emily was only using her own experiences to judge the actions of the character. She decided to make her own thinking transparent in order to help Emily reason an answer to the question. "I think you're partially right, Emily. She probably was thinking a lot about her mother, just as you would if your mother weren't with you. But, I'm thinking about the word 'worry' and wondering why Lucky might feel worried if her mother were gone. Certainly she would feel sad, but worrying is

a bit different from sadness, isn't it? Let's see if we can look back in the text to see if we can figure out what might have made Lucky feel worried."

Together the pair leafed through the pages that Emily had already read. As they did so, Mrs. Dahl asked Emily to discuss elements from that part of the story to see if they could discover the answer. At one point, Emily mentioned that Lucky often thinks that her guardian will leave her to go back to live in France. Emily's teacher knew then that Emily had not connected the potential leaving of the guardian to Lucky's feeling of worry. Emily did not have experiences similar to Lucky's and had difficulty making a self-to-text connection to better understand the story. In addition, the author probably had not explicitly written, 'Lucky was worried' in the text, instead planting clues for the readers to find and make inferences from. Therefore, Emily's teacher concluded that she needed additional coaching in making inferences.

As the conference continued, Emily's teacher made another attempt to "show" Emily her thinking. "Emily, when people worry they are thinking about something that might happen that would be unpleasant. You told me that the author has given some clues that Lucky's guardian might be moving back to France. As I think about what I know about Lucky, I can tell that she is feeling sad and alone in the world after her mother's death. She also has a guardian. However, she thinks that this guardian might be moving away, thus leaving her alone. Now, can you think about all of those clues and infer what might be worrying Lucky?"

With such strong scaffolding, Emily was easily able to determine that Lucky's worry was due to the fact that she was unsure of whether her guardian would be leaving her. They went on to discuss how Lucky's worry affected the rest of the story and how to use that information to make predictions about the ending of the story. Mrs. Dahl's ability to detect only a surface level of understanding in Emily's responses led to the scaffolding. This later enabled Emily to make an inference about the author's intent and understand the story more deeply.

Teachers must learn to make their thinking "transparent" to their students. Although this will often be done in Phase 1 through modeling answers to Bookmark questions, it should also be done with readers of all achievement levels in Phase 2. Please note, this is not a strategy reserved for use with struggling readers. All students will need some scaffolding and coaching if they are reading sufficiently challenging books.

GAUGING READING ENJOYMENT

Teachers should also use the conferences to gauge students' enjoyment of their reading. In most cases, teachers will begin each conference by asking the student, 'How do you like the story/book so far?' You will recall that the first goal in the SEM-R is to promote enjoyment of reading in students.

A sixth grade teacher's experience with her student, Tony, provides a good illustration of the importance of reading enjoyment. Tony was a struggling reader. He had low scores in reading throughout school and his reading interest scores, taken on his entry to sixth grade, showed that he did not enjoy reading. Early in the school year, Tony was having a conference with his teacher, Mrs. Karnes. During that conference, the pair was discussing the text, *Mick Harte Was Here* by Barbara Park. Mick's sister narrates the story and describes the fatal accident of her brother. Mrs. Karnes began the conference by asking how the character, Mick, had died. Although he was more than halfway through the book, Tony indicated to Mrs. Karnes that the character hadn't died. Though she had never read the book herself, Mrs. Karnes was able to deduce from the title of the story that Tony's comprehension had broken down somewhere along the way. The teacher worked with him to review the text and discover the sister's memories of Mick's death in the first few pages of the text. When Mrs. Karnes asked Tony if he was enjoying the book, he admitted that he'd never really gotten into it. She suggested that he find a book that he enjoyed. Later in the semester, Mrs. Karnes sat with Tony as he excitedly described to her the plot from the book, *Monster* by Walter Dean Myers. This time Tony knew every detail and plot twist of the novel, a novel that was more complicated than the other had been. When his teacher asked him if he was enjoying Monster, Tony emphatically nodded and indicated that he planned to read every book written by Walter Dean Myers.

Tony's situation could confuse any reading teacher. Why was it that he could read a more difficult text more successfully than one that was slightly below grade level? We would have expected that the more appropriate book for a struggling reader like Tony would have been the easier one. Since the word level, complexity, and subject matter were all more difficult in the second text than the first, only the interest level of the student seems to have changed. Interest seems to have complicated the matter of book match. In Tony's case, a simple formula involving word level and complexity and subject matter were not enough; finding an appropriate text for Tony also involved considering his interest in the text.

The lesson that we can learn from Tony's case is the guiding principle behind the SEM-R: interest often mediates ability. In other words, an otherwise struggling reader will be able to read a high-interest text that he or she could not normally access without the strong interest piece. Likewise, a perfectly capable reader may have lower comprehension of a text in which he or she is not engaged.

During conferences, we have found that teachers are more likely to make a connection with students when they share their own reading likes and dislikes. You might talk about the kinds of genres or types of characters that you enjoy. As you share your preferences, be sure to discuss the reasoning behind your preferences to demonstrate to your students some of the ways that you interact with the text.

SELF-REGULATION

Supported Independent Reading is most effective when all students are engrossed and interested in their reading. Experienced teachers know that there are always a few students who need additional support to stay on task. Advance planning and practice using techniques that can help students focus and regulate their learning can help to lay the foundation for success in reading for students.

Defining Self-regulated Learning

Successful students use self-regulated learning strategies to be more successful in school (Zimmerman, 1989). Self-regulated learning can help students develop a set of constructive behaviors that positively affect their learning. Several processes can be planned and adapted to support the pursuit of personal goals to change learning environments. Self-regulation skills can be taught, learned, and controlled by students and research on self-regulation (Zimmerman, 1990) has found that successful students use self-regulation strategies in three different categories: personal, behavioral, and environmental. Personal strategies involve how students organize information and include strategies related to: classifying and coordinating information, setting goals, and planning work. Behavioral strategies occur when students check their own progress or quality of work by examining what they do when they learn. Students must learn to independently evaluate the processes they use to learn and also to identify consequences for themselves. This means that students can arrange their own rewards to motivate themselves to meet their goals. They also can learn to use self-reinforcement and delay gratification until they have achieved their specific goals. Environmental strategies for self-regulated learning involve the use of other resources and the way that students change or adapt their own environment to achieve more positive results.

Developing Self-regulation

When introducing the SEM-R to a new group of students, Phase 2 should be implemented gradually. Eventually, most of the time you allocate to the SEM-R will be spent in Phase 2, but initially the students may not have the self-regulation necessary to read for long periods of time. In fact, our experience has shown that some students may not be able to read for more than 4 or 5 minutes at a time. This may be due to the type of challenging books you are asking them to read. Students may be able to read unchallenging books for long periods of time, but may not have developed the skills necessary to do so with more challenging texts. It may also be due to their inexperience with independent reading for longer periods of time. In this phase, students will begin to develop the self-

---

MINI-LESSON #3: USING THE SELF-REGULATION TOOLS

Goal: To increase students' self-regulation of their reading behavior

Objective: To develop students' ability to use the sun/cloud signs and sticky notes to identify reading difficulties during SIR time

Supplies Needed: Classroom set of sun/cloud cards, several sticky notes for each student, book for SIR time

Activities: Begin by discussing instances in which students may get off track in their reading. Ask students to share examples of times they have become confused.
- What do you do when you can't read a word?
- What do you do when you don't understand what is happening in the text?

Next, remind students of the need for them to self-monitor their reading. This is important because they may often be reading when no one is around to help (at home or while the teacher is conferencing with a classmate).

Next, role play two scenarios during which comprehension or fluency impede your progress in reading a text selection:
- Model the use of sticky notes to mark locations of unknown words in order to refer back to them in a conference.
- Demonstrate the use of the sun/cloud card to get the teacher's attention between conferences.

Discuss the possible benefits and drawbacks of each system with the students. Ask them to name instances when the use of one or the other might be better.

---

regulation necessary to read for sustained periods of time in self-selected, challenging texts. For some students, however, this will be no small undertaking!

When the SEM-R was first implemented, many students in some schools were only able to read for 3-4 minutes at a time during the first few weeks. After only a few minutes, they would begin to squirm and exhibit off-task behavior. When the teachers noticed that the students were getting off task, they ended Phase 2 and moved on to another SEM-R task, or another activity altogether. The teachers realized that once students were no longer attending to the task of reading, they were not developing the self-regulation necessary to participate successfully in SIR. When the majority of students are off task, it is best to end Phase 2 and move to more Phase 1 read-alouds or Phase 3 activities. The following suggestions can help you to manage students' independent reading and increase their self-regulation:

+   Proximity to students is the most proactive measure you can take to help them maintain their focus on reading. Rather than calling students to your desk for individual conferences, we suggest that teachers move throughout the room and sit beside students to conduct each conference. Your presence can help to keep

---

**MINI-LESSON #4: DEVELOPING SELF-REGULATION
AND AVOIDING READING DISTRACTIONS**

Goal: Support improvement of students' time on task with books

Objective: Identify reading distractions and self-regulation strategies

Activities : Begin with a discussion based on the following focusing question:

Have you ever been silently reading something and your mind wanders from "the story?" What happened? Why do you think this might have happened?

Some possible answers may include:

+   I got confused about . . .
+   I was distracted by . . .
+   I started to think about when . . .
+   I got stuck when . . .
+   Time went quickly because . . .
+   A word/some words I didn't know were . . .
+   I stopped because . . .
+   I lost track of everything except . . .
+   I figured out that . . .
+   I first thought . . . but then I realized . . .

---

your students on track and to provide other students with the opportunity to learn when they overhear your comments and suggestions to their classmates.

- You can share your SIR target time with your students and celebrate those days in which everyone exceeds expectations. Younger students in particular have a difficult time gauging the amount of time that they are actually reading quietly and on task. Providing students with a visual reminder of their goals (like a stop time written on the board, a timer, or a sticky note placed on the clock marking the end of SIR time) may help them to sustain a focus on reading throughout the designated SIR time.

- Some children may need to have their SIR time broken into smaller chunks of reading time. The goal is to build reading stamina with all students, but it will be necessary to make accommodations for some readers. For students who have great difficulty sustaining their reading for an extended period, you may want to give them the option of listening to an audio book for part of the SIR time, working with a buddy to read for a portion of the time, or on working on a written response followed by more SIR time.

- Encourage students to focus on one particular Bookmark or Bookmark question to provide a purpose as they begin their reading for the week. As students find evidence in the book to help them answer a question, they can either mark the spot with the Bookmark or make note of the page in their reading logs. They will then be prepared to discuss their ideas with you during the reading conference.

- Provide students with sticky notes or scratch paper on which they can jot questions, concerns, or unfamiliar vocabulary so that they can continue to read until an adult is available for a discussion or assistance.

- Many teachers have explained that during self-directed activities, they know that students cannot both raise their hand and continue to be productive at the same time. The sun/cloud cards can be used as an unobtrusive cue to indicate when a student wants assistance. The sun side indicates that the student is doing fine reading independently. The cloud side indicates that the student wants assistance. A template for the sun/cloud card is provided for you in Appendix D.

- Proximity to other students may be distracting to some children. Consider the spaces within the room where students will be reading. You may want to create some spaces that limit distractions, yet are inviting, for individuals to choose for their reading spot.

When introducing the SEM-R and SIR to students, it is important to engage them in several discussions that will set the stage for self-regulation in your classroom. These discussions will help students understand what is expected of them in terms of behavior during SEM-R time. Moreover, they will help you achieve the goals and objectives that you have set forth for the program as well. Two mini-lessons have been included in this chapter examples for this task.

Introduce the following strategies to help students focus on their reading and to self-regulate their behaviors.

+ Ask yourself why you are distracted.
+ If you are thinking of other things (like what you plan to do after school), write them down on a sheet of paper or a sticky note and set it aside on your desk.
+ If you don't know an important word, can you figure out what the word means from context clues? If not, you can look it up in the dictionary. You might also write the word on a sticky note to discuss with your teacher after she finishes conducting conferences.
+ If you are confused by what you are reading, you could re-read the paragraph. If you feel very confused, you may want to talk to the teacher about your book selection.
+ If your mind is wandering, try writing down what you think will happen next and then keep reading to see if you are right.
+ If you want to talk to a friend, ask yourself about what you are reading.
+ If you really aren't enjoying what you are reading, discuss your book choice with your teacher and ask for help in choosing another book.
+ Before reading for the day, have students decide which strategy they will try to use if they become distracted during SIR time.

Establish a Routine with Clear Expectations

One of the most important things to do when beginning to use the SEM-R is to create a structure with clear expectations. Establishing a routine will help the students understand what is expected of them during class period. Clear expectations will help students envision and imagine what it means to get into the groove of self-regulated reading while also providing a structure within which both you and the student can problem solve when difficulties arise.

Teachers should strive to give students all of the tools that will enable them to stay on task during their independent reading time. The following is an example of an expectations chart that could be posted in the SEM-R classroom.

Reading Behaviors Expected During SIR

- You must have a book to read at all times.
- If you aren't enjoying a book and have given it a fair chance (read at least 10 pages), ask the teacher to help you choose a new one.
- Select and remain in one reading area during SIR.
- Only reading is happening. (You may talk quietly with your teacher during conferences.)
- Do your best reading the whole time.

Managing Interruptions

There are times when students are more likely to be off-task, such as when they require teacher assistance, need permission to go to the bathroom, or want to select a new book. There are several management strategies you can use to keep students on track, even when they require your attention. First, you can develop a 'no interruption' policy during your conferencing time. Without such a policy, it is very likely that you will receive frequent requests from students for help with tasks that they could manage on their own. If students must ask permission to use the bathroom or get a drink of water, for instance, you are likely to be interrupted several times throughout the period.

Effective SEM-R teachers have developed systems in which students are able to excuse themselves without disturbing the teacher. For the purposes of most classrooms, it is important that the teacher is able to see at a glance which student is in the bathroom or at the drinking fountain. Therefore, some teachers developed systems in which students must hang a card with their picture on a hook when they are in the bathroom. This method is especially effective for large classrooms so that the teacher can immediately see who is not in the classroom. A sign-out log is also effective so that teachers can see if there are certain students who seem to make frequent bathroom and fountain trips as these are possible signs of inattentiveness to reading which may have many different causes.

You should establish procedures for using the classroom and school library during SIR. Without guidelines, it is possible that some students may abuse the privilege and use the library as an excuse to be out of their seats, rather than a resource for book finding. Additionally, some students may develop the habit of "book shopping" in which they choose a new book every period rather than completing books. If you find that you have a chronic "book shopper" in your room it will be necessary to diagnose the reason for the behavior and then apply an appropriate remedy.

For students easily off-task, it is important to try to figure out why they are not finishing or engaging in books. The books may be too challenging, too boring, too easy, or just not what they were hoping to read. Knowing the problem will allow for a solution. For instance, you might use the student's conference time to aid the child in finding appropriate books. You and the student might discuss ways to find books that are neither too difficult, nor too easy. You might also encourage the student to use different strategies, perhaps bringing several books back to his or her seat for reading time.

In some cases, however, chronic "book shoppers" do not easily shake the behavior! In such cases, it becomes obvious that students are less able to self-regulate their reading than their peers and teachers need to provide additional support. In some cases, teachers have require students to finish their books before they begin new ones. In other cases, students are asked to write a letter to the teacher requesting permission to abandon a book. Both strategies were helpful in lessening "book shopping" behaviors. Some teachers also discourage this behavior, as well as interruptions throughout the period, by having a rule that states that students can only visit the library during the first 5 minutes of the reading period.

Interruptions can also occur when students become confused by the text they are reading. At times they may get hung up on a word that they cannot decode, or an idea that doesn't seem to make sense. Teaching students how to deal with these type of content difficulties is an important step in teaching them to self-regulate in their reading. Therefore, if we continue to allow students immediate access to answers about these questions, it may discourage them from figuring out the answers for themselves. Thus independent processing is an important step in helping them become self-sufficient readers who will continue to enjoy the process long after they leave our classrooms.

Several teachers have developed strategies for dealing with students when they have questions during SIR. One fourth grade teacher allows her students to "phone a friend," a take-off from the popular game show, "Who Wants to Be a Millionaire." In her room, a student could ask a friend one question during the period. Some students might ask a friend to clarify the pronunciation or meaning of a word. Others might seek out a peer who has read the same book to get clarification on something that was misunderstood or to ask for a book recommendation.

Many teachers have employed the use of sticky notes. In these classrooms, each student has his own supply of sticky notes so that if he runs into something that doesn't make sense, he can mark the spot to ask the teacher in a free moment or during his own conference. Additionally, teachers have also asked students to use sticky notes to mark any sections of the text that illustrate their use of a reading strategy or that provides evidence to answer a Bookmark question. In addition, sticky notes can be used to mark the sections where a student made an inference or drew a connection, or raised questions for the reader.

Teachers can also use the time between conferences to answer questions for students. Teachers using the SEM-R have developed different management strategies that can be used to recognize which students are in need of some attention. In several classrooms, students alert teachers that they are in need of help by turning the "STOP" side up on a card, while the "GO" side is used when 'all systems are go' and reading is going smoothly. Such a system allows the student to indicate that the teacher's help is needed without interrupting his or her reading. In Appendix D, you will also find a pattern to make a similar sun and cloud indicator. When things are going well with their reading, the students display the sunny side and when they encounter a problem, they turn the card to the side with the cloud. Teachers have placed symbols on cardstock and laminated them for durability. With either symbol system, teachers can see with a glance across the classroom if a student needs help.

Managing Off-task Behavior

Students may also develop off-task behaviors for other reasons. They may be unable to concentrate on their reading for long periods of time due to the inability to manage their own behavior. There are many behavioral strategies that you can use to manage these issues for students in order to help them develop self-regulatory behavior for reading. Some students realize when they are becoming off-task and others do not. In any case, it is necessary to increase the student's metacognition of their off-task behavior. If he or she does not know that it is occurring, there is less chance that it will decrease. However, if the teacher is able to cue the child in to these interruptions, the student will be more likely to realize when it is happening and will learn to curb the same behavior in the future.

There are several things that teachers can do to increase students' metacognition of these behaviors. A simple tally system may be developed for students who occasionally become off-task. Every time students find themselves off task, they make a check mark or write the time on their paper. This system helps the students become aware of how often they are distracted and they may be able to determine whether some pattern exists.

For instance, they may become off task at the same time during each period. Or they may become off task more on certain days of the week. Such record keeping will raise the students' metacognition of their own self-regulation. If students are unable to redirect their behaviors, proximity may be used to remind them that you are aware of their actions and expect them to get back on task. It may even be as easy as walking to that side of the room or placing a hand on a shoulder.

Several options can be employed for students who require a more stringent system. Teachers may need to use behavior modification techniques, such as the behavior tally system described earlier to document the amount of time a student spends on task. Similar to when a student records, the teacher may check whether a student is on task at 5 or 10 minute intervals. There may be consequences or rewards based on the information that the teacher gathers. Another excellent strategy is to set time goals for individual students. Teachers can provide timers for these students so that they can see exactly how long they must read in order to meet their goal. After each goal is successfully reached, students can be provided with a rest break or other appropriate reward.

Time

Remember that the goal of SIR is to increase the amount of time that students are able to self-regulate their reading in challenging material. If you can increase their reading time gradually in small increments, however, it will make the additional effort of tackling appropriately challenging texts more manageable for students. Extending the reading time by a minute each day is one way to accomplish this. If at the beginning students are able to read for 5 minutes, by the end of one week of reading their time will be doubled. To illustrate this point, students can create graphs that show the amount of time spent reading daily or weekly. A template for graphing students' reading minutes is included in Appendix E.

Most teachers using the SEM-R have been successful at helping students increase their self-regulation of reading by including the students in goal setting. Each day, you should work with the students to set a reasonable goal for the day's reading period. After the students reach the goal, be sure to recognize their effort. By recognizing their effort, you show the children that at times this will be hard work and that it should be something that will challenge them. You also show the students that their success is the result of their behavior.

PHASE 2: INDICATIONS OF HIGH QUALITY

- Most students start to read without any reminders beyond initial direction.
- The teacher conducts conferences without interruption throughout Phase 2.
- The teacher communicates a purpose for each student's oral reading prior to listening to students read.
- The teacher extends discussion beyond the student's next book choice to address book selection habits in general.
- The teacher uses questions at multiple levels across conferences and uses one or more higher-level questions in every conference.
- The teacher diagnoses individual needs from student's oral reading, and integrates varied strategies clearly connected to demonstrated reading behaviors.
- The teacher provides verbal guidance and/or environmental reminders of self-regulation strategies for reading (e.g., verbal reminders at start of Phase 2, use of sun/cloud cards, self-regulation strategies posted in classroom). All or most students can self-regulate their behavior throughout Phase 2.

CHAPTER 4

PHASE 3: INTEREST AND CHOICE ACTIVITIES

BRIAN C. HOUSAND, SALLY M. REIS, REBECCA D. ECKERT, & ANGELA HOUSAND

What would happen if your reading classroom is a place where both individual and small groups of students explore new ideas while simultaneously building new literacy skills? Imagine the enthusiasm and learning that occurs when you and your students have the time and the freedom to work independently on projects based on interests and preferred styles of learning. In Phase 3 of the SEM-R, you can make these dreams a reality by creating opportunities for students to conduct investigations which will enhance their strengths and help them pursue and discover their interests. As a skillful guide for your students' discovery of joyful learning and the fun of literacy, you can work with students who are engrossed in challenging learning opportunities and who actually groan when the class period ends.

THE RATIONALE FOR PHASE 3

The ultimate goal of Phase 3 is for students to progress from teacher-directed extension opportunities to independent, self-choice activities. As students' self-regulation skills and enjoyment of reading develop during the first two phases of the SEM-R; they learn to select books in their areas of interest and many begin to have a desire to investigate these new topics and ideas. Phase 3 is the SEM-R component that utilizes this growth to encourage students to explore their personal interests through self-selected literacy pursuits. However, like other developmental skills, student independence does not happen overnight, or even at the same predictable rate for all of your students, making your role as a facilitator and coach vital during Phase 3 of the SEM-R.

With your help, students will use Phase 3 extensions to further understand, analyze, synthesize, and evaluate some of the information they have encountered in the books they have read during Phase 2. Although the options for Phase 3 are limited only by your students' creativity and interests, the information provided in this chapter will help you select a structure and successfully launch this third phase of the SEM-R in your classroom. Phase 3 may include a myriad of different options including: creativity training activities, reading on the Internet, book discussion groups, audio books, interest centers, independent or small group enrichment projects, Renzulli Learning activities, or a number of other creative explorations that require students to further extend their thinking. You may wish to review Figure 2: Components of the Schoolwide Enrichment Model Reading Framework in Chapter One as a visual reference. As you continue reading and begin to plan for your own classroom, keep the helpful acronym ICE in mind to remind us of the importance of Interests, Choices, and Explorations in Phase 3.

Interest

Activities in Phase 3 should be based on student interests because they provide motivation for students to tackle challenging work. Some students' areas of interest may have existed before they participated in the SEM-R. Alternately, students may have developed new interests based on books they have encountered during Phases 1 and 2. Quite often, students recognize the types of books or information they like and dislike, but they cannot always focus on an activity or exploration that requires them to do something with their interests and growing knowledge. This approach to teaching reading focuses on helping students become aware of how the books they are enjoying might relate to other literacy skills and explorations. Various questionnaires can be used to help students identify their interests as well as their learning and expression styles (Renzulli & Reis, 1997). One of these inventories, Reading Interest-a-Lyzer, is included in Appendix B. That inventory and others are also available in an electronic format summarizing their interests, learning styles, and product styles with a subscription to Renzulli Learning (www.renzullilearning.com). Information from these instruments will allow you to better understand your students' unique strengths and create opportunities for individual growth while simultaneously helping students better understand themselves.

Choices

SEM-R provides students with choices for exploring their interests in independent or small group work. This concept begins in Phase 2 as students read books of their own selection and it is more fully explored in Phase 3. As students are provided with additional choices, our goal is for them to be able to begin to develop independence in their exploration of interests. Phase 3 of the SEM-R creates a safe environment in which students may investigate their own topics and activities. Generally in the first few weeks of implementation, teachers have found that students are more productive and engaged when provided with structured extension activities designed to give learners practice in independent work skills such as task management, self-regulation, and creative problem-solving. As students (and teachers) become more comfortable with independence and student decision-making, Phase 3 activities expand to involve less teacher scaffolding and more student choice. The goal in Phase 3 is to promote creative productivity in the hopes that many students will choose to conduct their own self-directed activity.

Explorations

Often, a student's love for a book stays with them long after they finish reading the last page; however, time to act upon this passion in the school day can be a rare gift. During Phase 3, teachers who use the SEM-R make a conscious decision to create opportunities for students to investigate and explore what they love about literature. Rather than providing strict project guidelines or a format for a "book report," students are encouraged to use their own interests and skills as a map to guide their explorations; it is the developmental journey, not the destination, which is valued in Phase 3. SEM-R classrooms provide time for deep and meaningful investigations that build upon students' newfound enjoyment of reading and extend beyond the regular curriculum. Teachers can support and encourage students to delve deeper by providing the tools, scaffolding, and coaching necessary to help students explore and develop their interests.

IMPLEMENTING PHASE 3: STORIES FROM TWO CLASSROOMS

Perhaps one of the best ways to envision how interests, choice, and explorations can be coordinated during Phase 3 is to review the examples of two different SEM-R classrooms where all three are working in concert.

A Fourth-grade Class Using Phase 3 for 1 Hour Each Friday

In Mrs. Patrick's fourth-grade classroom, students participate in Phase 3 activities for one hour each week on Friday. At the beginning of Phase 3 time, students know exactly what they are supposed to do, and they begin working with little hesitation. According to Mrs. Patrick, having an extended time period enables students more time for getting the creative juices flowing and working on projects and less time spent on management of materials. After administering the "Interest-a-Lyzer" online using Renzulli Learning, Mrs. Patrick discovered that half of her students had interests in performing arts. Initially, she suggested that the students might be interested in the production of a class play, a suggestion that was greeted with both high levels of enthusiasm and outstanding results. One pair of students began writing a series of scripts based on books they had read during Phase 2, while a group of three students decided to use their talents and interests in creating set designs and learning about how professionals build props. Another group was interested in acting out the parts created in the student-written scripts. From this group, one student with strong leadership skills emerged as a director of the plays, while another group of students began designing playbills and advertisements for the productions.

Although the play eventually involved most of the class, some students demonstrated very different interests and their Phase 3 activities reflected this. One group of three students decided to create a project that highlighted the use of simple machines in everyday objects, while another group of four students scoured the Renzulli Learning websites for information and projects on topics ranging from starting a business to Mars exploration. Mrs. Patrick structured the classroom environment of Phase 3 to support the individual choices each of her students. This was accomplished by the use of learning management plans. This ensured that the students were aware of their tasks and timelines. The classroom was arranged to allow for multiple groups of students to simultaneously work together. To facilitate the management of group materials, each group also had their own stackable container

A Fifth-grade Phase 3 Implementation of 20 Minutes Each Day

After easing students into the SEM-R routine during the first two months of school, Mr. McMillian has since begun each hour of SEM-R with a ten-minute Book Hook that exposes his students to two carefully selected books. Then his boisterous fifth grade class reads for 30-35 minutes each day in Phase 2, and he usually reserves 20 minutes each day for Phase 3 Activities. At the conclusion of Phase 2, Mr. McMillian announces that it is time for students to wrap up their Supported Independent Reading (SIR) time. Every day Mr. McMillian quickly reviews the menu of choices, and each Phase 3 time begins with a proclamation that each student should "Go and do what makes you special!" With these words, students move with purpose and enthusiasm to their activity of choice.

When students are unable to put down their SIR books in Mr. McMillian's classroom, they are encouraged to simply continue reading during Phase 3. The four computers in the classroom are quickly occupied by students who want to continue their online independent projects using Renzulli Learning. In another corner, a group of four students have invested their time into playing a Stock Market game, and they use the remaining computer station to track the way their stocks have been performing.

In another part of the classroom, another group of students has gathered in the art center to continue designing board games based on their favorite books. Close by, a trio of students is playing a game that the group has previously created based on their favorite novel, *Eragon*. Finally, a group of five students are rehearsing a commercial they have written encouraging students to read more non-fiction. This commercial will be filmed for the library.

As students work on their chosen activities, Mr. McMillian circulates throughout the classroom to provide guidance and encouragement. Not only does Mr. McMillian answer questions, but he also asks students probing questions that extend their thinking skills, further developing their metacognitive strategies.

GETTING STARTED WITH PHASE 3

As mentioned previously, in the beginning of the SEM-R implementation, you may want to offer fewer choices during the start of Phase 3 and then expand the choices over time. Starting with a smaller number of choices will help students learn some of the skills (such as creativity training) that will be embedded into subsequent activities. This transition time should still enable students to make choices about activities, taking into consideration learning styles and interests. Some students may be able and willing to work independently for long periods of time, while others may not be ready to handle an unlimited number of choices, particularly if they have little experience with choosing work to do in school. For a successful implementation of Phase 3, in the beginning give specific choices of both group and individual activities and work up to a full-scale implementation with a choice of a broad menu of options. Many teachers have successfully introduced the process over a period of four to six weeks. The following timeline in Table 4.1 illustrates how this method of implementing Phase 3 might be organized.

Table 4.1. Timeline of Phase 3 Activities

	Duration	Activity	Instruction
Week 1	15-20 minutes per day	• Interest Assessment (Appendix B) • Self-Regulation Skill Lesson (Chapter Three)	Whole class participation and instruction
Week 2	10-15 minutes per day	• Creativity Training Activities	Whole class training, with follow-up free choice from three independent creativity exercises
Week 2-3	15-20 minutes per day	• Introduction to Interest Centers (Students rotate through each of three centers)	Teacher assigns and organizes small groups of students to ensure that each student explores all interest centers
Week 3-4	15-20 minutes per day	• Interest Centers • Creativity Activities • Computer Training (3-5 different choices each day)	Teacher directs students to sign up for one of the following choices: • Independent Reading • Art Interest Center • Poetry Interest Center • Animals in Literature Interest Center • Creativity Activities • Renzulli Learning
Week 5-6	15-20 minutes per day or 1 day per week	• Training on How to Develop Independent Activities • Free Choice of a Menu of Options	Students are guided to work independently or in small groups. Choices include: • Independent Reading • Audio Books • Buddy Reading • Poetry Interest Center • Animals in Literature • Interest Center • Renzulli Learning • Independent or Small Group Projects

A Continuum of Services

Students vary in abilities and interests, as well as levels of self-regulated behavior; necessitating a continuum of services (from very independent to very structured) for students. This continuum can range from simply allowing students to continue with their Phase 2 independent reading and listening to audio books, all the way to providing students with time to conduct independent investigations. In much the same way that a restaurant

Table 4.2. Phase 3 Menu Choices.

Phase 3 Menu Use for 15 minutes daily, or 1 period a week.		
Student Free-choice Activities	• Continued Independent Reading	Increasing Student Independence
	• Audio Books	
	• Buddy Reading	
	• Literature Circles or Novel Discussion Groups	
Teacher Directed Activities	• Creativity Activities	
Activities to Move Students toward Independence	• Investigation Centers • Independent Investigations • SEM-Xplorations • Renzulli Learning	

offers a menu of choices, the ideal SEM-R classroom will offer a menu of activities from which students can make selections. No one activity will satisfy all of your students' tastes. Moreover, while students may want to try particular menu items, it is unlikely they will be satisfied if they have to choose the same menu item day after day. At some point, they will want and will also enjoy some variety in their intellectual diet. You, as the academic chef, will want to prepare a collection of rich and inviting options for your students and establish a balance between standard menu choices and special Phase 3 opportunities.

What follows are some of the titles and descriptors of some of the most popular and successful Phase 3 options. This is not, by any means, an exhaustive list, and you should use your own creativity to develop and expand your own classroom menu (see Table 4.2).

STUDENT FREE-CHOICE ACTIVITIES

Continuing to Read

An easy choice to implement in your classroom is allowing students to continue their Phase 2 reading. Frequently, students can become engrossed in their SIR books and the thought of stopping troubles them; therefore, this choice should be included as part of Phase 3. Although many talented readers will be satisfied if they are able to continue reading a book that is both challenging and interesting to them, not all students will be able to maintain focused reading, making other options necessary as well. You should encourage all readers, at some point, to investigate topics of interest and extend their reading in varied ways. This allows them to see connections between reading and creative productivity.

Audio Books

In addition to serving as an effective scaffolding tool for struggling readers in Phase 2, audio books can provide an opportunity for students to listen as literature comes alive. Many of the more popular book choices for children are available in both unabridged and abridged audio versions. Teachers can encourage students to read along in the book as they listen or they can allow students to listen to a segment or chapter of the book as a pre-reading activity. In either case, listening to fluent reading and new vocabulary serve as both a scaffold and motivation which will further enjoyment of reading.

Portable CD players have become quite inexpensive and students may choose to listen independently or as part of a small group with the use of an auxiliary headphone jack. These small adapters are available from any consumer electronics store, and multiple headphones can be plugged into a single headphone jack to enable several students to simultaneously listen to the same book. To investigate affordable sources of audio and print materials, check with your school media specialist and local public librarian—you may be surprised at what you discover.

Buddy Reading

Many students want to share their reading experiences with their friends. A simple and effective option for Phase 3 is Buddy Reading. Rather than being assigned, students often choose to read a book aloud together. In fact, during one implementation of the SEM-R, two students spent the day reading a book to each other over the telephone on a day when the school was closed due to weather. While it may not be common, this strategy may serve as an excellent outlet for more social students and as a way to maintain a sense of purpose and order about reading in the classroom. We do suggest, however, that you try to help students select partners who have similar reading levels for buddy reading. For example, it has created conflict for some struggling readers to be paired with very talented readers, as the struggling readers have explained that they feel both embarrassment and angst in these situations. Therefore, some teacher guidance is needed for matching students that work well for buddy reading.

Literature Circles

Literature Circles also provide an opportunity for students to discuss either a book that they have read in the past or that they are currently reading. Initially, you may want to provide structure by offering a series of open-ended questions for students to discuss during their literature circles. There are many good books and articles that explain how literature circles should work in classrooms, but all seem to agree that they include the following characteristics:

+ students choose their own books
+ groups are temporary and based on the choice of book
+ different books are read by each group
+ students use written notes to guide their discussion on a regular basis
+ students choose their own discussion topics
+ conversation is open and natural and includes open-ended questions
+ students assume different roles over different days

A literature circle is created to develop an open conversation among students about a commonly read book. During literature circles, one student usually assumes the leadership position in the group. Other group members are assigned different roles with accompanying prompts that are used to enable each student in the group to respond to questions about the book. Everyone in the group then responds to questions raised by the other students leading to meaningful conversations. After this discussion, group members decide how much reading will be accomplished before the next meeting. Students in the group may write a response to the book discussion in their journals at the conclusion of the meeting.

The SEM-R Bookmarks can also serve as questions for discussion among a small group of students. As your students become more accustomed to conferences during Phase 2, literature circles will increase in complexity. Teachers can access more information about literature circles from the SEM-R website.

TEACHER DIRECTED ACTIVITIES

Creativity Activities

Creativity training activities can be used during the first few weeks implementing Phase 3, to provide teacher-directed activities that encourage students to expand their thinking and develop innovative ideas. The benefit of creativity training is two-fold. Students will develop skills that will help them explore new literary ideas. At the same time, teachers gradually create less structured opportunities in which students practice the problem-solving and self-regulation skills needed for a successful implementation of Phase 3. As students become more comfortable with independent work, the creativity activities will become one of the options available to students.

There is an introductory creativity training lesson in Appendix F for your classroom use. Additional creativity lessons can be found in the *New Directions in Creativity* Package (Marks A-3). (Renzulli, Callahan, Smith, Renzulli, & Ford, 2000). Above all, you should use your own creativity to modify these kinds of activities and lessons to meet the needs and to encourage the interests of your students. During these training exercises, establish guidelines for your students that will create an open, supportive, and non-judgmental environment. Additional activities are available at Renzulli Learning in the Creativity Activities section.

INDEPENDENT STUDENT ACTIVITIES

Investigation Centers

As students become more comfortable with working independently, Phase 3 activities can be expanded to involve more self-directed explorations. One possible way to ease the transition is through the use of classroom investigation centers. Investigation centers are an instructional component of the SEM-R designed to develop and create interest and enthusiasm about a particular topic or theme. The goal is to engage students actively in reading, thinking, and researching. Books, magazines, newspapers, computer technology, and specific exploratory activities can be included as part of a thematic collection of reading investigations designed for your students. Investigation centers can be as simple as a collection of high-interest, non-fiction materials based on student responses on the Reading Interest-a-Lyzer, or a space in the room devoted to accommodate audio equipment and a selection of audio books. Students' interests should be a driving force when creating investigation centers. For more information on creating investigation centers, see *Developing the Gifts and Talents of All Students in the Regular Classroom* (Beecher, 1995).

Independent Investigations

One goal of Phase 3 is to promote independence in students as they develop their interests. Ultimately, you want your students to progress to where they are conducting their own independent investigations. Rather than assigning a topic or project, you should encourage students to develop their own questions and goals. A step-by-step process can help you to teach students how to produce quality enrichment projects. This process, which has been applied in classroom and resource room settings, has evolved over several decades and countless activities. Two comments should be made on the steps themselves:

1) these steps do not have to be followed in the order given, and 2) some steps can be eliminated if students can accomplish the learning objectives in other ways.

Guiding Students Through Independent or Small Group Study

1. **Help students identify interests and connections to possible explorations.** Interest often drives effort; therefore, students should be encouraged to select topics in which they have an intense interest and investment. Book Hooks in Phase 1 and individual conferences during Phase 2 are an ideal time for teachers to help students uncover the connections between the content and form of the literature they are enjoying to create possible extension explorations during Phase 3.

2. **Help students with problem finding and focusing.** Consider what happens when you type in the term "Science" into an Internet search engine—you are faced with thousands of pages of pertinent information trough which to sift and locate useful details. However, if you used the same search engine to research "genetic engineering and biodiversity," the resulting Internet resources would be more relevant because you had focused your search to a more manageable collection of knowledge. This skill of winnowing down resources and ideas is essential to independent explorations. Nevertheless, most students have difficulty moving from a broad interest area to a specific one. One way to help young learners focus general historical, mathematical, musical, or athletic interests may be to translate their interests into a question or questions to research.

   Brainstorming a list of potential research questions will also encourage students to identify specific investigation topics. You can help students find "how-to" books to examine the methodology employed in specific fields of study. For instance, students who want to ask the right questions about problems in anthropology must start by looking at how anthropologists work and what kinds of questions they investigate.

3. **Make a plan.** Once students have brainstormed a question, they will need a plan to assist them in locating needed resources, identifying important tasks, and managing time. This plan should not be set in stone. Like assessing the "book match" in Phase 2, it needs to be revisited regularly so that scaffolding can be provided and modifications can be made to ensure student success. Many teachers have found success in using a learning contract, journal, or log.

An Example: Investigating Art

Begin by assembling a variety of resources to spark the curiosity of your students. Organize the materials so that students can easily peruse the resources and ponder. An art interest center might include the following:

Books

Biographies of famous artists such as Picasso, Van Gogh, Degas, and Frida Kahlo (see *Getting to Know the World's Greatest Artist* series by Mike Venezia)

Art Fraud Detective: Spot the Difference, Solve the Crime by Anna Nilsen

The Great Art Scandal: Solve the Crime, Save the Show! By Anna Nilsen

Who Can Open Michelangelo's Seven Seals? by Thomas Brezina and Laurence Sartin

Who Can Save Vincent's Hidden Treasure? by Thomas Brezina and Laurence Sartin

From the Mixed-Up Files of Mrs. Basil E. Frankweiler by E. L. Konisburg

A collection of art history reference books borrowed from the art teacher

How-to books

Discovering Great Artists: Hands-on Projects for Children in the Style of the Great Masters by MaryAnn Kohl, Kim Solga, and Rebecca Van Slyke

Introduction to Art Techniques by Ray Smith, Ray Wright, James Horton, Michael Wright and Royal Academy of Arts (Great Britain)

Career Ideas for Kids Who Like Art by Diane Lindsey Reeves

Looking at Art by Laurie Schneider Adams

Websites

National Gallery of Art for Kids http://www.nga.gov/kids/kids.htm
Take this virtual tour and learn all about different paintings located in the National Gallery of Art in Washington D.C.! Just click on any painting to begin, and see close-ups of many famous works of art housed in the museum, along with a description and history. You can also try the Art Zone, which lets you make interactive art online!

Museum of Modern Art: Destination Modern Art http://www.moma.org/destination/
Join a friendly space-alien in a journey to Earth to learn about modern art! On this website, you will guide the little alien as you both walk through the museum. As you look at each piece of art, you can use your senses to see the art, hear what the art may sound like, and use your hands to create your own art.

From Cave Art to Your Art http://www.sanford-artedventures.com/play/caveart/index.htm
This site is for those of you who like to create interactive art projects. Check out instructional videos about different art techniques. You can choose the ones your find most interesting or influential in your artistic life, add music, and a title page and then create your own informational video timeline of how art has evolved and how this has affected you as an artist.

The Louvre Museum http://www.louvre.fr/llv/musee/visite_virtuelle.jsp?bmLocale=en
Take a virtual tour of one of the greatest art museums in the world, the Louvre. Online exhibitions include Egyptian Antiquities, Greek, Etruscan, and Roman Art, Islamic Art, Sculptures, Paintings, and much more! Choose a tour from the list on the left of the screen to start.

4. **Work with students to locate resources and organize information.** Your students may not believe it, but there is a wealth of information and ideas beyond encyclopedias and Internet search engines. As you help students identify the many other available sources of information, you may also need to explain possible investigation techniques and the importance of keeping track of resources to avoid plagiarism. Remember librarians and media specialists can help steer students to sources beyond encyclopedic references and of varying degree of difficulty. Also encourage students to explore sources beyond encyclopedias and websites, to include atlases, letters, surveys, films, periodicals, and personal interviews can all serve as helpful sources of information.

5. **Identify final products and audiences.** A sense of audience is integral to students' concern for quality and commitment to their tasks. Students' attitude and attention to detail change when they know that their writing may be published in a children's magazine rather than simply remaining within the confines of the classroom. With that in mind, teachers should guide students in their identification of possible audiences and outlets for their independent explorations. Students should be aware that a job well done can bring more than individual expression and personal satisfaction; it benefits others by changing how they think or feel, or enhancing the quality of life in other, more tangible ways.

6. **Offer encouragement, praise, and constructive criticism.** Almost every student project can be improved through revision, rewriting, or closer attention to detail. When you convey this to students, be sensitive, as they should feel that the teacher's greatest concern is helping them achieve excellence, and understand that constructive feedback is vital to the process.

7. **Escalate the process.** Some students resort to simple or unimaginative research methods because they have not explored or experienced more advanced ones. You should assist students in phrasing their questions, designing research, gathering and analyzing data in an unbiased way, drawing conclusions, and communicating their results.

8. **Evaluate.** We discourage the formal grading of independent projects, since no letter grade, number, or percentage can accurately reflect the knowledge, creativity, and commitment students develop during an independent investigation. Nonetheless, evaluation and feedback do promote growth and should be used. The ideal process actively involves students and familiarizes them with the evaluative procedures. To

help students appraise their own work, we suggest a short questionnaire, such as the one below:

+ How did you feel about working on the project?
+ What did you learn through your study?
+ Were you satisfied with the final product? In what ways?
+ How were you helped with your project?
+ Do you think you might like to undertake another project in the future? Do you have any ideas what that project would be like?

SEM-Xplorations

Designed as a guide for students' exploration of a topic of interest, SEM-Xplorations provide a map for independent and small group investigations. These activities cover a wide range of topics from Building Bridges to Weather Forecasting. Each of these self-contained units encourages students to investigate a variety of resources. The units begin with a brief overview of the unit designed to pique student curiosity. In the "Charting Your Course" section, background knowledge is reinforced and resources for further information are presented. After developing their background knowledge, students are ready for the "Exploration" stage. In this section, SEM-Xplorations present a variety of short and long-term projects for the students to consider and create. Each unit focuses on helping students create something meaningful and putting their knowledge to work. While the students are creating a product, they consider how and why they will share it with a "real-world" audience. Each SEM-X project concludes with a "Treasure Chest of Tools" that features a list of books and Internet sites to help students locate resources that may prove helpful for their explorations. An example of a SEM-Xploration can be found in Appendix G. All of the SEM-Xploration projects have been loaded onto Renzulli Learning and are easily accessible.

Renzulli Learning

Renzulli Learning (www.renzullilearning.com) is an electronic search-engine and profiler that matches students' perceived interests, abilities, learning styles, and expression styles to thousands of enrichment activities. Renzulli Learning (RL) is based on The Enrichment Triad Model (Renzulli, 1977) and the Schoolwide Enrichment Model (SEM) developed by Renzulli and Reis (1985, 1997), representing over 30 years of research conducted at the University of Connecticut's Neag School of Education. In its original paper-based format, the SEM instruments that are now a part of Renzulli Learning have been field tested for over 20 years in thousands of schools. Currently, RL is being used in over 1,200 schools across 43 states.

Many teachers who have used the SEM-R have used Renzulli Learning (RL) as a part of their implementation. Renzulli Learning is an interactive online program that matches student interests, learning styles, and expression preferences with a vast array of educational activities and resources designed to enrich students' learning process. When using SEM-R, students were provided with RL, giving them opportunities to explore, discover, learn, and create using the most current technology resources in a safe environment. Many students spend hours reading independently on the Internet while using Renzulli Learning on a weekly basis, and new research indicates that the use of this online system can increase reading fluency and reading comprehension (Field, 2007).

Renzulli Learning uses a three-step procedure to identify talents and interests and promote advanced level thinking skills, motivation, creativity, and engagement in learning. Step One in RL consists of a computer-based diagnostic assessment that creates a profile of each student's academic strengths, interests, learning styles, and preferred modes of expression. The online assessment which takes about 30 minutes for most students to complete, results in a personalized profile that highlights individual student strengths and sets the stage for Step Two. Student profiles can also be used to form groups of students who share common interests.

The student profile acts like a compass for the second step, in which a search engine examines thousands of resources that relate specifically to each student's interests, learning styles, and product choices. These resources are grouped into fourteen various enrichment categories, including: virtual field trips; real field trips; creativity training activities; training in critical thinking; independent study; contest and competitions; interactive web sites; fiction books; non-fiction books; how-to books for conducting research; summer programs; research; videos and DVDs; as well as online activities. All websites are carefully selected and screened and matched to students' highest areas of interest, learning styles, and product styles, providing personalized and differentiated learning opportunities.

These resources are not merely intended to inform students about new information or to occupy them in spending time surfing the web. Rather, they are used as vehicles for helping students find and focus a problem or creative exploration of personal interest that they might like to pursue in greater depth. Many of the resources provide the methods of inquiry, advanced level thinking and creative problem solving skills, and investigative approaches. The resources also provide students with suggestions for outlets and audiences for their creative products. The resources available in Step Two also provide students with places where they can pursue advanced training in their strength areas and areas of personal interest.

Step Three in Renzulli Learning is an automatic compilation and storage of all student activity into an on-going student record called the Total Talent Portfolio. Teachers and parents can access the portfolio at any time allowing them to view student work and provide guidance to individual students. This feature also provides parents with information about students' work and opportunities for parental involvement. In this step, students can also pursue a variety of projects, using the Wizard Project Maker. Renzulli Learning includes dozens of previously written high-interest projects as well as opportunities to select and develop their own project ideas.

The Renzulli Learning Wizard Project Maker is designed to help students explore their interests and passions with varying levels of support. Students who are ready for independent study can create their own Wizard Projects, while those who need more support can start with a more structured Super Starter Projects. Using one of these two options, students can complete an interest-based project, using the steps outlined in both this chapter and in Renzulli Learning.

QUALITY INDICATIONS OF PHASE 3

Throughout the development and study of SEM-R, Phase 3 has evolved based on teacher, classroom, and students' varying needs and differences. While Phase 3 is focused on student choice and interests, there are common characteristics of highly effective interventions that have been observed in multiple classrooms. This list of characteristics is intended to serve as a benchmark of successful implementation of Phase 3. Developing a quality Phase 3 implementation is a process that takes time. By introducing the process gradually, the students will be able to make a natural transition. Creating a structure and organization for the phase by clearly communicating expectations to students is critical to success. A highly effective Phase 3 intervention includes the following:

+ Most students start to work without any reminders beyond the initial directions.
+ The activity choices offered include open-ended options and complexity to extend the challenge of previous phases.
+ The activity choices offered demonstrate responsiveness to specific student interests and varied expression styles in product development.
+ The teacher provides verbal guidance and/or environmental reminders of self-regulation strategies for activities (e.g., verbal reminders at start of Phase 3, self-

regulation strategies posted in classroom); and all students self-regulate their behavior throughout Phase 3.

- Most students demonstrate visible enthusiasm and task commitment for their chosen activity in Phase 3. The teacher enhances Phase 3 activities through existing physical organization and ease of student access to resources.

CHAPTER 5

INTEGRATING READING STRATEGY INSTRUCTION IN THE SEM-R

ELIZABETH A. FOGARTY, REBECCA D. ECKERT, & SALLY M. REIS

At first glance, one might get the wrong idea about the SEM-R. After reading about Book Hooks, individualized conferences, and exciting Phase 3 choices, one might mistakenly believe that the SEM-R was designed only to make reading a more pleasurable experience, rather than a learning experience grounded in research-based reading practices. The more experienced reading teacher, however, will have detected the inclusion of research-based reading methodologies that accompany the enrichment pedagogy and research and are embedded in all three phases of the SEM-R. In this chapter, we include an explanation of the reading strategies that are incorporated into the SEM-R, as well as explanations about how they can be integrated.

Reading strategies are used by students to integrate higher-order thinking skills such as questioning, making inferences, making connections, understanding one's own thinking processes, visualizing, determining importance, and synthesizing in order to make meaning of text. In our work with teachers we are often asked about the differences between reading skills and reading strategies. Teaching certain reading skills, like word-level decoding can be a pretty straightforward task for reading teachers because the skills are easily measurable; we can give a child a reading passage and determine how well he or she decodes. We can also teach students a set of vocabulary words, and then administer a quiz to determine how much they learned. The difficulty with teaching reading strategies, however, is that they are not clearly measurable and teachers must determine the extent to which students are able to use them in context.

In discussing comprehension Kintsch and Kintsch (2005) remind us that there are three separate and hierarchical levels in the process of reading comprehension. The first level called the decoding level is the process of the printed word transferring to meaning in the minds of readers. This process is different from the word-level decoding in which readers assemble letters into words and sentences. At the decoding level of comprehension, readers replace decoded words with meaning. The next level, a slightly deeper level of comprehension involves the blending of both literal and inferential levels of the text to be able to attend to the most important details of the text. These details are not necessarily those that involve direct recall of small details of the text. The important details usually include the bigger ideas that contribute to theme and author's message thus enabling the reader to have a whole-picture view of the reading. The final level of comprehension is the creation of the situation model when the reader's prior experiences and knowledge interact with the text. This includes the incorporation of the reader's emotions and visuals regarding the text as well. Reading comprehension should be defined, in the highest sense, as the complex integration of reader with text.

Several reading and literacy researchers have identified and defined reading strategies (Table 5.1) and as is suggested in this table, much agreement exists in the field of reading instruction about a common set of reading strategies, providing our rationale for their inclusion in the SEM-R. These reading strategies are embedded in both Phase 1 and Phase 2 of the SEM-R, and as teachers begin to plan and develop Book Hooks for classrooms, we hope that they consider how some of the following strategies can be used to enhance student enjoyment and understanding of the books introduced to students. The strategies can also be embedded within some activities that students pursue in Phase 3 activities, depending upon their choices and interests.

Table 5.1. Connecting Reading Strategies with the SEM-R

Paris' Strategies (Adapted from Paris, 2004)	Mosaic of Thought Strategies (Keene & Zimmerman, 1997)	Strategies that Work (Harvey & Goudvis, 2000)
Making Connections	Making Connections	Making Connections
Determining Importance	Determining Importance	Determining Importance
Questioning	Questioning	Questioning
Visualizing	Visualizing/Sensory Images	Visualizing & Inferring
Making Inferences	Making Inferences	
Summarizing	Synthesizing	Synthesizing
Metacognition		

READING STRATEGIES

We define any instruction that a teacher provides to connect a reader with a text for improved understanding to be a reading strategy. The following definitions of some of the strategies described in this chapter are included as a way to guide your thinking about how you can include these strategies in the SEM-R.

Making Connections

A reading strategy commonly suggested by reading researchers asks students to make connections so that they can more actively apply their own background knowledge and experiences to what they are reading. Asking students to make connections allows them to have some scaffolding toward a deeper understanding of the texts they read. Three types of connections allow students to relate their reading to their prior experiences. These include text-to-self (T-S), text-to-text (T-T) and text-to-world (T-W) connections.

Text-to-Self Connections (T-S)

By asking children to consider how the book they are reading may connect or relate to their own lives, we are asking them to use active reading strategies that compare and contrast their life experiences with the characters or situations in the book. They may also consider what they might do or what they would have done if they faced circumstance similar to those of the characters. This strategy helps struggling readers attend to the story by giving them a familiar context in which to think about the events. Advanced readers also benefit from making these connections as they are involved in more challenging literature.

A teacher may use a question such as *"In what way does this story relate to your own life?"* to begin a conference with a struggling reader. The conference might look like this:

> **Teacher:** *Good morning, Josh! I see that you're reading* Hoot. *How is the book going so far?*
>
> **Josh:** *It's going pretty well and I really like the story because the characters are always having adventures.*
>
> **Teacher:** *Really? Are any of the adventures that the characters have had similar to those you've had in your own life?*
>
> **Josh:** *(Student thinks) Well, the characters in the book are trying to stop a company from killing a bunch of owls, so they're doing all kinds of things to get them to stop the project. One of the things that they did was to put alligators in the porta-potties!*
>
> **Teacher:** *Wow! That would be a really big surprise. It sounds like they're trying to do a good thing by protecting some animals. Have you ever tried to protect something?*

Josh: Sometimes I have to protect my little sister on the bus. Sometimes she gets picked on by one of the other kids, so I have to think of ways to outsmart the bullies. That's a lot like what happened to Roy, the main character in the book. He was new and was constantly getting picked on by this bully and he had to stick up to him and also find lots of ways to outsmart him.

Teacher: It sounds like you and Roy have some things in common. Let's hear you read a page today. (Student reads and conference continues).

In this exchange, the teacher tried to get Josh to compare the actions of the characters to his own actions, perhaps as a way to understand the characters' motivations for doing what they do. If Josh could relate to the act of protection, he might better understand why the characters in the story were interested in saving the endangered owls.

Text-to-Text Connections (T-T)

A second aspect of the making connections strategy involves text to text connections (T-T). A text-to-text connection occurs when a reader makes a connection between two texts, defined as anything that is written (e.g., a book, a webpage, a poem, or a song). The goal is for students to begin to automatically integrate texts they have already read into their backgrounds as they compare them with the book they are currently reading. This action of comparing and contrasting enables students to ask themselves if there are similar characters, plots, settings or themes. Perhaps one event or one character in a book they are reading will remind them of an earlier book they have enjoyed, and a question such as *"How is this book similar to the last one you read?"* will enable them to read, reflect, and compare.

A reading standard common in many state curricula is for readers to be able to compare and contrast different works. The ability to make text to text connections enables readers to discuss the ideas among literary works, including poetry, prose and non-fiction pieces. Teachers might begin a conference by asking the student how their current book is similar to or different from the last book they read. They might also ask the student to comment on how their current book differs from other books by the same author. These questions should involve sophisticated levels of thinking far in a much more abstract manner than when using a Venn diagram to ask students to compare the characters or other surface level facets of the two texts. Teacher can use open-ended exploration of text to push their students' thinking to higher levels.

Text-to-World Connections (T-W)

A text to world connection occurs when the reader makes a connection between the text and something that either has previously happened, is happening currently, or that may happen in the future. Of the three making connections strategies, this may be the most complex because it requires students to have a rich understanding of the world around them in order to make sophisticated connections. For instance, a child reading a book about climate change and pollution may begin to consider how their own actions and conservation efforts could effect the environment now and years from now.

The amount of prior knowledge required to answer the question, *"How might your parents or friends react to living in the story setting?"* will vary based on the content of the text. When reading the book *The Watson's Go To Birmingham-1963* by Christopher Paul Curtis for instance, the students must be familiar with historical references surrounding the civil rights movement and the controversy that it brought. Many people, both culturally diverse and others, would prefer not to live in this tumultuous time in history. Alternately, students may be able to make judgments on the preferences of their friends or family based on what they know about the setting's features, rather than its historical significance. For instance, a boy reading the book *Anne of Green Gables* by L. M. Montgomery, which is set in the peaceful Canadian countryside may be able to deduce without ever having traveled to Prince Edward Island that his mother would love to live in the setting of the story since she enjoys the family's yearly vacation to a country cottage. He might make this determination based on knowledge of current events and the fact that Canada is a very peaceful place to live for Americans since we are allies.

Each of these connecting strategies enables children to use more active cognitive approaches to reading. Students, thus, transition from a passive mode of reading to thinking about what they are reading and using reading to learn, consider, reflect, and compare. In all three types of connecting strategies, the reader has applies his or her past experiences and knowledge in order to better understand and relate to the text.

Determining Importance

When asked to determine importance, students must evaluate material to decide which parts of a book or story are most meaningful or valuable in their understanding of the text. In doing this, students must consider their own interpretation of the text and their own belief about what are the most essential parts of the plot, setting, and/or characterization. Moreover, discussions about individual determinations of important aspects of a book help students understand that their own judgments are taken into consideration when they respond to questions.

> Example: *What were some of the most important parts in the story? Why?*

Teachers have long asked students to identify themes and main ideas of stories. Some talented and struggling readers, however, never have the opportunity to understand the importance of being able to determine the theme because the discussion stops once the theme is revealed. But the conversation must continue into why an author chose a particular theme. Students should also be able to relate the big ideas that an author is expressing to their own life.

Questioning

Self-questioning is when readers ask themselves questions about the text that they are reading. This may occur either while reading or at the conclusion of reading the book. In many adult books currently on the market, a readers' workshop or book club series of questions can be found at the conclusion of the book. Often, these questions help readers reflect on ideas that may not have occurred to them. Questioning strategies enable readers to consider one aspect of a book, such as setting or characterization, or there may be an overarching question that requires a synthesis of the entire book. The SEM-R Bookmarks can be used to encourage students to question what they are reading, enabling them to interact with the text, focusing on what they are curious about and what they want to learn and know. The use of sticky notes and/or reading journals may also encourage the reflective practice of self-questioning.

> Example: *What is one big question you still have after reading this book?*

In a study of the SEM-R that included over 80 hours of observation in reading classrooms across grades 3-7, the self-questioning strategy was used least often (Fogarty, 2006). Teachers in both SEM-R and regular classrooms rarely asked students to identify questions that they had while they read, or after they read. Most teachers probably believe that their students do this subconsciously, as practiced by most good readers. However, it is important to understand that struggling readers often suppress questioning as they read, believing that it will get in the way of their understanding of the text. Good readers know the opposite to be true and actively seek answers to the questions that come up as they read, but rarely have the opportunity to discuss these questions.

Often, however, books that are not sufficiently challenging for the reader will not cause him or her to develop questions during reading. Low-level texts with controlled vocabulary, for instance, may also require limited higher-order thinking to understand the text, thus requiring readers to ask themselves few questions. When talented readers read unchallenging books, they will, likewise, not develop and answer questions during reading. Either way, unchallenging text is less likely to promote the use of strategic reading that we hope to develop in students.

Visualizing

Visualizing involves making pictures in one's mind of what has happened in a scene or story that is read or heard. Many students, for example, visualize characters in their reading. One very precocious and talented reader explained that she did not want to see the Harry Potter movies because she had her own visualizations about the setting and the characters in the novel that she did not want to replace with the images selected by those who directed or produced the movie. Visualizing strategies are important to help students remember and understand important details or concepts in both fiction and non-fiction texts, thereby increasing comprehension.

Example: Which scene would you most like to illustrate? Why?

This strategy may be a difficult to teach children at first since it will require teachers to demonstrate this by making their own thinking transparent. During Book Hooks, you will need to model how you visualize the characters and scene based on the language of the text. This process helps students to make a mental running movie of the story that they are reading in order to better understand the book. A particularly effective way to do this is to listen to students read a section in which the author provides a thick description of a character, a scene, or an event. After reading, the teacher describes what he or she saw in his or her mind as the student read. After modeling this several times, ask the teacher can ask the students for their own descriptions. The students should also identify the part of the text that painted the picture for them.

Ms. Thomas, a fourth grade teacher, wanted her students to better use the visualization strategy. She began each Book Hook for one week by reading them excerpts of novels that provided thick, rich character descriptions and asked her students to visualize as she read. One day she read the following excerpt from *The Birchbark House* by Louise Erdrich:

> *"She was named Omakays, or Little Frog, because her first step was a hop. She grew into a nimble young girl of seven winters, a thoughtful girl with shining brown eyes and a wide grin, only missing her two top front teeth. She touched her upper lip. She still wasn't used to those teeth gone, and was impatiently waiting for new, grown-up teeth to complete her smile." (p. 5)*

She then asked the students to describe what they saw and all of the students were able to tell her that the girl in the description was small, healthy, and probably brown-haired. They were able to speculate about her clothing, as well as her heritage from just a short passage and their own visual image of the story.

Making Inferences

Inferences occur when a reader concludes something or gets an idea from reading that is not directly stated in the text. Good readers are able to make inferences about why events occur and why characters act in certain ways based on their knowledge of the supporting text. Students who read at higher levels and can be challenged to make inferences by using questions such as the one below:

> Example: *Why do you think that the author placed the setting of the book in this location?*

Good readers are constantly piecing together details from the story in order to fill in gaps in the author's writing or to use clues to solve little mysteries that the author has created. Struggling readers, on the other hand, do this much less frequently. These students, instead, learn to ignore the gaps or do not see that there are gaps in the information. These readers need to be taught to attend to the gaps in order to fill in the meaning themselves. Likewise, when talented readers read books that are insufficiently challenging, they will exercise the strategy less often and may be unable to make inferences when later faced with challenging reading material.

Readers of all ability levels should be asked questions that require making inferences. Teachers can model this kind of thinking in Book Hooks during Phase 1, as illustrated by the following example from Mr. Ortiz's class:

Teacher: Good morning students! Today we're going to have the opportunity to meet a brand new character. Some of you may even choose to read more about him. I'm going to begin by reading a bit of the story to you and then asking if you can make some inferences based on what I've read. Remember that readers make inferences when they have some of the information, but not all of it. Readers make inferences in order to fill in the blanks. (Teacher proceeds to read a bit of the story aloud, then asks students to tell him what they can deduce about the main character in the story, Bud, Not Buddy *by Christopher Paul Curtis.)*

Mr. Ortiz realized the open-ended nature of making inferences. He provided them with an excerpt of the story and gave a very open-ended prompt to his class. The students were able to make inferences about Bud just from the short excerpt their teacher read. Effective reading teachers will also ask students to substantiate their inferences with information from the text. This is also an excellent way to check for student understanding when you have not had the opportunity to read the relevant text during a student conference. Asking students about their impressions of the details in the text that led them to make a particular inference or conclusion will help them to be able to anchor their thinking in the text, rather than making arbitrary guesses.

Synthesizing / Summarizing

Synthesizing and summarizing, though similar, are not the same. Summarizing is a process of reading through a good deal of information to describe or retell the details as a salient, understandable whole. To synthesize requires students to be able to summarize in order to contribute some new thought or idea to answer a question or solve a problem. Synthesis, for example, occurs when students are asked to briefly explain how a main character may have changed over the course of the book.

Example: Compare the main character's personality at the beginning of the story to his or her personality at the end.

Initially teachers may ask their students summary questions in order to assess their general understanding of the text. Once they have ascertained the students' general comprehension, however, they can ascend into the higher levels thinking skills. These questions require students to use their ability to summarize in order to create new thinking on a question or topic.

The example below illustrates a conference between an average ability reader and her teacher. The student has been reading the book *When Zachary Beaver Came to Town* by Kimberly Willis Holt, in which two boys befriend an overweight boy who is part of a traveling sideshow.

> **Teacher:** *Have you been enjoying your book, Shannon?*
>
> **Shannon:** *Yes, sometimes; although sometimes this book is hard to read because you feel so sorry for Zachary.*
>
> **Teacher:** *What about the main character? Let's talk about him. Do you think that the main character's personality has changed at all from the beginning of the story to the end?*
>
> **Shannon:** *Oh yes, he has definitely changed. In the beginning of the story, Toby wants to see Zachary and maybe even make fun of him just like everyone else. He is also willing to do anything to do it. Later in the story, he doesn't want to just look at Zachary, he wants to try to be friends with him. He also becomes upset when people just stare at him. I think that he's become a more sensitive person throughout the story.*

This excerpt from Shannon's conference demonstrates her ability to synthesize. Initially she had to be able to summarize the story to remember what was happening, but once she had summarized the plot of the story, she was more able to draw out information to synthesize new ideas.

Metacognition

Metacognition involves thinking about your own thinking to better understand how you learn. Enhancing metacognition during reading enables the readers to consider and pay attention to the processes they are using. Metacognition in reading also enables children to be able to analyze what works best for them in the use of specific reading skills and strategies, and to consider how they can improve their focus and develop better self-regulation when they read. Some researchers liken this to monitoring. We have developed Bookmarks that teachers can use to enable students to actively use these strategies during their Book Hooks and these are included in Appendix A. An example about how to actively use metacognition is below:

Example: Has any part of the book confused you?

For many of the students in the SEM-R project, the use of metacognition was the most important reading strategy because it was imperative that their teachers help them to develop the behaviors associated with reading so that they can begin to develop the fluency and comprehension aspects of reading. These students needed to learn to attend to their thinking in order to determine things that might be holding them back from reading fluently or comprehending the text. Teachers might need to begin this process by asking students what they are thinking about as they read. These students may not realize that they are daydreaming and not thinking about the text as they read. Many struggling readers are able to read with excellent fluency and can read for pages and pages without comprehending the text. These students are reading purely at the most basic level—word-level decoding. To begin to climb the levels of comprehension discussed earlier in this chapter, these readers must begin to translate the text into meaning. To do this, these readers must learn that good readers think about each word and sentence in the text and add them to the previous ones in order to construct meaning.

The SEM-R is an especially effective program for working with "word callers"—both struggling and talented readers who are able to decode without a strong foundation of comprehension to support the text. Struggling readers often do this because they may be overwhelmed with decoding text and cannot expend additional cognitive energy for comprehension. Talented readers may surprise their teachers with this behavior, but usually do it because decoding, and reading in general, has become easy and they are able to set their brains to automatic pilot and decode without thinking about what they are reading.

Word callers must be engaged in thinking frequently as they read in order to break them of this behavior. They must be constantly reminded through questions like, 'What did you like about the section you just read?' or 'What ideas did you find challenging in the last chapter?' that ask them to focus on the task at hand.

BOOK HOOKS: EMBEDDING READING STRATEGIES

As part of both Phase 1 and 2 in the SEM-R, we have created a series of Bookmarks with embedded reading skills and strategies that can be applied across many different books. These Bookmarks include specific questions that require students to use and apply skills and strategies. The questions are arranged by literary elements or genre with cards on setting, characters, theme, non-fiction, poetry, biography, etc. Each card contains four generic questions that can be used to begin a conversation or make an assessment on that child's knowledge of the particular element or genre. The Bookmark questions also are developed to integrate the reading strategies discussed in this chapter. Figure 5.1 below includes notations that illustrate how reading strategies have been embedded into all of the SEM-R bookmarks.

Some teachers may ask why we do not just create a set of Bookmark questions arranged by reading strategy. After acknowledging the fact that this might make things easier, we follow up with the fact that it would also be impossible because the strategies vary by book. For example, in one specific book, a question might require an inference. A question in one of the Bookmarks above asks, "Do you think the setting for this story was real or imaginary? Why?" In some books, this might be an inference and require the reader to piece together information from the story in order to make an inference. In another story, however, the author might have used a real location, which would no longer require the reader to make an inference.

For that reason, teachers must understand what it is that they are asking students. Students should learn to make inferences and connections because one or the other might be important at any given time. In order to use the SEM-R, teachers must become familiar with their students' reading skill and strategy use, and be able to incorporate any missing knowledge into either the Phase 1 Book Hook or the Phase 2 conference.

THE CASE FOR SELECTING CHALLENGING BOOKS IN PHASE 2

In our work with the SEM-R, we have often found that readers tend to choose books that are not especially challenging reading during SIR time. This trend is especially true

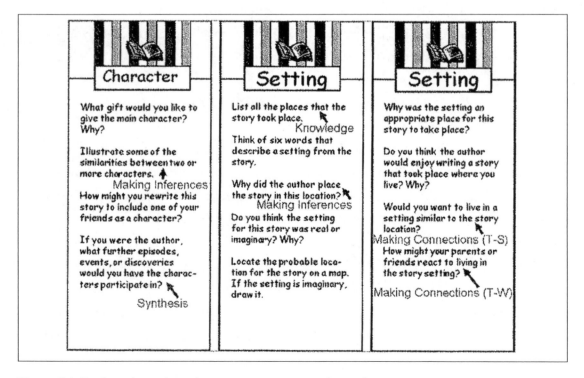

Figure 5.1. Bookmarks with reading strategies integrated into the questions.

among average achieving and above average readers who tend to choose something that looks appropriate as a grade level text, rather than something in a challenge range. Struggling readers are less often found to be using this behavior, as they tend to err on the side of too much challenge as they try to find books that appear to be similar to the books their peers are reading.

Regardless of achievement level, the problem is that many readers are not reading books that will challenge them at a rate that will help them to become better readers. When book choices are too easy, strategy use is not developed because students can comprehend without applying reading strategies. Easier and less complex texts do not require students to make as many inferences, or to develop questions as they interact with the text (Kintsch & Kintsch, 2005). A steady diet of books that are too easy will cause readers' strategy use to atrophy.

To promote increased comprehension in both fiction and non-fiction texts, teachers must provide adequately challenging reading material for students, as well as differentiated reading strategy instruction that supports each child in a more personalized manner. That is, not all of the students in the class will require the same types of strategy instruction at any given point. While some may struggle with determining importance, others may find it difficult to make connections between themselves and text. Teachers who have a strong understanding of the strategies discussed in this chapter will be better able to help their students' to these strategies to comprehend the challenging books in class, as well as in future reading endeavors.

CHAPTER 6

MANAGING THE SEM-R IN YOUR CLASSROOM: ORGANIZATIONAL STRATEGIES THAT WORK

SHEELAH M. SWEENY, REBECCA D. ECKERT,
& ELIZABETH A. FOGARTY

Similar to any other classroom endeavor, our experience has shown us that teachers who discover and develop their own comfortable system for organizing materials, structuring activities, and providing individualized support and guidance for students create a successful classroom environment for SEM-R. Many of the suggestions for implementing and using the SEM-R found were developed by classroom teachers searching for a practical solution to their own organizational dilemmas. Among the topics introduced are the creation of a classroom library and the ways in which you can organize your classroom to encourage enjoyment in reading. The management suggestions for each of the three phases have come from our most experienced SEM-R teachers. We want to remind you, however, that the SEM-R is designed to be flexible. We share these examples from elementary and middle schools to help you understand how some teachers have enhanced and modified this enrichment approach to reading according to the needs of their particular group of readers.

CREATING YOUR CLASSROOM LIBRARY

The creation of a classroom library is a very important facet of the implementation of the SEM-R. When teachers begin using the SEM-R, they often find that their students quickly outgrow a classroom library that was once sufficient when used as a supplement to a basal reading or guided reading program. However, a classroom library need not consist only of expensive book collections purchased out of pocket. A fabulous classroom library can be obtained through yard sale finds, trading books with another teacher, or by borrowing books from the school or public libraries. Especially when using the SEM-R, teachers may need to rethink their idea of the classroom library from a longstanding collection to something more fluid and able to change as the needs of readers change.

The composition of your classroom library that will be used to support SEM-R and other related reading activities should vary in genre, topic, text length, and reading level to meet the needs and interests of the students (Fountas & Pinnell, 2001). A library should include representation of different genres and a balance between fiction and nonfiction. When creating your classroom library, we suggest the inclusion of genres that will interest a vast array of readers. These genres include realistic fiction, historical fiction, biography, poetry, periodicals, graphic novels, informational text, and others.

Within each of these genres, we suggest that you also include some of the following to engage the majority of your students as well as to expose them to diverse and well-respected literature.

- Award winners (e.g., Newbery, Caldecott, Coretta Scott King, Pura Belpré, Robert Sibert, and Michael L. Printz awards)
- Classics (e.g., *Stone Soup*, *The Polar Express*, *Black Beauty*, *The Call of the Wild*)
- Picture books (e.g., *Amazing Grace*, *The True Story of the Three Little Pigs*, *Built to Last*, *Strega Nona*, *Art Fraud Detective*)
- Chapter books (e.g., *Anne of Green Gables*, *The BFG*, *Holes*, *Walk Two Moons*)
- Books in a Series (e.g., *Little House* books, the *Redwall* series, the *Eragon* series, *The Chronicles of Narnia*)
- Predictable and repetitive text (for students reading closer to a first or second grade level) (e.g., *Tikki Tikki Tembo*, *Why Mosquitoes Buzz in People's Ears*, *If You Give a Mouse a Cookie*)

As you select books for your classroom library, consider including books on social and cultural issues that will help to engage and involve all of your students. Children's engagement in literature grows when they discover books that contain characters and individuals with whom they can identify. Having access to books about people from a broad range of racial and ethnic backgrounds and with main characters of various ages and genders will enable you to, at times, match them with your students. Because of the independent nature of students' SEM-R reading behaviors, pay special attention to stereotypes in literature. Although we want to include classic books in our collections, we also want to avoid unguided student encounters with books that perpetuate hurtful or negative stereotypes or attitudes.

Often teachers encourage students to select books in which they can identify with or feel connected to the characters; however, skilled educators also recognize that engaging experiences with literature can help readers better understand people and cultures very different from their own. Ensuring a diversity of content, cultural representation, points of view, and author voices and languages in your library will help you and your students move beyond the boundaries of your classroom to learn about and celebrate the diversity in literature—and human nature, as well. For some of our favorite literature related to diversity, revisit the themed Book Hook recommendations in Chapter Two.

Another source for classroom library selections is your own reading history. If you want to include some of your favorite books from childhood in your library, consider the context of the story, plot, characters, and language. You may want to ask yourself if they are still relevant and understandable to students today, and use them as a Book Hook in Phase 1. Do not be disappointed if some of your students do not follow up and read the book, as our experience suggests that students in today's classrooms find many popular children's books from the 1950s, '60s and '70s too difficult to relate to and to fully understand. However, there may be talented readers in your class eager for the additional challenge or historical understanding readily available in older literature without the more mature themes or language found in some of today's adolescent literature. (See Chapter Three for more details.)

Organizing Your Library for Optimal Matches in Reading

Work in the SEM-R is undertaken with a clear goal: student choice in reading is supported by adult evaluation of independent performance. Therefore, two central challenges for teachers are to identify the correct levels of academic difficulty for each student, and to determine whether texts are appropriately challenging. As previously explained in Chapter Three, because students in your class will have very different reading skills and comprehension, there are no specific rules for deciding whether a book is a good match for SIR. Nevertheless, there are four general categories of guidelines to consider as you think about helping a student find the right book in your classroom library: readability, content complexity, subject matter appropriateness, and each student's interest.

In reading, educators usually determine the appropriateness of a text based on factors such as sentence length, vocabulary, readability, student skill development, and content. Graves, Juel, and Graves (2001) recommend fluency tests to judge readability, but this method does not specifically address content difficulty or students' interest in the text. The latter, student interest, has been emphasized as important in the process of finding the optimal student-challenge match and our recent research on SEM-R has found that students who make their own choices based on interests enjoy reading more (Reis et al., 2005).

Choosing challenging books requires sensitivity to a variety of factors that are individual to each student and environment. Readability tests provide information on difficulty, but the challenge of a text and its appropriateness for an individual student must be judged holistically. For example, if the content of a book is particularly difficult to understand, wading through difficult syntax may obscure comprehension. When a teacher selects texts using ongoing assessment of reading behavior, he or she can help to identify the text, provide scaffolding, teach background knowledge, engage student interest, and encourage students to make connections to personal as well as prior knowledge. Graves et al. (2001) agree that a key force in comprehension and finding the optimal match is helping students to access "prior knowledge" and experiences to bring meaning to a text, suggesting that if we support a child enough, he or she will be successful. In other words, there must be a "supported struggle."

With the variety and quantity of books in any classroom library, it may seem challenging to create an optimal match. There are methods to help both teachers and students in this process, and in our work on SEM-R, we found that teachers needed to consider three factors when assessing book match, including the qualities of the book, students' interests, as well as predetermined leveling systems. Considering these three in harmony with one another allowed teachers to help students choose appropriately challenging reading material.

There are many different systems currently used by publishers and reading experts for the leveling of books, as summarized in Table 6.1. Each system is designed to assist teachers and students in locating books that are appropriately challenging. Note that the second column in Table 6.1 indicates the SEM-R level of the book by designating both a color and a letter. The letter corresponds to the Fountas and Pinnell reading levels, but can be easily cross-referenced to either DRA or Lexile leveling systems by moving horizontally across the chart. The color designation, on the other hand, indicates the relative difficulty of the books in one range compared to another. For instance, the easiest books found in a third grade SEM-R study classroom will be coded green, whereas in the fourth grade classrooms in the study, the easiest books will be coded yellow. The yellow coding represents books that are slightly more difficult than those found in the green range, as designated by the ascending letter order.

Table 6.1. Different Leveling Systems for Coding Book Difficulty and Readability

Grade	SEM-R Color-Coded Level	Fountas & Pinnell Guided Reading Level	DRA Level	Lexile Level
Kindergarten		A	A	200-400
		B	1-2	
		C	3	
			4	
First Grade			A	200-400
		B	1-2	
		C	3	
		D	4	
		E	6-8	
		F	10	
		G	12	
		H	14	
		I	16	
Second Grade			6-8	300-500
			10	
			12	
		H	14	
		I	16	
		J-K	18-20	
		L-M	24-30	
Third Grade	J-K (Green)		18-20	500-700
	L-N (Yellow)	L-M	24-28	
	O-R (Orange)	N	30	
	S-V (Red)	O-P	34-38	
			40	
Fourth Grade	M-N (Yellow)		24-28	650-850
	O-R (Orange)		30	
	S-V (Red)	O-P	34-38	
	W-Z (Purple)	Q-R	40	
	Z+ (Blue)	S-T	44	
Fifth Grade	Q-R (Orange)		40	750-950
	S-V (Red)	S-V	44	
	W-Z (Purple)	W	-	
	Z+ (Blue)			
Sixth Grade	T-V (Red)	V	44	850-1050
	W-Z (Purple)	W-Y	-	
Seventh & Eighth Grade	Z+ (Blue)	Z		

(Fountas & Pinnell, 2001, p. 228; MetaMetrics, 2004; Scholastic, 1996-2007)

Some might wonder: why bother having a color coded system at all when it seems to be so random? The advantage to such a system can be illustrated by taking a look at Ms. Johnson's classroom. Ms. Johnson is a third-grade teacher whose students' reading abilities vary widely. Some of her third graders are quite proficient with both fluency and comprehension and have been reading novels for a couple of years. She also has students in her class who struggle with comprehension because they must devote so much effort to reading fluently. Using the SEM-R color coding system, Ms. Johnson is able to recommend books with green stickers to her students who would struggle to read fluently in a typical third grade level book. Likewise, she is able to recommend that a talented reader in her classroom browse through the books with red stickers to find an appropriate match. The color coding system enables teachers to provide students with a range of books that may be appropriate.

One informal method that you can use to understand the level of books in your existing classroom library is to gauge the reading difficulty level of the text based on the experiences of previous students or in comparison to grade level textbooks or other books in the classroom library. You might also want to work with other teachers or the school media specialist to divide the books into three or four general categories based on readability, complexity, and your own experiences with the text (e.g., on level, challenging). Though slightly narrower, these categories will still represent a range of options, and ease the process of book selection to give you and your students a head start for finding the right match. Once you are conferencing regularly, you will be listening to students read and talking to them about the books they are reading, thereby becoming even more familiar with the range of books in the library. Over time, using the Book Hooks and conferences with students, you will develop an even better knowledge of the books in—and the changing needs of— your classroom library. For those teachers who prefer a more detailed or specific approach to book leveling, there are many online resources available for checking the reading levels of books (see Table 6.2).

The selection of the right level of book does not have to be scientific, as we have found that finding the right match may often be accomplished by a hunch on the part of the student or the teacher. Common criteria for selecting a book include the overall length, the number of words on a page, font size, pictures that tell parts of the story or support the story, and the process of skimming a page for difficult words or new vocabulary. Our experience with the SEM-R has validated our belief and knowledge that children are astute observers who typically want to read more sophisticated or important books. Books with large print and few words, while appropriate for their readability for some students, will

Table 6.2. Resources for Leveling Books

Leveling Books	http://www.literacy.uconn.edu/month2.htm This site provides a summary of book leveling and a discussion of developmental reading levels and ways of matching readers to text. A variety of leveling systems are described.
Leveling Books Description	http://www.ciera.org/library/reports/inquiry-1/1-010/1-010.pdf The Center for the Improvement of Early Reading Achievement (CIERA) details leveling of books for first grade students. Nevertheless, useful information about the leveling process, which is applicable to many grade levels, is provided.
Book Leveling Database	http://registration.beavton.k12.or.us/lbdb/ This database allows users to search for a book and its corresponding guided reading level (in English or Spanish) by title, author, subject, key word, and publisher.
Lexile Levels	http://www.lexile.com/DesktopDefault.aspx?view=ed&tabindex=5&tabid=67 The Lexile Framework for Reading site allows users to search for the Lexile reading level for books based on title, author, Lexile level, or ISBN.

appear to be appropriate for younger children and may turn off some struggling older readers. Teachers should be sensitive to this and seek out high-interest/low-reading-level books that can be found in a formatted style to appeal to the older reader.

Looking up the challenge level of each book can be time consuming, and taking time to read each book, or at least a portion of it, also takes more time than most teachers have available. However, some time invested in becoming more familiar with the reading levels of the books in your classroom library before SEM-R implementation will actually save time once you are conferencing regularly with students in Phase 2. The goal, when helping students choose books, is to match each student's interests with a text at an appropriate reading level so that he or she becomes fully engaged in the process of reading. The use of a leveling system is intended to facilitate this process and to be used simply as a guide. Teachers and students should take care to understand that a book must hold the reader's attention, and even if a book is at the appropriate level of reading difficulty for a student, unless the subject interests the student, the book is not a good match.

The SEM-R framework is designed to provide teachers and students with dedicated time during the Phase 2 conferences to have conversations about the books students are reading. This time also provides teachers with the opportunity to listen to a student read to evaluate whether or not the book is at a reading level commensurate with the student's skills and reading ability. It is through these conversations and evaluations that the teacher and the student, working together, determine the best match of texts for the student as an individual reader.

PHYSICAL SET-UP OF THE CLASSROOM

Part of the planning for success during Phase 2 is developing a room arrangement that compliments and supports the self-regulation behaviors that students are developing during SIR. Ideally, the teacher should be able to see students from any area in the room so that help or guidance can be given quickly and easily. Therefore, consider how you can arrange furniture and reading areas so that students have the space they need and are visible to the teacher. You may also wish to designate or create special "reading areas" in your classroom, but be sure to also develop a corresponding system for managing fair access to the areas. For example, if you have a couch, a rug area, and comfortable pillows, you may want to make a chart that enables an orderly rotation of students in each area. Students may also read at their desk. The choice of reading space should be determined by your particular class setup, your style and preferences, and your students' behaviors and self-regulation.

As you consider how to organize your room for the best implementation of SEM-R, remember that students should have easy access to the book that they are reading, some ideas or lists about the next book they want to read, their reading log, and any other materials that they will be using on a regular basis, such as sticky notes and a reading response journal. Some teachers provide a book bin for each child, in which all these reading materials are located. Other teachers who have used the SEM-R have students keep all their materials in their desks. Or you may find that a central storage area for all reading logs and organized in alphabetical order is a good way to help students keep materials organized. Consider the space in your classroom, the organizational skills of your students, and ease of access when choosing a system for organizing these reading materials.

Most importantly, books should be easily accessible to students. Elementary school students are still very visual and they rely on the book covers to help them choose what to read. Bins or small boxes of books enable students to see the books available and to easily sort through titles. This system is usually preferable to keeping books shelved in the traditional manner in which the reader has to rely solely on the text on the book spine. Consider the height at which books are placed and make sure they are spread out so that students are not jockeying for access in tight quarters. Books can be arranged alphabetically by author name, grouped together by genre or series, by type (picture book, chapter book), by level, or grouped by some criteria determined by the teacher and the students, such as Class Favorites. The teacher or students can label the bins of books according to the chosen criteria. Students will need to become familiar with the range of titles and subjects in the classroom library. By enlisting students to help organize the collection, they will identify books in which they are interested and the process will also help them to feel some ownership of the library as an important part of their classroom community.

MANAGING CONFERENCES

The individual reading conferences during Phase 2 is where the majority of the reading instruction occurs. The conference is an opportunity for the teacher to provide one-on-one instruction, targeting the needs of each student in an atmosphere of support and collaboration. Having a conference with all students on a regular basis (two times each week) is quite possible, provided that the teacher puts certain supports in place.

Teachers should feel confident that the rest of the students are reading independently while reading conferences are underway. This will require teacher modeling and support at the beginning of the SEM-R implementation. Students will need to work up to reading for extended periods of time. The initial amount of time spent during Supported Independent Reading will depend on the age and reading stamina of your students. If they have not spent a good bit of time on independent reading, you should begin with 5-minute increments. Students who are accustomed to reading for longer periods can start out with a longer block of reading time. During this initial modeling and monitoring stage, the teacher should circulate through the room to make sure that students are actually reading. Teachers should encourage the students and provide them with positive feedback once the 5 minutes is completed. Students can record the name of the book they are reading in their Reading Log then begin with another 5 minute increment of sustained silent reading. At the end of the reading time, all students should record the total time spent reading and the pages they finished read. By breaking up the reading time into smaller chunks, the teacher can provide scaffolding for building more stamina for reading. The teacher is able to monitor students' time on the task of reading and ensure that students are properly recording their reading progress in their Reading Logs. This monitoring at the beginning of the SEM-R implementation helps to set the expectations for reading in the classroom.

On the second day of implementation, teachers should try to increase the first block of time by 2 minutes. By the third day, the teacher can consider holding one or two conferences during the blocks of reading time. During each subsequent day, teachers should lengthen the block of SIR time until the students are reading continuously for 30-40 minutes each day. Initially, it is important for teachers to circulate among the students to monitor their work and provide positive feedback to the students as they become more proficient at regulating their time on task and increasing their stamina as readers. Although this will limit the time you have available for formal conferences during the first weeks of SEM-R implementation, you must establish the "rails" of self-regulation and routine during Phase 2 before you can successfully set the "train" of conferences in motion. The following suggestions can help you to achieve the goal of meeting with each student several times each week.

Establishing a weekly record-keeping system will help you to keep track of the students with whom you have met, to remember the focus of the conference, and to keep other notes about the content of the conference and the student as a reader. This organization system is the first step to managing Phase 2 conferences. The style or preference of each teacher will determine the method chosen, but based on our experiences and what we have observed in successful SEM-R classes, we can offer a few suggestions:

1. Create a list of all the students in your class, with some space next to each name for your notes (we have included some samples of this type of list in our teacher log in Appendix H). Keep this list readily available (i.e., on a clipboard, in a notebook). Use this list to determine the next student with whom to confer. After you have met with each student, start a new list!

2. Put the name of each child in your class on a label on a full sheet of labels. Write your conference notes on the label, making sure to include the date. Once all the labels are full, transfer the label for each student to a page with that student's name. This will provide you with a record of all the conferences for that student. Once all of the labels from a sheet have been completed, repeat the process.

3. Create a "Conferencing" chart for your room using magnets or clothespins with the names of the students. Students can move their name to the bottom of the list once you have held a conference with them. This provides a visual reminder for you and the students.

4. Write the name of each student on a tongue depressor. Label two cups – Waiting to Conference and Conference Complete. Place all the names in the first cup. Draw names one at a time for a conference. Place the names of students whose conference is complete in the Conference Complete cup. Once all of the names have been drawn from the first cup, transfer the names back to that cup and repeat the process.

5. Use the sun and cloud cards (Appendix D) to enable a quick assessment of students who might be struggling so that time can be made to meet with a student or answer imperative questions.

Regardless of which management technique you use to select students for conferences, it is essential to keep some type of written record of the conference you have completed with each student. Some other suggestions for this task include keeping an index card for each student or including a note in the student's reading log (see Appendix I for a sample of the student log). The amount of time that teachers spend with each student during a conference will determine how many students are seen on a daily or weekly basis, but our suggestion is to keep each conference to approximately 5 minutes. Since the conference is the time during which meaningful instruction takes place, it is tempting to make these conferences last longer, but we have found that a 15-20 minute conference is less effective than conferences that are shorter and more frequent. As a general rule, one conference should not exceed 10 minutes and our target range is 5-6 minutes per conference.

Teachers should try to have a conference with each student at least twice each week. The key for success in conferences is to make the conference very specific. Focusing your conferences within that target range of 5 minutes and keeping them specific to each child's needs will enable you to have two to three opportunities to provide explicit instruction for each child each week. Some students, because of learning difficulties or behavioral concerns, may require shorter conferences more often or an additional planned conference rotation with a learning specialist or other support personnel to help them further develop self-regulation or reading strategies. See Chapter Seven for additional information.

When you first begin to conduct conferences, you may want to use a timer or stopwatch to keep track of the time spent with each student. Another strategy that you can use is to pre-determine the amount of time allotted for Phase 2, and divide it into 5-7 minute increments and schedule one student into each slot. This provides a couple of extra minutes of time for completing conference notes between conferences and checking on the reading progress of students as they read independently. Teachers should anticipate slightly longer conferences at the beginning of their use of SEM-R. As you become more accustomed to the process and knowledgeable about the specific reading needs of each student, the conferences can become shorter and more explicit.

HELPING WITH TRANSITIONS BETWEEN PHASES IN SEM-R

Smooth transitions enable teachers to optimize learning time in an increasingly hectic and busy school day and transitions are made easier when students have ready access to the materials they need and knowledge of the procedures to follow. Our experiences for managing the transition into Phase 1 for the Book Hooks include the following:

1. Designate one area in the class for Book Hook time and have students practice gathering in this area in a controlled, timely manner. Consider assigning some or all students to seats or places in the classroom.

2. If students have individual bins for their reading materials (e.g., Reading Log, books), consider placing these bins in close proximity to their desks. You might also consider placing the bins in two or three locations throughout the room to avoid having too many students trying to retrieve their bins from the same area at the same time. Students can get their bins when they enter the classroom at the beginning of the school day or prior to joining the class at the Book Hook area.

3. If all materials are kept in a central location, you can also assign two students to pass out the reading folders that include students' Reading Log and independent reading book. These can be delivered to students' desks while the rest of the class assembles in the Book Hook area.

4. If students are going to remain at their desks during the Book Hook time, you should establish guidelines to minimize distraction (desk cleared, hands on top of desk, etc.).

5. To facilitate the process when multiple students want to read a book from your Book Hook, consider how to create a way to manage sharing. Procedures that we have seen work well include:

    a. Placing all Book Hook books along the chalk tray or in a designated book bin. A student can take the book once he or she is finished with the book currently being read. Or you may choose to give the book to one student and ask that student to pass the book along to another classmate when he or she has finished the book.

    b. Creating a chart of books read during the Book Hook phase. Post this near the book bins where students can look for the books. You can also leave space for students to clip a clothespin with their name on it next to books they want to read.

    c. Putting a sticky-note with a list of the students who want to read the book inside the front cover. When one student finishes reading the book, it can be passed along to the next student on the list.

6. Desk placement, classroom library location, and additional reading spaces should be arranged to facilitate traffic flow as students move from Phase 1 to Phase 2. Try to avoid bottlenecks!

As you finish the Phase 1 Book Hooks, students will need to get their book and move to their designated reading spot to begin SIR. During the initial days and weeks of the SEM-R implementation, you will want to provide guidance, praise, and redirection to students during this transition. Make your expectations clear and easy to follow. You may also want to work with your class to create a list of guidelines to be followed during SIR. The list might look like this:

> 1. Have your book with you.
> 2. Keep your Reading Log and pencil with you.
> 3. Be settled and ready to read within 2 minutes!

Students will also need time to select the book they want to read during SIR—particularly in the first few weeks. You might consider allowing students to do this during other times in the day to minimize the amount of SIR time they spend looking for a book. There are several times in which students might be able to browse for a book including when they arrive in the classroom in the morning, when they finish with other work, or during designated free time. After the first week or so, it is not advisable to have several students selecting their books at the beginning of Phase 2 and so we recommend that students always have their next choice ready to read. If one or more students seem to always take a long time to select a book, you can take time during your individual conference with that child to discuss book selection strategies. Finding the optimal reading level match and interesting genre and/or subject should help alleviate a prolonged selection process in the future. Teachers who have used the SEM-R have found it useful to create the expectation that book choices must be made within 5 minutes.

You may want to assign jobs to students to facilitate the transition from one phase to another that might include:

+ Classroom librarian (makes sure books are returned neatly and to the proper place)
+ Book Hook manager (straightens up books returned to Book Hook bins, announces availability of titles to interested students)
+ Reading Folder technician (hands out and collects reading folders or Reading Logs)
+ Reading Area supervisor (straightens up special reading areas with pillows, mats, etc.)

+ Bookmark clerk (collects and organizes Bookmarks students have used during their reading time)

Each day at the end of Phase 2, students should be given time to write the name of the book they have been reading, the number of pages read, and the amount of time read in their student reading log (see Appendix I). This process will take less time as students become more familiar with how to record this information. You might also include extra time once each week, to ask students to prepare a written response in their logs, using a Book Hook question.

The ways that you manage the transition from Phase 2 Supported Independent Reading to Phase 3 Free Choice will depend largely on the choices that you offer during Phase 3. If you plan to provide direct instruction in creative thinking or some other process training skill, the transition will look different than if students are moving to pre-designated work stations or centers in the room. Moreover, managing student transitions and activities is also dependent upon whether Phase 3 activities are pursued each day or once each week.

You may want to distinguish among the different types of Phase 3 activities by using a posted schedule of options. In doing so, your students can sign up for the Free Choice options in advance or work together during Phase 3 to make decisions about their choices. An example of how this might look is presented in Table 6.3.

In highly effective SEM-R classrooms, the materials are easy to find and prepared in advance, teachers give clear instructions and expectations for transitions from one phase to the next, and they also plan a schedule for all phases in advance. In these classrooms, there are clearly defined work areas and materials are organized and easy to access.

INCORPORATING THE SEM-R INTO THE ELEMENTARY READING CLASSROOM

The SEM-R was initially designed to fit within the typical elementary school reading or Language Arts time block and was intended to be used as part of a daily 90-minute or 2 hour literacy block. The SEM-R is deliberately flexible to meet the educational needs of students and the scheduling demands of elementary school. The suggested implementation at this level involves 10 minutes devoted to Phase 1 Book Hooks, 30-40 minutes for Phase 2 Supported Independent Reading, and 10-20 minutes for Phase 3 Independent Choice time. Some teachers use their 90 minute literacy block in two parts: 60 minutes for SEM-R and 30 minutes for writing, spelling, or vocabulary work. Some teachers facilitate Phase 1

Table 6.3. Example of Phase 3 Sign-up Sheet

Phase 3 Sign-up for Thursday, March 24	
Choice #1: Participate in Reader's Theater	Mark Janelle Tammy Daniel
Choice #2: Use Renzulli Learning	James Sarah
Choice #3: Buddy Reading	Joy with Carolyn Louis with Dawn
Choice #4: Listening Station	Kristen Maria Tom Jack

and 2 four days a week for 1 hour each day, and provide Phase 3 Independent Choice time on the remaining day of each week for 1 hour at a time. Others use Phase 1 and 2 for 30 minutes for two days of each week, and then have 30 minutes for Phase 3 on those days, while doing Phase 1 and 2 for the entire 60 minutes the remaining three days of every week. Still others devote 1 hour every day to Phases 1 and 2 and then do Phase 3 for 20-30 minutes at another time during the day. The implementation is limited only by your ingenuity and should be organized according to your needs and those of your students.

ADAPTING THE SEM-R FOR USE IN THE MIDDLE SCHOOL

SEM-R in a middle school may require some adjustment of current approaches to Reading and English Language Arts instruction. The amount of time allotted to the SEM-R implementation in a middle school will be influenced by the length of class time. For example, in a 45-minute block, 10 minutes can be devoted to Phase 1 Book Hooks, 20 minutes for Phase 2 Supported Independent Reading, and 10 minutes for Phase 3 Independent Choice. Or each week could consist of four days of Phase 1 and Phase 2 instruction with a fifth day entirely devoted to Phase 3 explorations.

In many middle schools, Reading and English Language Arts instruction revolve around class studies of novels and writing instruction. The SEM-R framework represents a shift from whole-class to individualized instruction with a focus on the development of enjoyment of reading. Typically in middle schools, teachers use novel studies as a vehicle to teach various literary devices. Choosing one novel for a class to read can be problematic because even in classes that are grouped by ability, there exists a range of reading proficiency among the students. A book that will be a struggle to read for one group of students will be too easy for others, and it might be just right for those readers who read on grade level. Teachers can still teach specific literary devices when students choose books to read independently, but it requires that they think carefully about the skills that they want students to learn and how readers can demonstrate that they have learned these skills. Options for managing this process in any middle school class may include the identification of a genre or thematic book list from which students can select a text that interests them. Encouraging readers to choose an appropriately challenging book enables them to use the principles of SEM-R to select literature of different complexity and reading levels.

Another alternative might be to encourage independent reading after students have completed an assigned class book. Middle school reading or Language Arts teachers may want to alternate instruction, from teaching books of different genres or theme studies with periods of independent choice reading. Teachers can also enable students to use the SEM-R Bookmarks for conferences during two or three periods/classes a week in which Phase 1 and 2 reading strategies are implemented. During these periods, teachers can use Phase 1 Book Hooks to demonstrate how to recognize or apply a literary device, and then have differentiated Phase 2 conferences with students during SIR. Teachers may also implement this phase as originally designed by selecting several books for Book Hooks and using the Bookmarks as tools for engaging with text.

Phase 2 Supported Independent Reading in the middle school provides a unique opportunity for the teacher to meet with students individually to support their reading growth. Teachers may want to have a focus for conference discussions in advance so that students have time to prepare and reflect. As noted in previous sections, the teacher will want to record notes about the conference held with each student to better track reading progress over time.

During Phase 3 Independent Choice time, teachers may want to have students write a response to their reading that can relate to a theme or identified literary device. This task provides an ideal opportunity for students to apply higher-order thinking skills and to use examples from the text as evidence. This time may also be used for free writing in different genres. Teachers may consider using this time for students to discuss their independent reading with classmates. In this and other ways, middle school teachers have successfully implemented the SEM-R into diverse classrooms.

CHAPTER 7

CHALLENGING TALENTED & STRUGGLING READERS IN THE SEM-R

MARK E. OLIVER, SHEELAH SWEENY, SALLY M. REIS
& REBECCA D. ECKERT

*In the beginning, I did not realize how much middle-of-the-road reading instruction
I did and how few of my kids I really challenged. . . . I had not thought about the
stagnation in reading that occurred for kids at the middle and the top.*

- Fourth Grade SEM-R Teacher

Why is ensuring continuous growth in reading important? Educators and researchers agree that reading and literacy serve as the gateway to academic success (Burns, Griffin, & Snow, 1999; Moats, 1999; National Reading Panel [NRP], 2000). Being able to read fluently and comprehend written information is the foundation for many other skills taught in school. Furthermore, reading comprehension is key to solid performance on the standardized achievement tests that have quickly become the hallmark of U.S. educational accountability policies. Therefore, current legislation and reading policies focus on reducing the achievement gap between those who perform at the highest levels and those who perform at the lowest levels on standardized measures of academic proficiency with widespread support (and sometimes high-stakes pressure) from lawmakers and the public.

Unfortunately, there are no easy answers to closing this achievement gap, but the information in this chapter can help you to reflect upon the diversity of student needs in your classroom and the support and strategies you will need to capitalize on individualized instructional opportunities during SEM-R.

A RICH MIX OF STUDENTS

Today's classrooms include students with many different talents, abilities, and cultural backgrounds. This wealth of variation can enrich student experiences when educators are able to reflect on and refine their own instructional methods and strategies to address this diversity. Given the wide range of skills with which students enter a reading classroom, teaching all students using the same techniques and the same materials cannot foster increased reading achievement for everyone. These practices result in work that is too easy for talented readers—and too difficult for struggling readers—to provide opportunities for continuous growth. The report "National Excellence: A Case for Developing America's Talent" (U. S. Department of Education [USDE], 1993) suggested that enrichment programs, like the SEM-R, can make positive changes, as they have ". . . served as laboratories for innovative and experimental approaches to teaching and learning in the development of complex thinking strategies and problem solving" (p. 23) as well as sophisticated and alternative teaching strategies, and innovative curriculum approaches.

Although the development of the SEM-R was initially driven by concerns about the neglect of talented readers in classroom literacy instruction, it became apparent to us during our earliest pilot implementations of the SEM-R that the use of enrichment pedagogy and differentiated instruction benefited almost every student in the classroom, despite their level of skill. In our SEM-R research, we have routinely found a span of 8-10 grade levels in many of the classrooms in which we have worked and differentiated instruction (i.e., instruction designed to meet learners' individual needs within the classroom) has helped teachers better understand and further student growth in and enjoyment of reading.

The SEM-R enables all students, including those who read several grades above level, to select books they want to read, to read content that is above their current reading level, to engage and think about complex texts, and to extend conventional basal reading instruction, which too often is focused on reading appropriate for one specific chronological grade level. The SEM-R has been successfully used to challenge a wide range of readers, from struggling to talented, in elementary and middle school classrooms, including students from culturally diverse backgrounds and those with differing levels of ability (Reis et al., 2005).

READING STAGES OF DEVELOPMENT

Every classroom has a wide variety of students who have different reading needs. They may be at different stages of reading development, each of which has unique characteristics and requires use of specific strategies. There are four stages of reading development, as defined in work by Walker (2005). Knowing the characteristics of these stages can assist you during conferences and conversations with students. In stage one emergent literacy, students learn basic concepts about print; in stage two, students learn about letter-sound patterns in words and the organization of text; in stage three, sentence structure becomes more complex and the reader must use strategies to gain meaning from the text; and during stage four, the ideas are more complex, requiring the reader to determine what strategy or strategies are required to comprehend the text (Walker, 2005). Chall defined similar stages of reading, but included a fifth stage where the reader combines prior knowledge and new learning to create new knowledge (The Reading Foundation, 2005).

It is important to understand that these stages are not distinct; they overlap. Readers may exhibit characteristics of more than one stage. Higher levels of learning occur when students can move from one stage to the next (Walker, 2005), as is similar to Vygotsky's Zone of Proximal Development (1962) and the match that we call a supported struggle in SEM-R. Students become better readers when they are exposed to more complex reading tasks that require them to apply strategies they have already learned and to acquire and practice new strategies.

The Needs and Characteristics of Readers

As you become better acquainted with the characteristics and strengths of your students, the needs of individual readers will be more evident. Knowing some of the general characteristics of readers of differing abilities will help you choose a focus for selecting books or holding reading conferences. Common characteristics are summarized in Table 7.1.

As a group, talented readers are characterized as spending more time reading, and reading a greater variety of literature, even into adulthood (Collins & Kortner, 1995; Halsted, 1990). These students typically read at least two grade levels above their chronological grade placement, demonstrate advanced understanding of language, and have an expansive vocabulary (Catron & Wingenbach, 1986; Dooley, 1993; Levande, 1993). Research by Fehrenbach (1991) identified six strategies used by talented readers, "significantly more than average readers—rereading, inferring, analyzing text structure, watching or predicting, evaluating, and relating what is read to content area knowledge" (p. 15). If nurtured, all of these remarkable characteristics and skills enable talented readers to passionately pursue areas of interest and excel in academic endeavors.

Table 7.1. Reader Characteristics

Struggling Readers	Average Readers	Talented Readers
• Do not use strategies efficiently • Rely on limited number of strategies • Focus on the word reading level of the text, does not allow connections to own lives or other texts • Cannot easily monitor understanding • Internalize reading failures & disengage from process	• Use multiple strategies at once • Make connections • Monitor for understanding	• Use multiple strategies at once • Relate texts to prior knowledge and experiences • Have an expansive vocabulary and precocious use of language • May resist reading more difficult texts

In contrast, struggling readers often have difficulty in comprehending grade-level texts and making connections to life and literature because they must concentrate efforts on deciphering and identifying words rather than constructing meaning. Consequently, non-differentiated literacy experiences in the general elementary classroom are likely to reinforce students' negative feelings toward and beliefs about reading (Stanovich, 1986). The Committee on the Prevention of Reading Difficulties in Young Children identified the children most likely to experience reading difficulties throughout the course of their academic career as those who attend a chronically low-achieving school, have low English proficiency, are unfamiliar with standard English dialect, or live in communities of poverty (Burns, Griffin, & Snow, 1999). A number of factors, including classroom environments, play a major role in the lower rates of literacy and achievement often experienced by at-risk students. Research by Duke (2000) indicates all students must have experiences with a large amount of print representing a variety of genres and print types, as well as a sense of student agency (i.e., self-determination and choice) in their classroom reading experiences to promote successful literacy development and continued academic achievement.

In addition to understanding the characteristics of readers of different abilities, you should also be aware of students who are reluctant to read. A number of students may not be interested in reading because they experience reading difficulties, and others may avoid reading because of unpleasant reading experiences they have had in the past. Some students, however, may have adequate or above average reading ability and choose not to read, which is called alliteracy. You might try to motivate some of these students by helping them to identify and select high-interest books to read. Audio books can also motivate these readers. We have also found that self-selected Phase 3 projects can help to engage some reluctant readers, especially those who discover a passion for discovery in a certain topic or area.

In SEM-R, we focus on the necessity to include higher-level strategies for all readers. Struggling and talented readers both need the opportunity to discuss the strategies they are using and what they are thinking about a text. Moreover, all readers benefit from the development and practice of self-regulated behaviors that allow them to pursue and enjoy exciting and interesting literature.

MATCHING READERS TO TEXT

As discussed in Chapter Three, finding the perfect match of book for any reader can be a challenging task. The two keys to matching individual readers with the right book involve knowing your students' interests and skills as readers and thinking creatively about the type of books and literature readily available for readers. To try to match students to the right books, several of the characteristics below can be considered in combination:

- Reader (interest, background knowledge, preference, motivation)
- Reading level (challenge range)
- Content (subject, theme)
- Reader cognitive needs (reading support, differentiated, individualized reading strategies)
- Social/affective characteristics or needs (identity, emotions, connections to real life)
- Text (genre, structure, language, style, visual elements)

The Reader

One of the first things you can do to better implement the SEM-R is get to know your students' interests both in and outside of school. Information such as whether or not students participate in extracurricular activities, the types of reading material available outside of school, or a student's passion about a particular subject or topic may help you identify genres or authors that will spark a learner's motivation to read. Book discussions in Phase 1 and individual conferences in Phase 2 will also allow you to better understand and know your students' reading patterns and to track the growth of reading skills and strategies. Informal conversations and conference dialogues may prove helpful for gauging the depth of background knowledge each reader possesses. Using an interest inventory such as the Reading Interest-a-Lyzer (Appendix B) or the profile system in

Renzulli Learning can also help you gather and organize information about students as both individuals and readers.

As an enrichment-based program, the SEM-R offers challenge and choice as well as opportunities for imagination and creativity. In essence, tapping into student interests through formal and informal interest assessments and then providing choice in reading materials makes tackling an appropriately challenging book more palatable for many students at all performance levels. In describing the role played by interest in her success after a 12-week intervention with a fourth grade learning-disabled student, one SEM-R teacher explained:

> *He did not like to read and we hooked him. He was a success for me. We talked to him. We got him to read stuff he was interested in, and we found that when he was interested, he could really do well . . . . He is so successful now. He has made major gains in reading.*

The Reading Level

The second component of the right match relies upon teachers' abilities to make a determination about each student's current reading level. In many classrooms, this level is usually identified using quantitative information from various assessments at the school level or on state tests. These results can be a helpful starting point for you in the first few weeks of SEM-R implementation as you continue to learn more about each student as a reader. In our research on SEM-R, we have found school-based assessments, in particular, to be helpful in an initial examination of reading levels (e.g., Lexiles) that can be used to match students with appropriately challenging texts. However, it is important to bear in mind that interests and motivation have an impact on what students can and will read independently.

When you use the SEM-R, you will find that one effective way to determine students' reading levels is to encourage students to select books to read before they have their first individual conference with their teacher. During a subsequent conference, you can listen to your student read the book he or she has chosen, and then ask both skill-based literal and interpretive questions to determine student's levels of comprehension. If a student struggles with numerous words (either decoding or vocabulary), and/or has difficulty understanding the text, simply stated, the book is too difficult for that student.

In the SEM-R, we want all students to be challenged when they are reading during Phase 2, and we recommend that they select those books that are 1-1.5 years above their current reading level. To try to determine whether or not a book is at this level, we suggest that you listen to the student read. If the student is challenged by decoding a few words on each page, or struggles a bit to fully understand the meaning or content, then the book is most likely a good match for that student. We often praise students for reading quickly and with ease; however in our experience working with the SEM-R, we have found that when students are not challenged, their reading will not improve. In the SEM-R, we also want to encourage students to seek depth in ideas, in the new content in which they have an interest, and in the types of reading they want to pursue because of their interests. So while encouraging students to work and expend effort in their reading may seem counter-intuitive, it is by doing this that we can help them to improve and grow as readers. In addition to our suggested informal assessment of reading levels (which we believe works efficiently and will help you come to understand your students as readers), you may also wish to revisit the discussion "Organizing Your Library for Optimal Matches in Reading" in the previous chapter.

Content

A third criterion to consider when matching students with interesting and challenging books is the content—an area in which student interest plays the most important role. As mentioned previously, one important difference in SEM-R instruction is that students are able to choose what they are reading, with guidance and support from a teacher. Students with a great deal of knowledge about a topic can usually read more difficult books about a subject; however, they may struggle when they are asked to read books of similar difficulty about topics with which they are not familiar. The SEM-R encourages students to read books in their areas of interest, teachers are also encouraged to expose students to different topics and genres they typically would not chose on their own. This exposure is one important purpose of the Book Hooks that are used during Phase 1.

Familiarity with books in the classroom library can make the process of matching books easier for both students and teachers. When you are implementing the SEM-R, consider different organizational systems for displaying the books, concentrating on creating groupings that make book choice both inviting and practical for students. Books can be organized by genre, series, author, subject, theme, and we have found that teachers who involve students in the organization of their classroom books help these students to more actively identify books of interest for current or future reading.

Social/Affective

Another strategy to consider when helping students select a book is how the book can help the reader. Books can help students explore their feelings and deal with difficult events, and they can also serve as an important source of emotional support for students. If a student is new to a classroom or a school, a book about being a new student in school might make the transition easier. If two students are having problems in their friendship, books about how other friends deal with similar situations could be helpful. Good readers often make connections in their own lives to the lives of characters in books. Talented readers may also develop strong attachments to characters in books.

Nonfiction books can also help students feel more confident about their knowledge of a particular interest area that may also be useful when they begin to study other content areas in school. Books can help students cope with challenges they face and new experiences they encounter. Exposing students to a wide variety of books provides them with opportunities to better reflect upon their personal lives.

Finally, the conversations about literature that emerge during all three phases enhance students' ability to choose and recommend books while also building a sense of community literacy. Through conferences and conversations, teachers will learn the specific strengths and weaknesses of learners, as well as reading preferences. In addition, as the SEM-R program continues, students in the program will discover and discuss one another's reading preferences and interests and will be more likely to have conversations about the books they are reading. Teachers can also take advantage of students' expanding knowledge about books and encourage them to make suggestions for one another. In one classroom, the students were so in tune with their peers' reading preferences that they were able to make better recommendations than the teacher.

Text

The final characteristic to consider when matching readers and texts is the text itself. For a good match, you can consider the genre, the text structure, language and style, and visual elements such as headings, bold words, captions, illustrations, photographs, graphs, charts, and tables. Books that have a direct match between the text and the pictures are easier to read and are recommended for struggling readers. The length of a text or type of book does not automatically determine the text complexity. As an example, a picture book by Patricia Polacco has more sophisticated language and a different style than a chapter book in the *Horrible Harry* series by Suzy Kline. The pictures in a Patricia Polacco book support the more complex text, whereas the *Horrible Harry* books have fewer illustrations but more predictable text structure and vocabulary. For English Language Learners (ELLs), text with idiomatic phrases and figurative language can be difficult to comprehend without careful guidance or direct instruction. Organizational features such as headings and captions offer additional support for readers and can provide scaffolding of new learning.

TALENTED AND STRUGGLING READERS

Strategies for Talented Readers

The most common method of challenging talented readers in classrooms has traditionally involved providing talented students with more difficult and complex literature. While precocious readers need to be challenged by more difficult texts, supplying only books without supplementing more appropriate instructional support can isolate advanced readers and enable them to use reading as an escape rather than a learning opportunity for continued growth. Talented readers have the abilities to make sophisticated connections between texts, identify and synthesize multiple meanings contained in complex stories, and they also have the potential to analyze and evaluate the use of literary elements and techniques. The SEM-R provides teachers with the opportunity to maximize the potential of talented readers through appropriate levels of challenge and support.

A pervasive finding that has emerged from the limited research and discussions on instructional practices for talented readers is that regular reading instruction is often too easy for talented readers (Reis et al., 2004). Chall and Conrad (1991) also found that the talented readers they studied were not adequately served in school because their reading textbooks provide little or no challenge. Many students were aware of this, according to Chall and Conrad, who said that in interviews, students commented that they preferred harder books because they learned harder words and ideas from them, and SEM-R can provide that level of challenge. Consider the case study of Alex:

Alex, an 8-year-old third grader, was reading at an accelerated fifth grade level and had been previously identified as a gifted and talented student in his school. Alex lived with his mother and stepfather, and he explained that he enjoyed the company of both of his parents and that he was encouraged to read at home.

Alex was an energetic student who had difficulty with being still for any extended period of time. Although he could be quite focused when reading, Alex fidgeted and often had verbal outbursts during group activity. His classroom teachers had also noticed this heightened activity and reported that Alex was often distracted and lacked focus. They had provided him with a squishy ball to squeeze when he felt distracted, in the hope that this would help him focus better during group work or during any time that he could not be independently engaged in his own work.

In contrast to his behavior during group work, Alex was able to focus well when reading and could read quietly through periods of peer noise distraction. To ask Alex a question about his reading and gain his attention, we often had to call his name twice before he would take his eyes from the page. Although he was capable of reading on a fifth-grade level and despite being encouraged to read at a higher level, Alex's initial choices of books were always from the Goosebumps series, which was well below his challenge level. Alex liked some of the challenging books suggested to him, including biographies of baseball stars, but would discontinue reading if he perceived that he could not finish the book in a certain period of time, such as a half hour or 45 minutes. He could, for example, read one Goosebumps book in 45 minutes and initially seemed to need the extrinsic praise that he had been consistently given if he finished a book in that time period.

On his "Reading Interest-a-Lyzer," Alex indicated that he liked science books, fantasy, and comics, as well as writing activities and reading books of his choice before falling asleep. Alex also explained that he liked reading about spiders and frogs and often read children's science books he found in the library and the classroom. During the course of the SEM-R intervention, Alex began reading many novels that were suggested to him because of the match of interest and challenge level, but stopped reading shortly after he began almost every novel. If he chose a book that was well below his challenge level, he could usually read silently and independently for one hour. At the beginning of the SEM-R, when one of the researchers suggested a book in his interest areas of fantasy, sports, or science that was at an appropriate level of challenge, he would lose interest and become distracted after 15 minutes.

Toward the end of his first six weeks using the SEM-R, Alex needed to be in a separate space from his classmates to focus and had to be encouraged to take more frequent breaks. When the weather was pleasant, Alex asked if the group could go outside for a break. When granted permission, he ran the entire time, and he had to be cajoled to leave the playground to participate in the SEM-R. On some spring days, Alex simply seemed incapable of reading anything that challenged him in any way, and teachers were forced to let Alex read Goosebumps, or whatever books that might spark his interest. During the later sessions, when a book was suggested to Alex in his areas of interest, he would glance at the cover or read one page and dismiss it as boring. Despite having several conversations about giving books a chance and reading enough so that he could enter "the world" of the book, he did not appear to want to change his behavior. It was difficult to monitor his progress as he tried to read more challenging books because he asked to bring them home and would fail to return them to the program, saying he had forgotten them.

Based on some of his interests, science fiction or fantasy books (Harry Potter) were suggested to Alex, but he became frustrated with the unfamiliar names in the books and made fun of the sounds of the titles. He became discouraged about reading more challenging books when the title looked unfamiliar or the content was too difficult. For example, when the book, The Sands of Time by Michael Hoeye, was given to Alex, he immediately said the book was too hard. When Alex was informed that this book was special because it was the most challenging the program had offered any student, his interest was maintained a little longer as he read for 10 minutes, but then lost interest. He initially complained about the length of the book, but with further discussion, Alex explained that he had become accustomed to speed-reading at his comfort level and felt discomfort when he had to read higher content more slowly. After several hours of observation, it became apparent that Alex routinely read books that did not challenge him and he lost interest in or could not regulate his own reading of appropriately challenging material. When reading material was simpler, such as when a graphic novel version of Moby Dick was suggested to Alex, he read straight through the book for 50 minutes and finished the entire book. When asked comprehension questions about the content of the book, Alex remembered fine details and seemed to understand the plot. He also sped through The Little Prince, but initially seemed to have a limited understanding of this challenging text and the difficult issues raised within the pages. However, when asked additional questions after he had a chance to reflect more about what he had read, Alex was able to answer more in-depth questions, again suggesting that he may have initially lacked the experience to respond to challenging questions. Over time spent with the research team, he gained some skills in learning how to think through more challenging questions.

Alex's closest friends in the program were three boys from lower reading groups who were boisterous and also had difficulty focusing on reading. They were separated after the SEM-R Phase 1 read-alouds, but when they were together during this brief whole group time, these boys talked, touched, and kicked each other constantly, provoking reactions from each other. When separated into the advanced reading group, Alex moved constantly, but had fewer vocal outbursts. Throughout the entire SEM-R program, he repeatedly asked if the group could skip the whole group read-aloud sessions and move straight to the Phase 2 SIR. When asked, he admitted that he understood the larger heterogeneous Phase 1 was his most disruptive time. When Alex was asked questions about the section of the book or story read aloud, he usually answered accurately with details from the text, but would occasionally respond with a silly answer, causing the whole group to lose focus. When asked to write during the program, Alex wrote only occasionally and his writing was usually illegible. His letters were very large and lopsided, and he rushed through his writing assignments, often leaving out conjunctions and articles.

Intensive observations during the SEM-R intervention suggested that Alex was an academically talented student who had the ability to read challenging texts at the fifth or sixth grade level or higher if he had an interest in the content and could regulate his behaviors, but lacked the reading and self-regulation strategies to focus on new, more challenging material on a systematic basis. With enough support and with books in an area of interest, and if he was in a positive frame of mind, Alex could be encouraged to read at an appropriately challenging level for up to 50 minutes. This behavior occurred on only two occasions over the intervention, with a great deal of feedback and encouragement. If left to select what to read, Alex consistently read books below his chronological grade level, even though he understood he was reading material that was well below his skill level. He explained that he had learned over time that he could receive positive feedback for little effort, because his output exceeded that of the majority of his classmates.

Like Alex, some talented readers may not be accustomed to being challenged by more difficult text and high-level questioning, and may avoid reading or reading more complex books when possible. Conferencing with unmotivated talented readers on a frequent basis will help to promote reading as a valued activity and can help to prevent alliteracy. SEM-R teachers should also ensure that students are reading challenging books during

Phase 2 and encourage talented readers to take home books of interest that are too easy. To do this, simply explain to the students that, as the teacher, it is your job to make sure they are challenged. Suggest that students take the easy book home to read and while the students are at school and has your support, they should be engaging in material that is sufficiently challenging (i.e., 1 to 1.5 grade levels above their current reading level).

Alex's story also illustrates the need for thoughtful and flexible instructional grouping that has been successfully implemented with talented readers, resulting in increased understanding and enjoyment of literature (Gentry, 1999; Levande, 1993). In general, grouping academically talented students together for instruction has been found to produce positive achievement outcomes when the curriculum provided to students in different groups is appropriately differentiated (Gentry, 1999; Kulik & Kulik, 1991). To provide talented readers with multiple opportunities to discuss complex stories, SEM-R teachers may want to provide time for readers to discuss books together during Phase 3 or even as a featured option during Phases 1 or 2. Within groups of talented readers, each student can take a turn leading the discussion, and can use the Bookmarks to formulate questions for the reader sharing the book. It is the challenging content and instruction that occur within groups that makes grouping an effective instructional strategy (Kulik & Kulik, 1991; Rogers, 1991).

A differentiated reading program also enables students to interact with advanced content that has both depth and complexity (Kaplan, 1999), focuses on developing higher level comprehension skills (Collins & Kortner, 1995); and engages students with advanced reading skills instruction (Reis et al., 2004). In our research on the SEM-R (Reis et al., 2005), classroom teachers trained in this approach challenged talented readers with higher-level questioning that extended the depth of the students' contact with engaging literature. They encouraged the use of rich, complex reading that provided the possibility of multiple interpretations of literature that could challenge students at all levels. Talented readers also benefit from having multiple interpretations of text that encourage them to examine how they develop their own beliefs and respond to challenges that they seldom encounter in classrooms (Reis et al., 2005). The SEM-R also enables teachers to use reading strategies such as making connections, determining the importance of text, advanced questioning skills, visualization, inferences, summarizing, and metacognitive strategies (Paris, 2004) with talented readers.

SEM-R teachers should use a Book Hook to introduce at least one complex story line regularly during Phase 1, as stories featuring sophisticated plots and literary elements will challenge and motivate talented readers. Phase 2 also presents teachers with the opportunity to engage talented readers in extended discussions about literary devices and techniques (e.g., foreshadowing, use of metaphor), the author's intention, the relevance of the subject matter to the outside world, and the students' appraisal of the book's worth. Such discourse provides talented readers with the opportunity to develop higher-level reasoning skills through answering advanced-level questions. Talented readers may become excited by participating in challenging conferences and want to engage in prolonged conversations; however, it is important for SEM-R teachers to keep conferences brief. As discussed in the previous chapter, providing short but frequent conferences provides talented readers with the opportunity to discuss the complexity of a challenging book multiple times. If conferences are not scheduled on a regular basis, talented students may miss the opportunity to develop higher-level thinking, as they may finish the book before the next individual conference due to their pace of reading. If a talented reader is completing entire books between conferences, consider evaluating the student's choice of book as the content and reading level are likely to be too easy to encourage growth for this student.

Another lesson that can be learned from Alex is the necessity to challenge talented readers early in school. SEM-R provides opportunities for this level of challenge in all phases. During both Phase 2 and 3, talented readers can be given multiple opportunities to discuss complex stories together both with and without the teacher. Phase 3 also provides an ideal opportunity for talented readers to extend analytical thinking and creative-productive skills. The element of choice during Phase 3 offers the advanced reader the chance to pursue areas of interest related to books that they have read by working independently, or with a small group, to create a product for an audience. Some additional ideas to promote higher-level thinking for talented readers include the following:

- write a review of a book to be shared with a peer or to appear in the school newspaper
- hold a book award ceremony—students design evaluation criteria and judge books according (e.g., best picture book, best fantasy novel)
- adapt a favorite book into a class play
- complete a biography for their favorite author
- compose alternative endings for a book
- generate complex questions for books read that may answered by the next student to read the book
- use the Renzulli Learning System to generate and organize independent projects of interest

In summary, talented readers participating in the SEM-R can benefit from alternative challenging materials in reading based on their interests (Kulik & Kulik, 1991; Rogers, 1991). They can be assigned appropriately challenging substitute books that offer depth and complexity and themes similar to those of books provided to readers at or below-grade-level to facilitate whole class discussion of themes across books (Kaplan, 2001). Talented readers can also be given opportunities to complete different creative products and participate in alternative writing assignments (Reis & Renzulli, 1989). Talented readers can be encouraged to bring prior knowledge and insight into their interpretations of challenging text. They can use technology to access web sites of authors, read challenging books online, and interact with talented readers from other schools using literature circle discussion strategies. Technology can also be used to access advanced content, to create concept maps and other technological products, to write and revise stories, chapters, and even books (Reis et al., 2004).

The SEM-R uses differentiation to address the variations among learners in the classroom through multiple approaches that enrich, modify, and adapt instruction and curriculum to match students' individual needs (Renzulli, 1977; Tomlinson, 1995). Differentiation of instruction and curriculum suggests that students can be provided with materials and work of varied levels of difficulty through scaffolding, enrichment, acceleration, diverse kinds of grouping, and different time schedules (Tomlinson, 1995). Differentiation must be started early for talented readers, as indicated by current research by Reis and Boeve (in press) who found that at-risk talented readers had difficulties participating in above grade level reading, due to an elementary school reading program that was consistently too easy. These talented readers were accustomed to expending minimal effort and had few self-regulation strategies to employ and few advanced reading strategies that they could use when they were asked to read material that was slightly above their grade level. Although talented readers can benefit from appropriately challenging levels of reading, they seldom receive it.

STRATEGIES TO SUPPORT STUDENTS WITH READING DIFFICULTIES

After learning more about students' reading levels and interests, you may wish to conduct further assessments to identify the specific nature of the difficulties experienced by students. Additional assessment can provide information that will help teachers choose instructional strategies to meet the needs of individual students. The source of reading problems experienced by students, as described by Walker (2000), can be due to issues associated with print processing (decoding) and/or meaning processing (comprehension).

Problems with print processing are usually detected by conducting informal reading inventories to determine reading behaviors (e.g., the degree of self-correction, frequency of skipping words/lines, mispronunciations, etc.) and by using word-recognition and spelling tests to determine decoding skills (e.g., phonological knowledge). Meaning should be assessed using both oral reading analysis and silent reading analysis. Oral reading analysis involves asking the student to read a passage aloud, and stopping the student regularly to answer comprehension questions about the text (both literal and interpretive). A student may struggle to complete this task; however, this does not always mean that the student has a problem with comprehension. Reading aloud places additional demands on memory that can compromise understanding. You can therefore follow-up with a silent reading task analysis, where the student is asked to read a passage silently and is stopped periodically to answer literal and interpretive questions. If the student successfully answers questions, this will indicate that the student can process the meaning of text when he or she does not have to read aloud. If the student fails to respond appropriately to questions in the silent reading analysis, the student does experience problems processing the meaning of text.

Using the information gathered from the assessment described above, the teacher may choose instructional strategies to support the specific problems experienced by individual students. You may want to use time during Phase 2 or 3 as an opportunity to implement specific instructional strategies to individually support struggling readers. Suggested strategies for print and meaning processing problems are listed below:

Print Processing Instructional Strategies
- **Echo Reading** is where the novice reader echoes the reading of a proficient reader. This strategy helps students to learn sight words, improves reading fluency and phrasing, assists readers to read text that is too difficult for them to read alone, and develops reading confidence.
- **Chunking** involves the grouping of words in a sentence into short meaningful chunks (usually 3-5 words). Chunking helps students to read in meaningful units (as opposed to word-by-word reading), which assists students to improve both fluency and comprehension (Walker, 1996).
- **Paired Reading** involves the student and teacher reading together in synchrony, and then after some time, the student continues to read on his own. The teacher commences reading again when the student experiences difficulty decoding the

text. On average, children involved in paired reading make three times the normal reading progress in reading accuracy and five times the normal progress in reading comprehension (Topping, 1995).

- **Repeated Readings** involves students reading the same book several times. Familiarity with text after repeated readings improves fluency and reduces the demands placed on working memory, therefore students can dedicate more attention to comprehending text on subsequent readings. Young, Bowers, and MacKinnon (1996), for example, found that the use of repeated readings improves the reading rate, accuracy and comprehension of students with reading difficulties.

- **Word Walls** involve creating an area in the classroom where students can display unknown words that they encounter while reading; students add to the wall after the completion of Phase 2. Teachers select words from the wall during Phase 1 and define the words to develop vocabulary and sight word recognition.

- **Readers Theater** develops the reading fluency and expression of students. Using a familiar book, small groups of students read a story, fable or play to an audience. The general rules of Readers Theater include students' minimal use of gesture, keeping feet still, and a focus on using voice and facial expression to enrich the retelling of the story. Many students enjoy participating in Readers Theater, and it can be a motivational activity for students who experience reading problems.

Meaning Processing Strategies

- **Cloze Instruction** is an instructional technique where words are deleted from text (covered by the teacher), and students are asked to insert words that would "make sense." Cloze instruction encourages students to make predictions and monitor for meaning while reading and is particularly effective for students who read fluently but struggle to comprehend text.

- **Directed Reading-Thinking Activity** is an effective method of improving students' prediction skills. After reading the title and cover of the text, students make initial predictions about the content of the book (plot, characters, settings, etc). Students then read a section of the book, stop, and then review their initial predictions (i.e., were their predictions accurate; what happened that they did not predict?). The students then make new predictions as to what will happen next in the story. The students then recommence reading, stop, and check their predictions. This pattern continues during the reading conference, and throughout independent reading as students develop self-regulation skills.

+ **SQ3R** is an instructional method that assists students in comprehending and retaining information that they read. This strategy is primarily used with non-fiction texts, but may be applied to fictional works. The first step in SQ3R requires a student to *Survey* the chapter and develop an idea of the main ideas presented by the text. The student then generates *Questions* about what he/she wishes to know (the student may record these in writing). Next the student *Reads* the chapter to learn the content of the text. The student then *Recites* his/her understandings of the text by discussing the chapter with others, or by making summaries of the information that he/she learned. The final step involves a *Review* of the chapter and notes the following day (or several days) to reinforce learning.

+ **Triple Read Outline** assists students in identifying the main idea of a passage and the details that support the main idea. Though there are several forms of this technique, the goal of the first reading is for students to identify the main idea of the passage. The second reading of the passage requires students to identify the details that support the main idea. The students then read the passage a third time to confirm their outline of the main idea and supporting details. Students may then use their outline to write a summary of the passage or engage in a discussion about a pre-selected Bookmark question. This instructional strategy helps students develop comprehension and study skills.

+ **K-W-L-H Technique** is a strategy that helps students activate prior knowledge before reading and ask questions that will promote engagement with reading material. Students first list what they KNOW about the subject matter of the text, then they record questions about what they WANT to learn. The students then read the text and look for answers to their questions. After the conclusion of the reading, the students discuss or record what they LEARNED about the subject from reading and then list HOW they could learn more about the subject (e.g., read other books about the topic, conduct a web-search to find out more information).

When you are having a conference with struggling students, it is important to use high-interest and personally challenging books, keep conference times brief and focused on strategy use, and provide specific feedback about reading performance. Finding books for struggling readers can be difficult, but school librarians and reading specialists can help locate suitable texts. It is important to keep conference times to a minimum when teaching struggling readers. Short but frequent conferences help you provide regular feedback about reading strategies and words of encouragement that can be powerful motivators for struggling readers. Increased levels of motivation to read may see the struggling student read for longer periods independently, which should be positively reinforced by teachers.

All three phases in the SEM-R can be successfully used with struggling readers, however they may be somewhat modified to meet individual needs. During Phase 2, some students with similar patterns of reading difficulties may be occasionally grouped together to provide specific mini-lessons about print- or meaning-processing strategies. This action should not however become the norm, as conferencing with individual students to provide differentiated instruction and encouragement is essential. You can also support students who are not able to maintain independent reading throughout Phase 2 by offering alternative activities (e.g., audio books, computer programs that reinforce reading skills and strategies). Teachers should, however, set a goal for the amount of time students spend reading independently, which should be increased on a weekly basis for struggling readers. It is essential that you assess students with reading difficulties during each conference, and, when appropriate, promote the students to a higher reading level. Frequently increasing the difficulty of text encountered by struggling readers just beyond their comfort zone will improve reading skills and confidence.

Struggling readers may view reading as a chore and often miss out on participating in fun activities, as they are required to complete remedial work. It is important to offer choices during Phase 3 for struggling readers, as pursuing areas of interest related to books they read can improve motivation to read. Struggling readers can experience success by completing independent and small group projects though they may also benefit from participating in more structured activities such as Readers Theater and Paired Reading to improve specific reading skills.

Students with reading problems may continue to experience difficulties despite the efforts of the SEM-R teacher. Teachers should consult a reading specialist for advice about additional strategies and resources; further assessment and support may be warranted in some cases. Teachers should be aware of common signs that may indicate more serious problems. Students who persistently make visual errors (e.g., reversal of letter/words, skipping words and lines of text) may experience problems with visual processing and students who commonly mispronounce and misspell words may experience problems with auditory processing. Students who exhibit difficulties comprehending text and verbal instructions may experience problems with language processing. All three problems should be referred to the reading specialist and/or special education teacher for further assessment.

CHAPTER 8

IMPLEMENTING THE SEM-R IN AN AFTER-SCHOOL SETTING

CATHERINE A. LITTLE, SALLY M. REIS, KATHERINE L. RINALDI, & ASHLEY H. HINES

The flexibility of the SEM-R framework allows for application in a variety of contexts beyond the regular reading classroom. A number of schools have experimented with SEM-R in out-of-school time, specifically during after-school programs. For some schools, the after-school setting may be a more feasible option for SEM-R implementation because of curricular and administrative requirements during the school day. On the other hand, schools that use SEM-R during the school day might consider also offering it after school at a different time of year, for different grade levels, or in a different combination of students from the school day application of the framework.

SEM-R in the after-school setting follows the same basic structure as it does during the school day, with time allocated to each of the three phases and central emphases on reading for enjoyment, reading at challenging levels, and developing self-regulation. However, implementing SEM-R after school involves some logistical questions that differ somewhat from the school-day application, raising different kinds of challenges and opportunities. Also, because an after-school SEM-R program likely will meet less frequently (i.e., on fewer days per week), teachers must make instructional decisions around phase scheduling to ensure continuity for the students with the books they are reading. This chapter will explore special considerations for implementing SEM-R after school, including details of scheduling, staffing, program resources, and instructional planning. Near the end of the chapter, several existing after-school SEM-R programs will be profiled as examples of implementation.

Scheduling the Program

In planning an after-school SEM-R program, one of the first issues to be determined is program duration—the number of sessions per week, the length of each session, and the number of weeks in total. Scheduling options for incorporating SEM-R after school vary and depend largely on the resources available.

How Many Days Per Week?

Schools that have implemented SEM-R after school to date have generally scheduled sessions twice a week. If the program only occurs once a week, it is difficult for students to maintain continuity with the books they are reading during Phase 2. Indeed, two days a week presents a fairly limited timeframe for continuity as well. However, an after-school SEM-R program that meets more than 2-3 times per week may run the risk of inconsistent attendance because of other after-school commitments among students, and administrators may find it more difficult to staff a program that meets more frequently.

Another consideration in determining how many days per week to run the program is the issue of avoiding "overload." Reading instruction is an expected part of every school day, so a five-day-a-week schedule for SEM-R works for regular reading time in school. However, SEM-R after school should have greater feeling of something enjoyable, a treat, or a special enrichment experience that becomes more exciting if it is a little less frequent. Keeping in mind that enjoyment of reading is a central goal, planners of an after-school SEM-R program must recognize that even students who already really like reading might not want to spend an additional 90 minutes reading at school beyond the regular school day. With an after-school SEM-R only two to three days a week, students (and teachers!) are more likely to maintain enthusiasm longer. (Naturally, this is not to say that students shouldn't be reading every day after school— just that they might not need a special program for it every day!)

In some cases, SEM-R might be implemented as a part of an existing after-school program that serves as child care for children at the end of the day. If such a program meets five days a week, administrators should still consider running SEM-R formally two to three of the days, although making reading a part of the program every day is recommended as well.

How Many Hours Per Day?

Existing after-school SEM-R programs generally run about 75-90 minutes per session. This length of time allows some flexibility with incorporating all three phases as well as key elements of an after-school program that might differ from reading class, such as time for a snack or some movement activities. A 90-minute session also allows Phase 2 to be lengthy enough each day that students can make good progress in their books each week, despite only meeting on two days.

Again, if an SEM-R program is incorporated within an existing after-school program, planning for the length of time devoted to SEM-R should take into account the other goals of the after-school program and the amount of time students may need to complete homework and other expected after-school activities. It is important to keep SEM-R activities separate from the time students spend on their homework, to maintain focus on reading and enjoyment.

A key consideration in determining the length of an after-school SEM-R program is transportation availability. If students are to be taken home via a school-sponsored method, such as a late bus, obviously the program must fit into a time frame that allows students to board the bus at the time it is available. However, if parents will be picking students up from the program, the ending time is somewhat more flexible, within the range of available times for parents.

How Many Weeks at a Time?

The first pilot implementation of an after-school SEM-R program ran for 6 weeks, twice a week. This time frame allowed the students to become accustomed to the program, to begin to demonstrate some of the expected enjoyment and self-regulation, and to have opportunities for multiple reading conferences. Subsequent after-school programs extended the overall length significantly, however, to allow greater exposure to all aspects of the program and more opportunity to develop habits in reading. Most of the after-school programs using SEM-R to date have run for 10-12 weeks at a time, with a weekly schedule of two 75-90 minute sessions. Schools might consider running the program for the entire school year as well, depending on resource availability. The existing SEM-R after-school programs have involved college student volunteers as a central part of the staffing model, so the program schedules were designed to fit within the fall and spring college semesters. This arrangement resulted in a 10-12 week program run twice a year, approximately from late September to early December and from late January to early April.

These program schedules have resulted in approximately 30-36 hours of contact time with students for each implementation of SEM-R after school. A recent review of evaluation literature on out-of-school time literacy programs suggested that the highest levels of growth in reading achievement have been associated with programs that run between 44-84 hours (Miller, Snow, & Lauer, 2004); by this calculation, the existing SEM-R programs have been somewhat below the recommendations. Nevertheless, our results have suggested some evidence of reading gains from participation in after-school SEM-R (Little & Hines, 2006; Reis & Boeve, in press), and student and teacher enthusiasm seemed strongest in the programs that lasted about 10 weeks. However, it is important to consider how to make the program long enough to have the potential for positive outcomes for students.

Some additional variables to consider in determining the schedule for an after-school SEM-R program are as follows:

- Are other programs going to overlap with the SEM-R schedule in ways that will affect participation and attendance? For example, at one school we saw significant attrition 8 weeks into a 12-week program when a spring after-school track club started. The following year, we rescheduled SEM-R so as not to overlap with track and thereby force attrition or nonparticipation in one program or the other.

- What is the staffing budget, and how will compensation per session vary for different program lengths? Although volunteers can make significant contributions to an after-school SEM-R program, it is important to try to hire paid professional staff to ensure both consistency and strong instructional implementation. Staffing and related budget questions will be discussed further below.

- Will the program rely on volunteers from local colleges or high schools? If so, are there elements in the college or high school schedules that should be considered in scheduling dates for the SEM-R program? (e.g., exam schedules, sports season schedules, college semester start and end dates)

STAFFING

Educational Professionals

During the school day, teachers take primary responsibility for implementing SEM-R and use their expertise in reading instruction and instructional differentiation to support student growth. Because of this expertise, after-school programs using SEM-R should

122

also involve teachers as primary instructors and facilitators. Ideally, the program should be facilitated by teachers with some expertise in reading instruction; however, after-school programs also offer great opportunities to reduce the student-teacher ratio with the use of volunteers and support staff. Moreover, the teachers who work in an after-school SEM-R program do not necessarily have to be the same teachers who would be able to implement SEM-R during the day. For example, our previous after-school SEM-R programs have included a kindergarten teacher and a teacher who works with students with severe disabilities; teachers from a wide range of teaching assignments might be interested in getting involved in students' reading experiences through an after-school SEM-R program.

One of the challenges of staffing SEM-R after school is the question of using paid staff versus volunteers (or some combination of the two). Most school activities that employ teachers beyond the school day, such as coaching, do provide some additional compensation beyond teachers' salaries. Therefore, planning an after-school SEM-R program requires consideration of acquiring funds to pay teachers, and determining how much they should be paid. Some school districts have funding for extracurricular programming that might be tapped for paying teachers; there are also an increasing number of grants available to support after-school programs that might be explored (see Table 8.1).

In addition to the teachers who facilitate the instructional portion of the program, larger programs incorporating SEM-R after school should also consider employing a coordinator to handle administrative and organizational tasks. An SEM-R after-school coordinator might be a teacher, administrator, or other employee of the district, or it might

Table 8.1. Selected Funding Resources

After-school Alliance: http://www.afterschoolalliance.org
This advocacy organization works to raise awareness of the importance of after-school programming and to provide resources for programs. This site includes a page on funding and sustainability, with suggestions for how to search for funding and a database of funding sources.

National After-school Association: http://www.naaweb.org
This organization accredits after-school programs and advertises itself as the leading professional association in the field. The website includes a resource page with links to information and funding sources.

For information on more localized resources, both of the websites listed above also include listings of their state affiliates, .

be someone hired from outside the district to administer the program. This person can be responsible for student recruitment, acquisition of materials, and arrangements for snacks, transportation, and communication with parents. In addition, a coordinator can substitute for a teacher who might need to be out on a given day from the program, thereby preventing the program from having to be cancelled if the regular teacher is unavailable.

In a school implementing an after-school SEM-R program with multiple classes, it is useful to have one person serving as the coordinator across the classes. In a district implementing SEM-R across multiple buildings after school, it is also possible to have one person serving as a coordinator across buildings. The responsibilities of the coordinator, as of the teachers, should be clearly delineated in planning the program.

Planning an after-school SEM-R program also requires considering who in the building will serve as the responsible representative of the school district; in other words, who will make sure all the children are picked up and who will contact parents who might be late arriving; who will be in charge should any emergencies arise or if a child is sick or hurt during the program, etc.? In many schools, a principal or other administrator remains in the building as long as any after-school programs are running. However, if an administrator cannot or does not remain, he or she should designate someone to be in charge—ideally the SEM-R coordinator if such a position has been established. Furthermore, even if a program is staffed largely by volunteers or others who are not employed by the school district, a district employee should be in the building at all times overseeing the program and enforcing school rules and policies.

Teachers and coordinators who are going to serve as the staff for an after-school SEM-R program should participate in professional development around SEM-R just as teachers implementing it during the school day. In addition, teachers should have access to the same kinds of resources for the after-school program as they would during the school day, including bookmarks, CD players with headphones, and reading logs. More discussion of program resources will appear in later sections of this chapter.

Volunteers and Other Support

An after-school SEM-R program is a great context for involving volunteers from the local community in a school-based activity. Volunteers help to reduce the child-adult ratio, which means even though the program may only meet twice a week, each child can likely still have a conference every two to three sessions. Moreover, the reduced ratio and the involvement of multiple adults allows the program to have a focus on developing strong staff-student relationships, which is a key aspect of successful out-of-school-time programs

(Hall, Yohalem, Tolman, & Wilson, 2003; Halpern, 2003). Involvement of multiple adults from different backgrounds and experiences also invites varied experience and expertise, which contribute variety and depth to the exposure provided in Phase 1 and the activities and options provided in Phase 3.

The existing after-school SEM-R programs have used university students as the main source for volunteers. Most universities have a central unit for student activities that likely includes volunteer options, and an after-school program can be advertised through this venue. Advertisements can also be sent to such programs as an Honors program, a school of education, and a child development department as opportunities for students (see sample advertisement). Similarly, high school students may be invited to volunteer in an after-school SEM-R program, with the opportunity advertised through a high school's National Honor Society affiliate, a future educators' club, or the high school newspaper. Finally, parents might be invited to serve as SEM-R volunteers through a school newsletter, parent teacher organization, or similar vehicle.

Volunteers provide wonderful support and enthusiasm for a program using SEM-R after school, and their presence is an added attraction for the children who participate, particularly if the volunteers are young adults. However, as with recruiting teachers and students, program planners must consider the incentives for volunteers to participate and the logistical issues that might prevent or facilitate their participation:

- Transportation: When college students are invited to participate in an after-school program in local schools, many times transportation can become an issue. Many college students with sufficient time to volunteer in such a program are in their earlier years in college and may not be permitted to keep cars on campus. Therefore, recruiting volunteers must involve transportation considerations (e.g.,

---

Volunteer Opportunity!

Do you like working with kids? Do you love to read? Come volunteer in an after-school reading program for elementary and middle-school students. Help classroom teachers in local schools work with kids to strengthen their enjoyment of reading and their understanding of what they read. We are looking for volunteers on Monday, Tuesday, and/or Thursday afternoons for about an hour and a half each visit, starting in mid-September and finishing in early December. We will provide training on the specific program activities before you begin, including tips on how to ask challenging questions about books and how to help kids choose books they might enjoy. Please contact _____ if you think you might be interested in volunteering.

Figure 8.1. Sample advertisement for volunteers.

setting up carpools or making sure volunteers have access to vehicles). Sometimes, if a program can be established as an "official" partner program with a university, transportation may be available through a university outreach or community service program.

+ Scheduling: Volunteers may be limited in their ability to participate based on conflicts in scheduling between their other activities and the after-school program. As noted in the scheduling section above, program planning should consider major events, holidays, and start and end dates of key activities involving the volunteers to the extent possible.

+ Time Commitment: Often, a volunteer may be interested in participating in the program but may only be available one day a week instead of two, or for the first eight weeks of a program but not the last two or three, etc. In program planning, schools must weigh the relative advantages and disadvantages of requiring fulltime participation from volunteers or allowing more volunteer flexibility (and simultaneously creating more inconsistency in the program for the students).

+ Training: SEM-R volunteers are less likely than certified teachers to have a strong basis in reading instruction, child development, or questioning. Therefore, their training for the program will need to involve more of a basic-level overview of some key ideas regarding asking questions about books, helping children with reading, and recognizing when a book is more or less difficult for a child to read. In addition, the SEM-R program should be a situation with "on-the-job" training, with teachers observing and supporting the work of the volunteers (especially regarding conferences). Program coordinators should also communicate expectations to volunteers for their work in the program; both in terms of specific tasks and general conduct (for example, see "Expectations for Volunteers" [Figure 8.2] and "Conferencing with Students: Guidelines and Suggestions" [Figure 8.3]).

RECRUITING STUDENTS

Careful consideration and discussion must be given to recruiting students for SEM-R after school. Although the framework is designed to support reading growth in any student who is capable of reading independently for at least a brief period, it is questionable whether an after-school SEM-R program is appropriate for a child who is a very reluctant reader, or for a child who may have difficulty continuing an academic program beyond the school day because of a need for more physical movement or a change of activities. SEM-R after school is probably best suited for students who already enjoy reading somewhat, at least when they are able to make choices in what they read. The program is less effective if the students do not want to be there. The program is also very appropriate after school for talented readers who may not be challenged by the reading instruction they receive during the day. Many after-school programs emphasize responding to individual needs for remediation through homework help and tutoring; however, this emphasis may limit the challenge provided for more advanced students and the opportunity to focus on strengths. Special programs for students who are advanced in a given area can provide, instead, the kind of challenge and above-level tasks that they may not experience frequently in school.

Schools have approached recruitment for SEM-R in a variety of ways. A school might choose to prepare an invitation letter to send home with all students at relevant grade levels, giving the option for students and parents to express interest in participating, and then program staff may select from the total responding group through a review or lottery process. In such a circumstance, the letter of invitation should clearly communicate that the program is not intended to be a remedial program or one for highly reluctant readers. A school might also choose to conduct a rolling recruitment strategy in which they begin by inviting students who have been specifically recommended by their teachers or based on scores, and then broadening recruitment as space allows. Part of the determination for how this recruitment should go forward is an understanding of the school community; in some schools, opening up a program such as this might lead to a flood of interest and the need to establish a lottery or waiting list. In other schools, a wide net might need to be cast in order to bring in enough students to make the program worthwhile to run.

Part of the student recruitment process also involves determining policies or guidelines for attendance. Before advertising the program to students and parents, SEM-R program planners should establish some attendance guidelines to be shared with parents and students from the beginning. Attendance guidelines are important for a successful implementation in general, and also for ensuring that selection for the program is fair and identifies students who will be able to attend the most of the program. A general guideline is that students should not miss more than three program sessions (within the 10-12 week, 2-day-per-week schedule); if a program has a waiting list and certain students are consistently absent, their spots may be given to other students who wish to participate. The following are some sample questions and scenarios that have arisen regarding program attendance, with the decisions that the schools made and an explanation of the rationale:

* The program will run on Mondays and Thursdays. One student interested in the program already has another after-school activity scheduled for Thursdays but could participate on Mondays. Can he participate one day a week instead of two?

  Decision: No. Participation only one day a week is likely too inconsistent for the program to have any effect, and the student will have difficulty maintaining any continuity in what he is reading and in the relationships he is developing. (Note that this attendance decision for students differs from the guideline given above for volunteers.)

* The program runs from 4:00 until 5:30 on Tuesdays and Thursdays. One student has a karate lesson on Thursdays at 5:30 and would have to leave at 5:15. Can he participate?

  Decision: Yes. In this case, the staff decided to allow the student to participate because the program time missed would be relatively brief.

Expectations for Volunteers

Please be at the schools when you say you will be there! The teachers and the kids are very excited that you are volunteering to help them, and they are depending on you to stick to your set schedule. If you cannot go to your school on your scheduled day, please e-mail or call _____ as far in advance as possible so we can let your teacher know.

If the school district has an early dismissal because of the weather, the program is CANCELLED for the day. _____ will e-mail you to let you know of any closings, so please check your e-mail! You may also check the school districts' websites for closing info.

Just a few reminders about visiting schools:

Please dress appropriately. You might be sitting on the floor, bending down, etc., and you don't want the kids to see more than your outer layer of clothes.

Make a conscious effort to watch your language while you are at the schools.

You are a pre-professional representing the University, so please remember professional conduct.

When you arrive at the school, please check in at the main office; checking in might involve signing into a book and/or wearing a name badge.

Ideas you can contribute to our project…

If you have ideas for class activities, especially for Phase 3 activities, please let us know!

The teacher you work with may ask you to do a Book Hook during Phase 1. If you have a favorite book that you'd like to share, let your teacher know!

Figure 8.2. Sample list of expectations for volunteers.

Conferencing with Students: Guidelines and Suggestions

1. When you begin a conference, sit down with the student and ask him/her to tell you a little bit about the book.

2. Ask the student to describe how he/she likes the book so far, and why.

3. Ask the student to read a little bit of the book aloud to you, starting wherever they stopped when you dropped in. Have the student read about 2 pages or 1-2 minutes.

    a. If the student comes to a word he/she does not know, wait a few seconds and then tell the student the word. Allow the narrative flow to keep going, rather than interrupting with too much time spent trying to figure out the word.

    b. If the student is missing so many words that it is impossible to keep the narrative flow up, stop the student and suggest that maybe this is a book he/she wants to save to read later on, when he/she has had a little more time to practice reading. Have the student write the name and author of the book on the sheet "Books I Want to Read Later," and then help the student choose a new book.

    c. Pay careful attention to how the student reads the passage. Listen for about how many words are difficult for the student, for expression, and for other indications of comprehension.

    d. Also pay careful attention if the book seems to be very easy for the student to read. If the student is able to read every word on every page, with clear indication that comprehension of the book is also very easy for the student, the book may be too easy for reading time in the program. See #7 for further discussion of this issue.

4. When the student finishes reading, offer some praising comment. Try to be specific (e.g., "I really liked how you used different voices for the characters!" or "I liked how you went back and corrected yourself on a word that you missed!"), then ask the student a few follow-up questions about the reading. You may want to use one of the Bookmarks as a guide, or you may want to ask some questions that are more specific to the passage itself.

    a. Try to ask questions that go beyond just recall of what happened in the text. Ask "why" questions, and ask students to support answers with details from the book.

    b. Try to ask questions that are challenging for the particular student. Different types of questions are more appropriate for different students.

    c. You can ask the student to talk about what he/she likes or does not like about the book, but do not limit your questions to that! The goal of the conference is to challenge the student to think about the book more deeply and to develop stronger skills at reading and interpreting the text.

    d. One good source of questioning is the connections that can be made with the text. We can classify connections questions as "text to text," "text to self," and "text to world."

5. The follow-up questioning time is also a good time to revisit words that the student might have missed. Go back and point out some words that were a little challenging and ask the student how he/she might have tried to figure out the words. Talk about strategies for figuring out words, such as using context clues, using pictures, and looking for parts of the words that are familiar.

6. The questioning portion of the conference should take just 3-5 minutes. The overall conference should take only about 7-10 minutes at most. *continued on next page*

Figure 8.3. Conferencing guidelines and suggestions.

Conferencing with Students: Guidelines and Suggestions (continued)

7. In some cases, the reading and discussion portions of the conference, together or separately, might indicate that the book is too hard or too easy for the student. If this is the case, encourage the student to try a different book. In the case of books that are too easy, talk to the student about the importance of reading challenging books while at school where someone can help. Encourage the student to read the easier book on his/her own time. In the case of books that are too hard, encourage the student to save the book for later, as noted above. In either case, offer to work with the student to choose a more appropriate book, and spend some time talking about ways of choosing books. Check the child's "Books I Want to Read Later" and also the "Completed Books" list for some indication of the types of books that might appeal to this particular student.

8. Record details of the conference into the "Conference Log" in the student's reading log. Indicate the main area(s) of focus of your conference (e.g., character, theme, word attack strategies, selecting books, etc.), and jot down any notes that would be useful to you or another volunteer or teacher for this student's next conference. Ask the student to display his or her "Conferenced Today" card as a signal to other adults in the room, and thank the student for sharing some reading time with you.

Figure 8.3. Conferencing guidelines and suggestions (continued).

* The program has been meeting for two weeks already, and one enrolled student has yet to attend. School records indicate that she has been out sick for those two weeks. Should she be removed and her spot given to another student?

  Decision: No. In general, the program is linked to the attendance policy of the school. If a child is in school on a given day, that child should attend the after-school program; if a child is absent from school, the absence from the after-school program would not count against him or her.

These decisions represent samples of what existing programs decided regarding attendance, not hard and fast rules. The two main considerations in establishing attendance guidelines are (a) will the student be attending enough to receive the benefit of the program? and (b) are there other students waiting for a spot that is taken by a student who does not frequently attend? In schools with lower participation rates in general, attendance guidelines have tended to be more relaxed than in those schools with waiting lists; however, students who attend the program infrequently do have difficulty maintaining consistent focus in their reading.

In addition to attendance guidelines, those planning an SEM-R program should also consider the behavioral expectations within the program and the kind of program outcomes that will be communicated to parents. Presenting some of these details as part of an invitation to the program or confirmation of registration helps with keeping the program goal-focused and organized. It also gives parents and students advance understanding of key elements and expectations (see sample guidelines letter in Figure 8.4).

IMPLEMENTING THE PROGRAM

Scheduling the Phases

In general, the organization and presentation of the three SEM-R phases should follow the same pattern after school as during the school day. Sessions should begin with one or more Book Hooks and potentially some related discussion and/or reading strategy instruction, followed by time for Supported Independent Reading, concluding with choices of interest-based activities for Phase 3. The length of each of the phases depends, naturally, on the length of the program sessions, and on students' capacity for reading independently for an extended period of time. In some cases, depending on how student recruitment is conducted and who is selected for the program, an after-school SEM-R program may begin with students already capable of maintaining independent reading for 30 to 40 minutes or more; in other cases, the independent reading time may have to be built more gradually over time.

Teachers implementing the SEM-R after school should consider a couple of key questions as they plan the program schedule. First, will students have enough time in Phase 2 to maintain continuity of attention to the books they are reading? Second, will students have enough time in Phase 3 to accomplish the kinds of projects they wish to explore? These considerations may influence the types of options offered for Phase 3 and the guidance teachers provide to students in selecting their books to read in Phase 2. In most cases, a 90-minute after-school program does not actually mean 90 full minutes of SEM-R time, because of the need to include time for snacks and to prepare for a late bus or parent pick-up. As noted in earlier chapters, some teachers choose to implement "Phase 3 days" in one day of the week during school-day SEM-R programs so that Phase 3 time is not shortchanged. This schedule can be accommodated in the after-school setting as well, but teachers who choose to do so must recognize that if a session is devoted entirely or primarily to Phase 3, students will only have one day in the space of a week to continue their independent reading books.

Dear Students and Parents/Guardians,

Thank you for your interest in the Expanding Horizons reading program! This letter will inform you of some of the rules and expectations of the program. Please read carefully, and sign and return the bottom portion of the letter.

Attendance and Transportation
- The program will run as scheduled from the week of January 16 through the week of April 24, except for scheduled school holidays.
- On days when school is cancelled or dismissed early for weather, the program will not run. If all after-school activities are cancelled due to weather, this program also will not run. Snow days in the program will not be made up.
- The program cannot provide transportation for students. Parents must arrange transportation home as with any other after-school activity.
- Students in the program are expected to attend on any day that they attend school. If a student misses more than three (3) program sessions on days that he or she does attend school, the student will be asked to leave the program to make space for another student.

Program Expectations
- The program invites students to spend extra time enjoying reading after school. The program is not intended to be a homework help program. Homework will have to be completed after students leave the program each day.
- The program will provide all books and materials for students and a small snack each day. Students may bring a snack from home if they prefer. Snacks including peanut products should be avoided.
- No grades will be assigned based on the program. Students will complete a reading log to demonstrate their progress and activities.

Program rules are as follows:
Respect others.
Follow directions.
Stay with program staff at all times.
Arrive at the program ready to read!

Consequences for not following the rules are as follows:
1st offense: Warning
2nd offense: Time-out
3rd offense: Call home
4th offense: Asked to leave program

— — — — — — — — — — — — — — — — — — —

Please sign and return to your child's school.
Child's Name: _____
We have read and understood the program guidelines presented above.
Parent Signature: _____
Child Signature: _____

Figure 8.4. Sample guidelines letter.

PROGRAM RESOURCES

Planning for an after-school SEM-R program requires consideration of several resource questions. As described in previous chapters, the program makes use of a large library of books as its primary resource and also additional materials such as reading logs, CD/tape players with headphones, computers with Internet access, and art supplies for some Phase 3 activities. Some of the resource issues to address in planning an SEM-R program after school are as follows:

- **Program location:** Will the program be held in classrooms or in some other place in the school building? To some degree, the answer to this question may depend on how the program is staffed. In past implementations of SEM-R after school, the program has generally occurred in the classrooms of the teachers facilitating it. In some cases, if the teachers traveled from a different building to run the program, the sessions might instead be held in the library/media center.

- **Books:** Other than stipends for staff members, books are generally the largest expenditure for an after-school SEM-R program. Such a program may be able to use some of the books already in the school or in the classrooms of teachers conducting the program, but implementation will be smoother if a collection of books is available and reserved for after-school program participants. Just as in the school-day version of the SEM-R, the book collection should include a wide array of topics, genres, and reading levels, and although many books should be available at the beginning of the program, a portion of the book budget should be reserved for adding to the collection based on students' expressed interests as the program progresses. Planning an after-school SEM-R program should also involve a conversation with the school librarian to determine the level of access students may have to the library after school; indeed, schools might consider inviting the librarian to help to coordinate the program, thereby creating better opportunity for access to library materials.

- **Reading logs:** Again, just as in a school-day implementation of SEM-R, reading logs should be used as a record-keeping mechanism for both students and teachers to keep track of reading progress. It is especially important to use a conference log within the reading log in an after-school program; with multiple adults conducting conferences with students, the conference log provides a method of communication among the adults as to a particular child's progress and the focus of different reading conferences. Obviously, reading logs for an after-school version of SEM-R should be tailored to include log space for students matching the schedule of the program, rather than for a five-day-a-week format.

- ◆ **Snacks**: A 90-minute after-school program is a significant addition to the school day for children. Some kind of healthy snack is important for helping students to maintain energy and focus. Often, snacks for an after-school program may be arranged through the school's existing food service program, or they may be purchased and brought in separately for the program. Either way, snacks are an important component to incorporate into a budget for an after-school program.

VARIATION FROM THE SCHOOL DAY

One of the recommendations from evaluations of after-school programs is to be sure that they are different from what kids experience during the school day (Hall et al., 2003; Halpern, 2003). An after-school version of the SEM-R should maintain the challenge and integrity of the framework, but should be different from what students experience during their school-day reading class. In many cases, this distinction may be in the framework itself, if it is significantly different from students' regular reading class experiences. In other cases, the variation may occur through the involvement of volunteers or through some aspect of the choices and options available to students, especially in Phase 3. After-school SEM-R programs also offer opportunities for flexible grouping, including cross-grade grouping, to allow students to share reading time with students from other grade levels and classes, with whom they may not normally interact during the school day.

Movement activities represent another component that helps create distinction from the school day while also promoting healthy activity and exercise. Given the widespread concerns about weight and related health issues in children, it is important to consider how to get students up and moving after school, even though much of the program time is devoted to sitting and reading! Movement activities may include walking with friends to discuss books they are reading during Phase 3; dramatic activities that involve taking on the roles of characters in stories and acting out scenes; or even a short physical warm-up before the program gets started each day.

EXAMPLES OF AFTER-SCHOOL IMPLEMENTATIONS OF THE SEM-R

Throughout this chapter, existing after-school SEM-R programs have been mentioned with some details about how they have implemented the framework. In this last section of the chapter, three school programs will be described more holistically to demonstrate how several sites have put all of the pieces together. Each of these program descriptions will discuss (a) recruitment of students, (b) organizational and instructional details of the implementation, and (c) special features and challenges regarding the implementation at each site.

Four Corners School

This elementary school implemented the SEM-R roughly in its original form in one classroom during the after-school time. The teacher who facilitated the program, a fourth-grade teacher at the school, had previously implemented SEM-R during his regular reading instruction, so he was familiar with the framework and able to transfer it smoothly to the after-school setting. Most of the participants in the program were fourth graders, the highest grade level served by the school, although a few third graders were also invited to participate. Students were selected by the team of fourth-grade teachers and invited to the program, and then third-grade teachers selected a few students for the remaining spaces. All of the students selected were fairly strong readers. They included a few students who were strong readers in their native Spanish but not in English, but because the teacher and some of the other students were bilingual and a number of books in Spanish had been purchased for the program, these students were able to participate.

A class of about 20 students met in "Mr. C.'s" classroom after school from 4:00-5:30 twice a week. During each session, two to four volunteers also attended, including college students and a parent helper. One volunteer was able to attend twice a week, while each of the others attended once a week.

Each session began with a snack, and Phase 1 usually began while students were finishing their snacks. Mr. C. conducted most of the Phase 1 Book Hooks himself, but also occasionally invited the volunteers to lead, emphasizing that they should choose books to share that they themselves had enjoyed as children.

Phase 2 found the students scattered around the classroom to read, while the teacher and volunteers conducted conferences. Phase 2 usually began by about 4:20 or 4:25 and lasted until about 5:00, except on a few days when extra time was needed for special activities in Phase 3.

Mr. C. made use of his volunteer support to conduct Phase 3. He and the volunteers collaboratively determined several options based on students' expressed interests, and then each adult took responsibility for one of the options. When Phase 3 began each day, usually about 5:05 p.m., students moved to their groups and worked on projects with facilitation by the adults. Phase 3 activities included research on the origins of names and the origins of mathematical terms, learning about dissection through online demonstrations and diagrams, writing and performing a mystery play, and participation in a "Stock Market Game." Occasionally, about once every two or three weeks, Mr. C. would bring the whole group together for a special activity during Phase 3 rather than dividing the class into groups. For example, he shared with the whole class an online "field trip" to a rain forest, projecting images from the screen at the front of the room and involving the class in make-believe travel. Mr. C. used technology resources extensively, allowing students to listen to audio books, to read online, and to use the Internet for many of the Phase 3 options.

Mr. C. also began and ended each session with a conversation with the whole class, keeping a strong emphasis on building community. Through these conversations, students as well as adults shared observations about their reading and about the program as a whole, so Mr. C. was able to evaluate the program on an ongoing basis and make necessary adjustments.

This school is a good example of the benefits of involving volunteers in a program, thereby allowing Phase 3 activities to be fairly extensive despite limited time. Mr. C. made it a point to meet with his volunteers regularly to talk with them about program progress and to ask them about their reactions and their own interests and how those interests might be put to use in program activities. Nevertheless, the intensive involvement of volunteers also presented challenges for this program if, for example, a volunteer was unable to attend on a given day; also, because most of the volunteers were only able to attend one of the two days per week, there was some difficulty in maintaining continuity in the Phase 3 activities. The teacher's strong management of the program activities was important in alleviating the difficulties that might have presented themselves around Phase 3 activities.

Another special feature of this school's implementation was the involvement of students who were English language learners. The program gave them a safe space in which they could participate by reading books in their native Spanish or try reading books in English, with support for either. Overall, the sense of community in the classroom made this school's program a unique setting and a very popular one with strong student attendance and little attrition from volunteers.

Northend School

This intermediate school implemented a slightly modified version of the SEM-R during after-school time, slightly altering the schedule of the phases to fit within a challenging program schedule. The program served four classes of students, one at each grade level 3-6, and used four teachers as classroom facilitators and one teacher as a coordinator. With large numbers of students across the program and varied interests among the participating teachers, this school had students spend Phases 1 and 2 in grade-level groupings and then allowed regrouping across classes for Phase 3.

To recruit interested students, the school district mailed home letters at the beginning of the school year explaining the program to all families with students at the relevant grade levels, with a form to be returned to indicate interest in participating. A meeting for interested parents at the school allowed parents to learn more about the program and ask questions before deciding whether to enroll their children. The school, planning to run both a fall and spring session of the program, asked parents to indicate a scheduling preference. The team of program teachers then reviewed the forms and placed the students in the fall or spring sessions. If a question arose as to whether the program was a match for a particular student, a discussion was held with the student's classroom teacher and parents before a decision about the student's participation was collaboratively made.

By sending out the invitations at the beginning of the year, the school avoided having to create a waiting list despite large numbers of interested families at grades 3 and 4. The students at these grade levels were assigned at the beginning of the year either to the fall or spring session, and each interested student was accommodated. In grades 5 and 6, interest was somewhat lower and a second letter of invitation went out in December to invite students to the spring session. Those students who wished to continue for a second semester were also allowed to do so.

Each grade level class of approximately 10-15 students met after school from 3:00-4:30 twice a week. During each session, 2-6 college volunteers gave their time to the program. When at least 4 volunteers were available, each classroom had an available teacher and volunteer to work with the children; when fewer volunteers attended, they were generally assigned to work in the classrooms with younger students, which tended to be the larger classes.

Every session began with the students convening in the cafeteria for a snack. The coordinator supervised this time, while the program teachers were dismissing the rest of their classes to the intermittently arriving buses. Upon finishing snack, the students went to their classrooms, grouped by grade level. As noted above, this school ran the program from 3:00-4:30; however, because of the school's lengthy dismissal period and the process used for distributing snacks and then moving the students to their classes, Phase 1 usually did not begin until 3:20. Therefore, after first trying to fit all three phases into a short period every session, the teachers made a modification and decided that most sessions should include only Phases 1 and 2, with every fourth session devoted to Phases 1 and 3.

Phase 1 was usually conducted by the program teachers, though occasionally volunteers provided the Book Hooks as well. Phase 1 was usually completed by about 3:35 or 3:40, at which time Phase 2 would begin on three out of four days and Phase 3 on the fourth day. On Phase 2 days, students would remain in their grade level groupings for reading and conferences. On Phase 3 days, each teacher would offer a different option, and students would move to different classrooms for their Phase 3 activities. This allowed some regrouping across grade levels and encouraged teachers to share their own interests with students. During one SEM-R Phase 3 session, a student might work on an artistic piece reflective of the theme of a book he recently read. At another time, the same student might participate in readers' theater or in development of a puppet show. On yet another day, the student might go online in a computer lab to explore topics of interest.

Students in this school enjoyed the variety of Phase 3 days, and the teachers were satisfied that the alternating schedule offered sufficient reading and conferencing time for students while also giving them solid blocks of time for Phase 3 activities. Thus, the teachers at this school used their limited time productively to provide an array of activities for the students. Collaboration across multiple classrooms and teachers in this school also created a strong sense of camaraderie and program ownership among the teachers, including the coordinator, who played a crucial role in keeping the large program organized and running smoothly.

Parent involvement is very strong overall at this school, so the parent meeting to discuss the program and ongoing communication efforts from the coordinator were critical to the program's success. This school was also able to provide transportation home for students on a late bus at the end of the program each day, which also helped with the positive response to the program. Of course, the positive response also limited the length of time the younger students, at least, could be involved in the program. This school experimented across several program sessions with class sizes, discovering ultimately that with somewhat limited volunteer support, the teachers wanted to keep class sizes under 15 to provide sufficient individual attention. Such attention did allow the teachers to get to know their students well, and to respond to their needs; the teachers at this school were also vigilant about consistently adding new titles to the program library to respond to student interests.

Gunther Hill School

This school also modified the SEM-R framework slightly in application because of a combination of limited time and highly talented and focused readers. The program at this school involved two teachers and 25-28 third and fourth graders, and sessions lasted from 3:45-5:00 twice a week. Each day, two to five college volunteers also participated.

At this school, the principal and teachers decided that the program would primarily be intended as an enrichment program for talented readers, and they first invited fourth grade students who scored in the top 20th percentile of various reading assessments. Additional open spaces were offered to third grade students who also scored in the top 20th percentile on their tests. Individual teacher recommendations were also taken into consideration when extending program offers; the two teachers conducting the program represented two-thirds of the fourth grade team in this small school, so their familiarity with the students was helpful in determining participation.

Each session began with all the students gathering in one of the two classrooms to eat a snack and participate in Phase 1. The teachers presented the majority of the Phase 1 Book Hooks, but they also extended the opportunity to the volunteers to occasionally conduct Book Hooks if they felt comfortable. At the conclusion of Phase 1, the two teachers invited the students to go to either classroom to do their reading and Phase 2 began. With students moving from one classroom to another on different days and with a large number of volunteers, the teachers at this school implemented a conference documentation system that was quite effective. They posted a chart with a list of the students and columns for each program date on the wall between the two classrooms. Each time a teacher or volunteer conducted a conference, he or she would initial the chart on the appropriate date. This allowed a quick visual reference for which students had been conferenced with most recently or most frequently, and prevented too much interruption of individual student reading to check their reading logs for recent conference details.

The program at this school was designed as enrichment for the highest-achieving students at a high-achieving school, and almost all of the students were voracious readers; therefore, Phase 2 usually lasted for almost the entire program session, beginning by around 4:00 at the latest and lasting until students began packing up at about 4:55. Rather than representing a separate phase for the whole group, Phase 3 activities were intertwined into Phase 2 on a highly individualized basis. Each time a student finished reading a book, that student would be invited to work individually with a teacher or volunteer to select an activity for "celebrating" that book. Some students chose to write to the author to discuss the novel in greater detail, others opted to create and share an artistic piece or poem to commemorate the book, and others chose to conduct Internet inquiries to gather more information on a topic of particular interest. Furthermore, just as in the general recommendations for Phase 3 students may have the option of continuing to read, at this school students could choose not to do a book celebration, but rather to start reading their next selection.

The decision to conduct Phase 3 in this manner at this particular school was made based on the students' own interest in having as much reading time as possible. Most of the students were content to read for the majority of the time they spent in this after-school program. This model might not be appropriate for all settings or all students, but in this case it worked quite effectively. The concept of "book celebrations" for a modified Phase 3 was also an excellent fit for this school, matching the students' high-interest in reading and supporting development of strong interpersonal relationships between students and adults around the celebration of books.

Assessment was a particular challenge for this program because most of the students were so highly fluent that little change could occur in their reading fluency. Most assessment had to occur through conferences, and the volunteers at this school had to work to learn high-level questioning that was sufficiently challenging for the advanced readers.

EXPANDING THE VISION

After-school settings represent a good context for implementing SEM-R in a way that thoroughly promotes enjoyment of reading and allows a little more latitude and flexibility than might be available during the school day, in terms of staffing, timing, and other aspects of implementation. After-school settings are by no means the only out-of-school time options for SEM-R; schools might also consider whether a summer or Saturday SEM-R program might be feasible, or whether a modified version of the program might be presented as a "lunch bunch" activity or an elective/enrichment class at the middle school level. The flexibility of the SEM-R framework allows it to be applied smoothly across a range of settings, and out-of-school time provides a special context for students' reading experiences to go beyond the school day.

"Just the knowledge that a good book is awaiting one at the end of a long day makes that day happier." (Kathleen Norris, *Hands Full of Living*, 1931)

CHAPTER 9

SUPPORTING IMPLEMENTATION: THE SEM-R COACH

CATHERINE A. LITTLE

As teachers begin to implement a new instructional framework, such as the SEM-R, questions inevitably arise about how best to make the strategies work within their own classrooms and with their own students. For example, a teacher might ask herself, how will I be sure to cover all the elements in the reading standards? How can I ask students challenging questions when they are reading a book I have not read? What kinds of reading strategies should I be teaching when working with highly advanced readers? What kinds of options can I provide for Phase 3? This guidebook is intended to answer some of these questions, but having the support of other collaborative professionals can be vital in helping teachers become more comfortable with new ideas and instructional strategies.

Literacy coaching is becoming a popular support and professional development model in reading education generally, and the idea of coaching has many applications within the SEM-R framework. This chapter explains the roles and responsibilities of an SEM-R coach.

An SEM-R coach is a professional in the school environment whose role is to support implementation by facilitating SEM-R teachers' goal-setting, classroom practice, and reflection. Coaches work with teachers during and outside instructional time to understand the framework, find answers to questions that arise during implementation, and develop activities and resources. Coaches are not supervisors or evaluators, but rather colleagues who can offer another perspective on classroom practice and assist in seeking resources and answers.

Recommendations for coaching SEM-R are grounded in more general strategies for literacy coaching as well as experience with the implementation of the framework in a number of different school settings. The following are some examples of an SEM-R coach's activities:

- gathering a group of teachers together to discuss how SEM-R relates to their current reading instruction
- documenting alignment of SEM-R with district and state expectations in the area of reading
- working with school administrators and librarians to find ways to add to the school's collections of books
- modeling a Book Hook or conference in a particular classroom with a follow-up debriefing conversation with a teacher
- working collaboratively with teachers to plan Phase 2 conferences and Phase 3 activities to respond to a student with special needs
- covering an SEM-R teacher's class to allow him or her to observe another colleague implementing the framework
- helping teachers search for books to meet special interests or ability levels of some students

Through a combination of these types of supports, our experience has demonstrated that the SEM-R coach can help make implementation of the SEM-R easier and more effective by supporting teachers as they develop their own sense of efficacy and by linking the SEM-R to the overall reading instruction program of the school.

ROLE OF A COACH

Who is the SEM-R Coach?

A literacy coach is not the same thing as a reading specialist, although many literacy coaches are also or have been reading specialists. The main distinction between the roles is the primary audience for the work that they do in facilitating reading. While reading specialists generally focus on students including small group or individual instruction for struggling readers, literacy coaches focus primarily on supporting teachers (Toll, 2005).

An SEM-R coach's primary responsibility is to help teachers to implement the program effectively; the coach does this by facilitating teacher goal-setting and reflection, by modeling and discussing classroom activities, and by helping teachers to link the framework authentically into their existing repertoire of skills. The following research-based characteristics and skills (IRA, 2004; Toll, 2005) are important ones for an SEM-R coach:

- strong background and experience in teaching reading
- comprehensive knowledge about the SEM-R
- thorough knowledge of reading strategies, including foundational strategies to more advanced strategies for critical reading
- understanding of the special needs of students with exceptionalities, including struggling readers and advanced readers
- experience with facilitating discussions among groups of teachers
- strong habits of reflection
- ability to model goal-setting and reflection
- well-developed skills at observing classroom activities and problem-solving related to classroom events
- experience with providing feedback to colleagues in a collaborative manner that facilitates reflection and problem-solving

Although the SEM-R coach will take on a leadership role in implementation, the coach can also be someone who is just beginning to develop expertise in the SEM-R framework through professional development activities related to the program. The person who is going to serve as an SEM-R coach in a school must have dedicated time within the school day assigned to the role, to allow for classroom visits as well as meetings with teachers individually and in groups during planning time. In our research with the SEM-R, reading specialists, administrators, and gifted resource teachers have volunteered or been assigned to assume the role of SEM-R coach in their schools.

Although most coaches will have other responsibilities beyond what they do to support SEM-R, it is important that the coach not be someone with the responsibility for supervising or evaluating the teachers implementing the framework. While it is important for coaches to spend time in classrooms, working with teachers and becoming familiar with their practices, that time should not be viewed by coach, teacher, or administrator as an evaluative experience. The evaluative role can limit the development of the professional relationship needed for collaboration (Joyce & Showers, 1995; Toll, 2005).

Why is a Coach Necessary?

Part of the reason for the genesis of the coaching model is the difficulty in transfer of skills presented in professional development workshops to changes in classroom practice. Professional development research has consistently demonstrated that without follow-up after new strategies are presented to teachers, classroom implementation tends to be limited (Joyce & Showers, 1995). The coaching model responds to this issue by having a professional support person who is knowledgeable about best practices in reading, well-versed in the new strategies that are being implemented, and able to assist teachers in changing classroom practice. In-class coaching promotes the transfer of newly learned skills or ideas into classroom practice, in part because of the opportunity for coaches to guide teachers in recognizing the linkages between past practice and new strategies. Coaches also work to develop confidence and comfort with changes in practice. As teachers begin to try out a new program, coaching can provide validation of what the teachers are doing, as well as support and feedback for areas in which teachers might be struggling or unsure. During and following the implementation of new strategies, a teacher and coach can talk together about what worked, what could have gone better, and how to improve (Joyce & Showers, 1995; Toll, 2005).

Defining the Coach's Role

One of the difficulties related to the literacy coaching model is the ambiguity that exists related to the definition of the role. Dole (2004) discussed the many questions that persist related to literacy coaching, such as the issue of whether the coach should primarily be working with groups or individuals and the question of how much time should be spent in classrooms demonstrating lessons versus co-teaching or observing. The literature on coaching has consistently highlighted the importance of establishing a clear understanding between coach and administration as to the nature of the coaching role, the expectations for time spent in various activities, and the importance of avoiding a supervisory role. The expectations of the roles of both coach and teacher must be clearly communicated among all involved, to promote relationships of trust and clarification that the coach is not an evaluator (Toll, 2005).

Much of the previous discussion has highlighted the coach's work with individual teachers; coaches should also focus on working with groups of teachers, to foster professional learning communities around the teaching of reading. Coaches must recognize, however, that merely getting groups of teachers together to talk about their reading instruction does not necessarily foster professional learning communities. Rather, once again, collaborative groups must be formed around specific questions and directions for reflection and growth, and coaches must work to recognize and respond to the different needs of teachers within a group and to use their understanding of different individuals to facilitate productive conversation. One of the most effective ways coaches may support the implementation of best practices among a group of teachers is to give teachers opportunities to visit one another's classrooms to observe instruction. A coach may take over a teacher's classroom to provide release time for this, and can facilitate the process by helping teachers to determine who would be the best match for them to observe.

Getting Started with Coaching in the SEM-R

In a school planning to adopt the SEM-R across a diverse range of classrooms, a coach should be involved in the process from the beginning. As a group of teachers prepares to implement the SEM-R, the coach can provide support and leadership with consideration of the following elements of professional development and logistical planning.

- **Understanding the SEM-R.** The coach must take the lead role in developing a thorough understanding of the SEM-R, through such activities as careful reading of this guidebook, exploration of the SEM-R website (www.gifted.uconn.edu/ semr), and participation in professional development activities.

- **Making linkages to the SEM-R.** Beyond understanding the model itself, the coach should also take the lead on aligning local expectations for reading instruction to SEM-R. This includes identifying elements in adopted textbooks or curricula that may transfer easily to the SEM-R classroom and recognizing how reading standards may be achieved within SEM-R, through such aspects as instruction during Book Hooks and Phase 2 conferences. It also involves identifying elements of local expectations that do not link directly to the SEM-R, in order to determine how best to attend to these standards.

- **Documenting how state and district standards will be addressed and integrated.** To clarify the connections between local reading expectations and the SEM-R for all stakeholders, the coach may create written documentation that explains how reading standards will be addressed and assessed. Such a written document will help alleviate any concerns of teachers, parents, or administrators about how the framework fits within the larger picture of the school's reading goals.

- **Facilitating teachers' goal-setting.** As teachers prepare to implement the SEM-R, they should be purposeful and proactive about their own professional development by setting specific short- and long-term goals for how they will enact the framework in their own classrooms. Careful goal-setting helps teachers make a new program more manageable, and it also facilitates ongoing reflection on progress. An important responsibility of the literacy coach is to facilitate goal-setting and reflection. Prior to beginning to implement the SEM-R, the coach may meet with teachers individually and in groups to review the framework, discuss questions, and develop goals. The coach should not dictate the teacher's goals. Rather, the coach may ask questions that help teachers recognize their own areas of strength and interest and determine what they will focus on as they begin implementation.

+ **Collecting resources.** The coach should work collaboratively with administrators, media specialists, and classroom teachers to collect the resources needed to begin SEM-R implementation. This task includes helping teachers assess their current classroom libraries to determine "gaps" in their book collections in terms of genres, topics, and levels of difficulty. The coach should also lead a discussion about the kinds of options they would like to provide during Phase 3, to ensure that any necessary resources for Phase 3 activities are available.

+ **Communicating to parents.** Depending on a school's current reading program, the SEM-R may represent a departure from the norm, and it is important that parents understand how the program works and how they may work in partnership with teachers to support reading development at home. In a school-wide implementation of SEM-R, coaches should take the lead in preparing parent letters and, possibly, organizing parent meetings about the program and its implications for student learning in reading.

+ **Developing relationships.** The effectiveness of the coaching model is grounded in collaborative, collegial relationships between coach and teachers. Before implementation even begins, coaches must be proactive about building those relationships and about establishing the routines to be followed during SEM-R.

COACHING DURING ALL SEM-R PHASES

SEM-R coaches work with teachers throughout all aspects of implementation, and often their main areas of focus will be determined by what each teacher and group of teachers may identify as goals or areas of concern. However, there are some specific activities within each phase that coaches may wish to consider in planning their support role for SEM-R.

Coaching for Phase 1

During Phase 1, coaches may on occasion demonstrate how to lead a Book Hook, sharing one or more selections of their choice with students and providing some brief reading instruction as part of the process, as described in more detail in Chapter Two. This process enables the coach to model Book Hooks for other teachers and also adds some variety to the students' listening experience and their learning from the reading habits of others. If teachers specifically request that a coach watch an individual classroom teacher's Book Hook and provide feedback, coaches may also use these experiences as a basis for follow-up conversations with teachers about Phase 1 activities, with a clear understanding that the observation does not take on an evaluative slant.

Another way coaches can support teachers in Phase 1 is to talk about and model how best to incorporate targeted reading instruction within the Phase 1 context. Because coaches are often reading specialists themselves, or have a strong reading background, they can guide teachers in identifying areas of need for strategy instruction for students and best practices to implement such instruction. For example, a coach may work with a teacher to select discussion questions to help assess students' predicting skills during a Phase 1 discussion. Or, a coach and teacher might work together to select several reading selections that demonstrate the patterns that characterize a particular genre or tradition in literature. Further, because the coach works with teachers across a range of classrooms, he or she can facilitate a sharing of what works in Phase 1, including both instructional activities that are embedded within the read-alouds and particular book selections to make Book Hooks both educational and enjoyable.

Coaching for Phase 2

Phase 2 is perhaps the most critical part of the SEM-R framework, as it is the phase in which teachers provide differentiated and individualized instruction and foster one-on-one relationships with students around reading. Coaches offer several aspects of support during this phase, including direct interaction with students, although it is critical for coaches to maintain focus on supporting teachers as their central emphasis.

Coaches can hold conferences with students during Phase 2 to model good practices as well as to assist teachers with students of various levels of reading achievement and self-regulation. By conducting these conferences themselves, coaches can help adjust the teacher-student ratio more favorably and enable more students to participate in conferences on a regular schedule. This strategy may prove particularly helpful in the first few weeks of implementation when SIR reading times may be short and both teachers and students are still adjusting to new instructional goals. As noted, though, coaches should primarily be focusing on supporting teachers in their professional development and appropriate implementation of the framework by modeling conferences and offering guidance to teachers about the conferencing process.

Several aspects of conferences that are more challenging and may require more coaching support include the length of conferences and the types of instruction provided, particularly to more advanced readers and other students with special needs. As discussed in Chapter Three, conferences should be brief and efficient; yet often, our research has suggested that teachers are tempted to work with a given student for a longer conference, thereby reducing the total number of students who can have conferences, as well the time certain students spend reading and developing their self-regulation skills. As coaches visit classrooms and notice the ways in which teachers interact with students, coaches should remain aware of issues, such as the length of conferences and which students are receiving more or less frequent conferences, as they can then help teachers to focus and balance their attention. Our research suggests that direct observation of teachers' conferences followed by positive and constructive feedback is most beneficial in helping teachers improve their implementation of SEM-R.

A second area for coaches' attention during Phase 2 is the guidance provided to readers with particular needs during conferences. Because the coach may have a more comprehensive background in reading, he/she should be able to guide teachers in recognizing the individual reading strategy needs among students, from students who struggle with fluency to students who have advanced fluency and comprehension in reading. Conferences are intended to provide a context for strategy instruction and for encouraging and modeling critical thinking about the texts students are reading. Often, teachers are well-prepared to provide individualized strategy instruction and questioning attention for readers who tend to struggle. However, they may wrestle with how to provide appropriate levels of challenge for those readers who are more advanced and do not seem to need specific guidance with standard decoding and comprehension strategies. Coaches can model conferences with advanced readers to encourage critical thinking questions, challenging these readers to take on books that are sufficiently difficult for them, and suggesting advanced skills in reading strategy use that warrant instructional attention. Such modeling can help teachers in implementing similar conferencing strategies with other advanced students. Coaches can also work with teachers to use the Bookmarks to support critical thinking and to encourage their own development of additional Bookmarks that target specific skills for students in their classes.

One strategy for making coaching around Phase 2 more effective is to ensure careful documentation of student progress during conferences. When teachers make notes in a student's reading log immediately following a conference, they provide both themselves and the coach with important information that can serve as a basis for discussion about individual students and a class as a whole. Student logs can be used to help teachers remind themselves in later discussions about strategies that seemed particularly effective and questions raised in their own minds as they worked with students.

Coaching for Phase 3

Each phase of the SEM-R framework reflects the individual characteristics of teachers and the students in their classrooms, but none more so than Phase 3. The options provided by teachers for choice and exploration during Phase 3 reflect the particular interests of the teachers and of the students, as well as the teacher's management style and classroom environment in general. Coaches can help teachers explore possibilities for Phase 3 that will match both their individual strengths and interests, as well as those of the students. Coaches can also support implementation and facilitation through modeling and goal-directed conversation as occurs during the other SEM-R phases.

Some SEM-R teachers, depending on their teaching backgrounds, may be less familiar than others with the idea of establishing centers in the classroom and having multiple groups of students engaged in different kinds of activities at the same time. SEM-R coaches can assist teachers in developing ideas for Phase 3 choices as well as managing those choices with students. This task may involve finding resources online for students to access, organizing materials for a particular type of project or creative exploration, or even helping teachers establish a system for selecting activities.

Depending upon the size of a school, the interests of students, the scheduling of reading classes, and the organization of SEM-R within the overall schedule of a day, teachers may wish to increase their Phase 3 options by making choices available simultaneously to students across multiple classrooms. This arrangement could be successful if all teachers implementing the SEM-R decided to use one day each week (for at least an hour) during SEM-R reading time to offer Phase 3 activities simultaneously. A group of teachers may choose to capitalize on their individual strengths by offering different options for students in different classrooms and then allowing students to move among the classrooms to select their activities. Coaches can help by organizing time for teachers to meet and plan their range of Phase 3 options and then help coordinate the movement of students across classrooms. The coach may also bring particular interests of his or her own to share with students during Phase 3 time, and volunteer to work with groups of students who are pursuing a particular interest or activity. In this way, again coaches can help reduce the teacher-to-student ratio and provide students with different choices and perspectives on what they are learning.

Ongoing Professional Development and Classroom Support

Throughout the SEM-R implementation, coaches provide attention to organizational and material details, support and facilitate teachers' classroom practice and professional development, and guide collaborative efforts among teachers. It is recommended that coaches develop a regular but flexible schedule that will allow them to interact with each SEM-R teacher during each phase on a regular basis, but also to find regular times to respond to specific teachers' requests for in-class support or release time. In addition, coaches work on SEM-R beyond their activities in specific classrooms. Within and beyond classrooms, our experiences suggest that the SEM-R coaches' work usually involves some combination of the following activities:

* direct instruction and interaction with students
* modeling and/or co-teaching
* supporting reflection and offering feedback to teachers
* creating contexts for teacher interaction and collaboration
* obtaining and developing support materials
* serving as a primary liaison among teachers, administrators, and parents.

This section will highlight some of the tasks that SEM-R coaches have been asked to do in addition to the time they spend working with teachers on the various SEM-R phases in particular classrooms with specific teachers.

During the SEM-R, coaches serve as the primary contact persons for the program, playing the role of liaison between teachers and administrators and between teachers and parents. They can communicate teacher needs and concerns to the administration and request support in the form of planning time, materials, etc. They provide ongoing information by communicating with parents about the SEM-R and its progress in the school. Coaches can also work with both administrators and teachers to document the ways that the SEM-R framework enables progress toward local goals for reading.

These efforts to promote communication reflect a larger, central element in the most important work of an SEM-R coach: a focus on developing relationships. The first and most significant of these relationships concerns interactions between coaches and teachers. Coaches need to be proactive in their efforts to develop trusting relationships with teachers, with a focus on honest, open communication about classroom practice. Each teacher relationship will be different, and different teachers will want and need different kinds of support from the coach. The coach must consider carefully how to encourage, guide, and support each teacher, using each teacher's own professional goals as a central focus of the relationship. Coaches must also actively explore how to foster collaborative relationships among teachers implementing the framework.

Other important relationships that the coach can foster to facilitate SEM-R implementation include good relationships with school librarians and media specialists as well as with local librarians, as these individuals can provide invaluable support in implementing the SEM-R due to their knowledge of children's literature and access to books and other resources. Supporting student needs in all phases of SEM-R also requires careful attention to students with special needs, so involving resource teachers in special education and gifted education is important to effective implementation. The coach can integrate these specialist teachers into the program to both support and work directly with students in all SEM-R phases.

Coaches also work as "scavengers" of both books (of all types) and equipment (tape players, CD players, computers), always on the lookout for more resources to with students. They can also support teachers by acquiring books in response to particular student needs. For example, if a certain genre or author inspires great interest in a given classroom, the coach can work to find additional books within that genre or by that author, either in the school or other schools in the district, or by purchasing them with reserved funds that enable them to invest in materials that will contribute to fostering higher levels of student interest. Coaches can work to provide books at either lower or higher levels of challenge as needed for individual students. Moreover, in cases in which individual students show a particular strength, interest, or need that is not met by the current classroom library, coaches can seek out books that respond to these children's particular needs.

Assessment is a key element in any instructional program, and the SEM-R integrates both formal and informal assessment conducted on an individualized level and on an ongoing basis. Coaches can assist with both formal and informal assessment in a number of ways. For example, a coach's assistance with fluency testing at the beginning and at the end of the SEM-R implementation eases the classroom teacher's burden of the time spent. More importantly, however, coaches can assist with ongoing assessment through the conferences they conduct with students and their subsequent discussions of these conferences with teachers. Coaches can assist teachers with the use of assessment information gleaned from conferences with students. Working collaboratively with groups of teachers, coaches can help with the interpretation of assessment data for instructional planning, and with decision-making about the ways in which student work in SEM-R can and should be used for grading purposes.

Finally, beyond these varied continuing efforts to support SEM-R implementation, coaches should also consider ways to celebrate and acknowledge the progress of teachers in implementing the SEM-R. For example, increasing levels of student engagement and self-direction in reading might be highlighted. Acknowledging good work can be done in several ways. A teacher luncheon might be held during which teachers reflect upon and celebrate progress toward goals or progress might be highlighted in an SEM-R newsletter sent to each classroom that includes individual teacher updates or articles about effective implementation of SEM-R. Several schoolwide special reading events might be scheduled, such as author visits or character costume days. Naturally, the teachers implementing SEM-R should also be involved in decisions about which combination of these events can be used to celebrate their success, but the coach can coordinate and facilitate these events and activities across classrooms that bring parents, students, and teachers together to celebrate the work that has been done.

Coaching in Action: Sample Situations

In the previous pages, we highlighted many roles and responsibilities of the SEM-R coach, including "phase-specific" activities as well as efforts related to more general support. In this section, a few concerns of teachers who have implemented the SEM-R are highlighted, as is a discussion of how coaches might respond.

Situation 1: A group of teachers is interested in implementing SEM-R and excited about the program, but they are concerned about the state standards in reading and whether their students will be prepared for the state tests if they participate in the SEM-R. Teachers and administrators raise the concern with the coach both individually and in groups during meetings about planning SEM-R implementation.

To ease this concern and to facilitate communication and understanding among teachers, parents, and administrators, coaches can carefully review the existing expectations for reading and systematically align the SEM-R with them. In most cases, many of the goals of a reading program can be met using the SEM-R framework, but the instruction will be different because of the individualized nature of the format used. The SEM-R does not incorporate formal guided reading in the same way as other current reading programs, yet the individualized conferences provides a method that is intended to accomplish the same goals. Therefore, it is important for someone to review existing goals and objectives and demonstrate clearly how they will be met with the SEM-R reading instruction. For example, one coach worked with teachers to develop Bookmarks that specifically incorporated the types of questions in state tests; these Bookmarks helped to demonstrate to teachers how they might incorporate the same skills within SEM-R that they used with other reading programs. As has also been discussed, the SEM-R is not intended to be a complete Language Arts program, as spelling and writing activities are not an integral part of this approach to an enriched and differentiated experience in reading.

Some specific efforts that will enable a coach to respond to this situation are as follows:

+ Carefully review SEM-R and local/state reading documents to find alignment of goals and outcomes. Read the SEM-R background information that demonstrates evidence of student achievement in reading fluency and achievement (no difference or higher reading achievement in the SEM-R group when compared with a control group). Create a document that highlights the ways in which SEM-R supports local expectations.

+ Meet with administrators to clarify expectations about reading instruction and to document any specific expectations regarding time devoted to particular instructional activities and documentation of student progress. Give administrators materials that demonstrate the alignment of SEM-R with local reading goals.

+ Meet with teachers (preferably with an administrator present) to assure teachers of administrative support for the SEM-R implementation. Clarify for all present the expectations for reading instruction within the school, and initiate a discussion of overall expectations and areas of flexibility.

+ Meet with teachers to discuss in detail the alignment of SEM-R with other standards and expectations. Discuss scheduling and lesson planning at a macro level (i.e., year or semester plans) and at a micro level. Consider developing a sample plan to cover one to two weeks of reading instruction, highlighting how other expectations are weaved into SEM-R, as well as a sample course plan for a year or semester demonstrating how to coordinate SEM-R with other reading and language emphases. Discuss how teachers might plan a continuum of assessment to chart and document student progress.

- Work with individuals or groups of teachers to develop materials that support local reading expectations within SEM-R (e.g., Bookmarks using specific types of questions, Phase 3 writing or other creative activities that support specific objectives).

- Prepare a parent-friendly explanation of how SEM-R meets reading expectations and will support students with the types of skills needed for state testing.

Situation 2: A coach senses, based on teacher comments and body language, that teachers are concerned that the coach is evaluating teachers' implementation of the SEM-R. Some teachers appear to be uncomfortable while the coach is in the room.

Teachers are often unaccustomed to observations that are not evaluative in nature, and they generally have had very limited opportunities to visit one another's classrooms. Therefore, a relationship that involves extensive time with another professional in the classroom may initially feel uncomfortable to teachers. For many teachers, it is not the norm to have someone in a resource role in the classroom who may also be available to give non-evaluative feedback about students' progress or lesson planning. Additionally, because the SEM-R represents new learning that may be a departure from a teacher's previous practice, he or she may be uncomfortable having someone there to experience the initial trial and error process of a change in instruction and classroom organization and management. Therefore, a coach needs to be proactive, organized, and open about classroom visits and what they will involve, and the role of coach as non-evaluative support person must be consistently communicated by all who are involved.

When a coach enters a classroom, whether at the specific invitation of the teacher or through another arrangement such as a rotating visitation schedule, it is important for the coach to know why he or she is going into that classroom (Toll, 2005). In other words, purposeful classroom visits can help to clarify the coaching role and may lead to more productive interactions with teachers. Coaches and teachers may together develop important questions that will help to identify the purpose of a classroom visit, including an emphasis on how certain teaching practices will affect particular students or groups of students, the content and timing of the lesson, and how each of these interact with a variety of coaching strategies (Blachowicz, Obrochta, & Fogelberg, 2005). These questions or plans for classroom visits should be linked directly to the individual teacher's goals for professional growth related to SEM-R implementation, as these linkages help to give the teacher more control about the visit, creating greater comfort for the teacher. Following a classroom visit, purposeful debriefing is important, again with the emphasis on facilitating reflection through questioning.

The in-class portion of coaching might also include team teaching or small group work, enabling the coach to gain a sense of what is happening in a classroom as a basis for facilitating feedback without specifically conducting an observation. During a classroom visit, a coach may also conduct a portion of the lesson while the classroom teacher observes (Joyce & Showers, 1995). Either way, observations should serve as the basis for generating reflection and conversation; feedback should be given in a way that encourages the teacher to reflect on his or her own practice with the coach as a facilitator of that reflection and a sounding board for asking further questions.

The following suggestions and considerations can help coaches make teachers feel more comfortable during SEM-R classroom visits:

- Reflect carefully, before even discussing classroom visits with teachers, on what can be accomplished through time in the classroom and which coaching strategies you want to use as an individual coach. Also, prepare a flexible, general schedule for visiting all classrooms, with time and space for additional classroom visits as requested or needed.

- As part of a meeting or training session with teachers prior to implementation, include classroom visits on the agenda for discussion. Share what you consider to be goals of these visits in general, including the critical issue of helping teachers reflect on progress and their individual goals.

- Create and share a set of options for your role during classroom visits. These might include modeling a strategy within one of the phases, co-teaching, or making notes on a particular practice or activity identified by the teacher. Discuss the suggested schedule for classroom visits, emphasizing that even scheduled visits will be preceded by a conversation in which the teacher and coach work together to identify the purpose for the visit and the format it will take. Explain that teachers may also request classroom visits.

- Share an additional option for teachers by which they can request a classroom visit to cover their classes while they go to observe another teacher. Emphasize that these other observations should also be purposeful and goal-directed.

- Following the group meeting, plan individual meetings with each teacher to discuss goals and questions or concerns about classroom visits and the non-evaluative methods. Keep notes and reflect on each teacher's areas of concern, to facilitate appropriate responses on an individual level.

- When conducting initial classroom visits and follow-up discussions, encourage the teacher to take the lead in discussing and debriefing the time spent in each classroom. Throughout the conversation, you should emphasize a focus on each teacher's goals and reflections upon their implementation of SEM-R.

- Think about the ways you can provide specific feedback, through questions and more direct comments over time. Be sure to offer praise as well as giving suggestions for growth.

- Make discussions about classroom visits a part of regular group meetings with the SEM-R teachers. Encourage teachers to talk about what they expect of classroom visits and to share their experiences with one another in ways that might be productive for group growth.

Situation 3: A group of teachers consistently raises the concern with the coach that they do not have time to read all of the books students are reading, and that they are not sure how to conduct conferences without prior knowledge of the books.

Many teachers are used to developing and using questions that are specifically tied to the group novels or readings they have used in the past with students. The concern about conferences with unfamiliar books is particularly important because of a strong emphasis in reading instruction on having students refer specifically to the text in responding to questions. Without comprehensive knowledge of the book, teachers are often uncertain about how to conduct interviews and give differentiated instruction to their students. Prior to implementation of the SEM-R, through informal conversations or in more formal workshops or meetings, coaches can try to ease this concern by discussing the types of general questions that can be asked about books. They can also offer a context for practicing questioning skills with books that teachers have not read. The Bookmarks developed for SEM-R provide samples of the kinds of general questions that can be asked, and groups of teachers can work collaboratively to develop their own additional bookmarks. By encouraging teachers to work together and by facilitating contexts in which teachers can share their experiences after implementation begins, coaches can help to alleviate this concern. Other suggestions for how to address this concern include the following:

- Incorporate conferencing practices into initial SEM-R training sessions. Encourage teachers to bring children's books or other books they are reading to a training session and have them role-play conferences with each other and debrief about how they selected questions to ask.

- ◆ Conduct a mini-workshop with teachers in which Phase 2 questioning is the primary focus. Include time for teachers to identify types of questions to ask, to develop sample generic questions about books, and to discuss their concerns about this area with time for group problem-solving or suggestions.
- ◆ Encourage all teachers to incorporate questioning into their individual SEM-R goals. As noted previously, coaches should not set teachers' goals, but a general suggestion to the group to keep a focus on questioning would be appropriate.
- ◆ Build time for discussion about questioning into every group meeting of SEM-R teachers. Encourage teachers to discuss regularly what has worked and what has not, and to pay attention to their questioning skills with unfamiliar books and with students with specific kinds of needs. Individual conferences are a central core of the SEM-R and should be an integral part of professional development throughout implementation.

Situation 4: Several teachers in a school have raised concerns about how to implement Phase 3 effectively, with management issues as a central focus of discussion. Teachers who generally have not had multiple activities occurring at once in a classroom are uncomfortable with getting Phase 3 started, and uncertain about whether students will remain focused and engaged.

The variety of activities that should occur during Phase 3 can make a teacher uncomfortable if he or she has generally fostered a more teacher-centered, whole group learning classroom environment. Coaches can help teachers gain greater confidence in their Phase 3 management through assistance in planning and implementation. As a group, SEM-R teachers can review Phase 3 options suggested in this guidebook and brainstorm additional activities they want to offer, and individual teachers can subsequently select the ones that suit their particular styles from this larger set of options. A coach may wish to create several sample Phase 3 choices to share with teachers in a planning meeting or training, and to incorporate a collection of options that range from easiest to implement to those that require greater amounts of planning or flexibility.

Coaches should work more closely with those teachers who are most concerned about implementing Phase 3 to classify different options based on the amount of supervision they would require, and the space, materials, and preparation needed. Following this classification, the teacher and coach can work together to plan out a start-up set of options that involve minimal preparation, with perhaps only one option that requires extra supervision. Once these options have been implemented, teachers can consider broadening the options or trying new ones that might be a little more ambitious in terms of preparation or student activity. Coaches should also encourage these teachers who are more concerned about Phase 3 to select this as a major goal for their own growth in SEM-R implementation.

Coaches can also facilitate discussion among teachers about Phase 3 management strategies, including signals for quiet or for clean-up time, guidelines for students in selecting a Phase 3 activity, methods of documenting student work in Phase 3, and classroom setup. Coaches should encourage those teachers who have more experience with learning centers and other strategies similar to Phase 3 to share their experiences and perhaps some of their materials with teachers who are more uncertain.

Some specific strategies for discussing Phase 3 concerns include the following:

- Encourage teachers to start small and remind them that the goal of Phase 3 is to move gradually from teacher-directed and selected options to student selected options as everyone gains the strategies and skills needed for independent learning. Identify a few "low-preparation" Phase 3 activities (e.g., Buddy Reads, Audio-Books, or Internet Exploration) that teachers may implement with limited preparation and limited classroom "busy-ness." Encourage teachers to start their SEM-R implementation with just a few of these strategies, and to build their bank of options for students over time.

- Identify and acquire ready-made materials and equipment that can support Phase 3, including listening centers for recorded books, bookmarked websites for student access, and resources such as plays for reader's theatre. Also, identify others in the school with specific interests and expertise who might be able to guide or work with teachers to plan a particular Phase 3 exploration.

- Provide release time for teachers to observe one another's Phase 3 activities, with follow-up discussion about effective management strategies and encouragement of engaging activities.

- Encourage teachers to work together to provide Phase 3 options across classes that build on teachers' own strengths.

Key Strategies to Becoming an Effective Coach

The SEM-R coach helps ensure the success of the program with a community of teachers by facilitating teachers' goal-setting and professional growth, answering questions and serving as a resource for responding to implementation challenges, and assisting with the logistics of implementation. The following key strategies about effective coaching summarize this chapter and can also serve as indicators of a high-quality SEM-R implementation:

- Be supportive and encouraging, not evaluative. The coach is not an evaluator, but a facilitator of growth and reflection. Through a combination of affirming successful implementation efforts, working collaboratively to identify areas for growth, and pushing teachers to take on new challenges, coaches provide teachers with a resource for supporting professional progress.

- Keep the focus on student learning and growth. In conversations with teachers about their implementation of SEM-R, coaches should guide the discussion to focus on how and why students are reading and growing in their skills, and they should encourage teachers to explore evidence of that in the conferences they conduct and the conversations they have with students. In both group and individual meetings with teachers, coaches should use specific evidence of student work in reading as a basis for discussion about how SEM-R is working in classrooms.

- Help teachers to be goal-oriented about their work. In addition to helping teachers examine evidence of student growth relative to program objectives, coaches should also facilitate discussion of how teachers' progress links to their own individually determined goals for growth. As noted previously, coaches should not set teachers' goals for them, but rather facilitate the process of goal-setting and self-evaluation regarding progress.

- Provide opportunities for teachers to validate their own professional growth and judgment. Teachers' concerns about whether they are implementing the framework appropriately may be alleviated through giving them opportunities to observe other teachers or to discuss what they are doing with one another. Coaches can provide these contexts by helping with release time and by organizing group meetings to discuss the progress of the SEM-R program. Furthermore, through reinforcing a clear focus on student learning, as noted above, coaches can help teachers recognize that their efforts are making a difference for students.

- Define the role. The coach's role should be clearly defined for the coach, as well as for administrators and teachers. The coach must engage in thoughtful reflection on the responsibilities of the role and communicate his or her own understanding of the role to teachers and to supervisors. Coaches should also encourage teachers to help in defining which support activities would be of greatest assistance to them.

- Build trusting relationships. The coach is a guide, a facilitator, and a liaison, all of which require emphasis on communication and trust. Coaches should actively promote purposeful communication among teachers about the program, and should work to be regarded as supportive, collaborative professionals whose arrival in the classroom is welcomed as an opportunity for interactive professional development and conversation.

- Remember that the focus is on enjoying reading and taking on new challenges and pursuing interests. Coaches should help teachers to understand the connections between the goals of SEM-R: to support enjoyment of challenging reading—and their own opportunities for enjoying professional growth and challenge.

REFERENCES

Anderson, R. C., Wilson, P. T., & Fielding, L. G. (1988). Growth in reading and how children spend their time outside of school. *Reading Research Quarterly, 23*, 285-305.

Beecher, M. (1995). *Developing the gifts and talents of all students in the regular classroom: An innovative curricular design based on the Schoolwide Enrichment Model.* Mansfield Center, CT: Creative Learning Press.

Blachowicz, C. L. Z., Obrochta, C., & Fogelberg, E. (2005). Literacy coaching for change. *Educational Leadership, 62*(6), 55-58.

Burns, S. M., Griffin, P., & Snow, C. E. (Eds.). (1999). *Preventing reading difficulties in young children.* Washington, DC: National Academy Press.

Catron, R. M., & Wingenbach, N. (1986). Developing the potential of the gifted reader. *Theory Into Practice, 25*(2), 134-140.

Chall, J. S., & Conard, S. S. (1991). *Should textbooks challenge students? The case for easier or harder textbooks.* New York: Teachers College Press.

Collins, N.D., Kortner; A.K. (1995). *Gifted Readers and Reading Instruction.* Bloomington, IN: ERIC Clearinghouse on Reading, English, and Communication. (ERIC Document Reproduction Service No. ED379637).

Dole, J. A. (2004). The changing role of the reading specialist in school reform. *The Reading Teacher, 57*, 462-471.

Dooley, C. (1993). The challenge: Meeting the needs of gifted readers. *The Reading Teacher, 46*, 546-551.

Duke, N. K. (2000b). For the rich it's richer: Print experiences offered to children in very low and very high-socioeconomic status first grade classrooms. *American Education Research Journal, 37*, 441-478.

Fehrenbach, C. R. (1991). Gifted/average readers: Do they use the same reading strategies? *Gifted Child Today, 35*(3), 125-127.

Field, G. (2007). An experimental study using Renzulli Learning to investigate reading fluency and comprehension as well as social studies achievement. Unpublished doctorial dissertation, University of Connecticut, Storrs.

Fogarty, E. A. (2006). Teachers' use of differentiated reading strategy instruction for talented, average, and struggling readers in regular and SEM-R classrooms. Unpublished doctoral dissertation, University of Connecticut, Storrs.

Fountas, I., & Pinnell, G. S. (2001). *Guiding readers and writers grades 3-6: Teaching comprehension, genre, and content literacy.* Portmouth, NH: Heinemann.

Geffner, D., Lucker, J.R., & Koch, W. (1996). Evaluation of auditory discrimination in children with ADD and without ADD. *Child Psychiatry & Human Development, 26,* 169-180.

Gentry, M.L. (1999). Promoting student achievement and exemplary classroom practices through cluster grouping: A research-based alternative to heterogeneous elementary classrooms (RM99138). Storrs, CT: The National Research Center on the Gifted and Talented, University of Connecticut.

Graves, M. F., Juel, C., & Graves, B. B. (2001). *Teaching reading in the 21st century* (4th ed.). Boston, MA: Allyn and Bacon.

Hall, G., Yohalem, N., Tolman, J., & Wilson, A. (2003). How after-school programs can most effectively promote positive youth development as a support to academic achievement: A report commissioned by the Boston After-School for All Partnership. Wellesley, MA: National Institute on Out-of-School Time.

Halpern, R. (2003). *Making play work: The promise of afterschool programs for low-income children.* New York: Teachers College Press.

Halsted, J. W. (1990). Guiding the gifted reader. ERIC EC Digest E481. Retrieved November 20, 2001 from http://kidsource.com/kidsource/content/guiding_gifted_reader.html

Harvey, S., & Goudvis, A. (2000). *Strategies that work.* Portland, ME: Stenhouse.

International Reading Association. (2004). The role and qualifications of the reading coach in the United States: A position statement of the International Reading Association. Newark, DE: Author. Retrieved November 15, 2006, from http://www.reading.org.

Joyce, B., & Showers, B. (1995). *Student achievement through staff development.* White Plains, NY: Longman.

Kaplan, S. (2001). An analysis of gifted education curriculum models. In F. A. Karnes & S. M. Beane (Eds.), *Methods and materials for teaching the gifted* (pp.133-158). Waco, TX: Prufrock Press.

Kaplan, S. (1999). Reading strategies for gifted readers. *Teaching for High Potential, 1*(2), 1-2.

Keene, E. & Zimmerman, S. (1997). *Mosaic of thought.* Portsmouth, NH: Heinemann.

Kintsch, W., & Kintsch, E. (2005). Comprehension. In S. G. Paris and S. A. Stahl (Eds.), *Children's reading comprehension and assessment* (pp. 71-92). Mahwah, NJ: Lawrence Erlbaum Associates, Inc.

Kulik, J. A., & Kulik, C.-L. C. (1991). Ability grouping and gifted students. In N. Colangelo & G. A. Davis (Eds.), *Handbook of gifted education* (pp. 179-196). Boston, MA: Allyn and Bacon.

Levande, D. (1993). Identifying and serving the gifted reader. *Reading Improvement, 30*(3), 147-150.

Little, C. A., & Hines, A. H. (2006). Time to read: Advancing reading achievement after school. *Journal of Advanced Academics, 18,* 8-33.

Moats, L. C. (1999). *Teaching reading is rocket science*. Washington, DC: American Federation of Teachers.

MetaMetrics, Inc. (2004). The Lexile Framework for Reading, FAQ. Retrieved February 26, 2007 from http://www.lexile.com/DesktopDefault.aspx?view=ed&tabindex=6&tabid=18

Miller, K., Snow, D., & Lauer, P. (2004). *Noteworthy perspectives: Out-of-school time programs for at-risk students*. Aurora, CO: Mid-continent Research for Education and Learning.

National Reading Panel. (2000). *Teaching children to read: An evidenced-based assessment of the scientific research literature on reading and its implications for reading instruction.* Washington, DC: Author.

Norris, K. T. (1931). *Hands full of living: Talks with American women*. Garden City, NY: Doran & Co.

Paris, S. G. (2004, July). How to teach and assess reading comprehension. Seminar conducted at the CIERA Summer Institute.

Park, B. (1995). *Mick Harte was here*. NY: Random House.

Reis, S. M., & Boeve, H. (in press). How academically gifted elementary urban students respond to challenges in an enrichment reading program.

Reis, S. M., & Fogarty, E. A. (2006). Savoring reading, schoolwide. *Educational Leadership, 64*(2), 32-36.

Reis, S. M., Gubbins, E. J., Briggs, C. J., Schreiber, F. R., Richards, S., Jacobs, J., Eckert, R. D., & Renzulli., J. S. (2004). Reading instruction for talented readers: Case studies documenting few opportunities for continuous progress. *Gifted Child Quarterly, 48.* 309-338.

Reis, S. M., Eckert, R. D., Schreiber, F. J., Jacobs, J., Briggs, C. J., Gubbins, E. J., Coyne, M., & Muller, L. (2005). The Schoolwide Enrichment Model—Reading Framework (RM05214). Storrs, CT: The National Research Center on the Gifted and Talented, University of Connecticut.

Reis, S. M., & Renzulli, J. S. (1989). Developing challenging programs for gifted readers. *The Reading Instruction Journal, 32,* 44-57.

Renzulli, J. S. (1977). The enrichment triad model: A plan for developing defensible programs for the gifted and talented: II. *Gifted Child Quarterly, 21*(2), 227-233.

Renzulli, J. S., Callahan, C. M., Smith, L. S., Renzulli, M. J., & Ford, B. G. (2000). *New directions in creativity: Marks A-3.* Mansfield Center, CT: Creative Learning Press.

Renzulli, J. S., & Reis, S. M. (1994). Research related to the schoolwide enrichment Triad Model. *Gifted Child Quarterly, 38*(1), 7-20.

Renzulli, J. S., & Reis, S. M. (1985). *The schoolwide enrichment model: A comprehensive plan for educational excellence.* Mansfield Center, CT: Creative Learning Press.

Renzulli, J. S., & Reis, S. M. (1997). *The schoolwide enrichment model: A how-to guide for educational excellence* (2nd ed.). Mansfield Center, CT: Creative Learning Press.

Rogers, K. B. (1991). Grouping the gifted and talented: Questions and answers. *Roeper Review, 16*(1), 8-12.

Scholastic, Inc. (1996-2007). Leveling Resource Guide. Retrieved February 25, 2007 from http://content.scholastic.com/browse/article.jsp?id=4476.

Stanovich, K. (1986). Matthew effects in reading: Some consequences of individual differences in the acquisition of literacy. *Reading Research Quarterly, 24, 7-26.*

Taylor, B., Frye, B., & Maruyama, G. (1990). Time spent reading and reading growth. *American Educational Research Journal, 27,* 351-362.

The Reading Foundation. (2005). Stages of language and reading development. Retrieved March 7, 2007, from http://www.thereadingfoundation.com/stages.html

Toll, C. A. (2005). *The literacy coach's survival guide: Essential questions and practical answers.* Newark, DE: International Reading Association.

Tomlinson, C. A. (1995). *How to differentiate instruction in mixed-ability classrooms.* Alexandria, VA: Association for Supervision and Curriculum Development.

Topping, K.J. (1995) *Paired reading, spelling and writing: The handbook for teachers and parents.* London and New York: Cassell.

U.S. Department of Education, Office of Educational Research and Improvement. (1993). *National excellence: A case for developing America's talent.* Washington, DC: U.S. Government Printing Office.

Vygotsky, L. S. (1962). *Thought and language.* Cambridge, MA: MIT Press.

Walker, B. J. (2000). *Diagnostic teaching of reading.* Columbus, OH: Merrill Publishing Company.

Walker, B. J. (1996). *Diagnostic teaching of reading: Techniques for instruction and assessment.* Englewood Cliffs, NJ: Merrill.

Walker, B. J. (2005). *Techniques for reading assessment and instruction.* Upper Saddle River, NJ: Pearson Merrill Prentice Hall.

Young, Arlene R., Bowers, P. G., and MacKinnon, G. E (1996). Effects of prosodic modeling and repeated reading on poor readers' fluency and comprehension. *Applied Psycholinguistics, 17*(1), 59-84.

Zimmerman, B. J. (1989). A social cognitive view of self-regulated academic learning. *Journal of Educational Psychology, 81*(3), 329-339.

Zimmerman, B. J. (1990). Self-regulated learning and academic achievement: An overview. *Educational Psychology, 25,* 3017.

APPENDIX A

BookMarks

Character

If you had to choose to be one of the characters, who would you choose? Why?

Does one of the characters remind you of someone that you know? Why?

How would you feel if you were one of the characters in the book? Explain.

How do the actions of a character tell you about his/her personality?

Create a new problem for one of the characters.

Character

Who is the antagonist of the book? How do you know?

Which actions of one of the characters confused you?

How would the book be different if it were told from another character's point of view?

Does the protagonist force the antagonist to change? If so, why and how?.

Describe the appearance of your favorite characters.

Character

Do any of the characters display the trait of honesty?

Were you surprised by the actions of any of the characters? How?

Describe a decision or choice made by one of the characters? Do you agree with this decision?

Who is the protagonist of the book? How do you know?

Character

If you could change the behaviors of any character, which one would you change? Why?

Would you like the main character as a best friend? What qualities does the character display that lead you to that decision?

Did the main character (protagonist) change during the story or did he/she stay the same throughout?

Would you want to read other books about these characters? Why?

Character

How does the setting of the book influence the characters?

Which character in the book faces the biggest problem? Why?

Tell one event in the story from another character's point of view (besides the narrator).

What trait do you admire most in a character in the story? Why?

Character

Describe the scene in the book when a character's thoughts differ from his/her actions? Why do you think this happened?

How would the characters behave differently if the story were set in a different place or time?

Compare two characters in this book. Tell which one you think is a better person and why?

Plot: Basics

What do you think was the most important event in the story?

Where and when does the story take place?

Who are the main characters? What makes them the main characters?

What has happened in the story so far?

What is the problem or main situation in the story?

Character

If you could eliminate one character from the story, who would you choose? What effect would that have?

What gift would you like to give the main character? Why?

How might you rewrite the story to include one of your friends as a character?

If you were the author, what future events or discoveries would you have the characters pursue?

How does the main character stand out from other characters?

Character

How does the personality of one character contribute to his or her eventual success or failure?

Who narrates the book? Why do you think the author made this choice?

Describe two events that portray the main character's personality?

Order the story characters from your favorite to your least favorite.

If you had been one of the characters, would you have done anything differently?

Plot

What problem exists in this book? How is it solved?

Would this book work as a movie? What might have to be changed?

What do you consider the strongest part of the book? The weakest?

What did you learn from this book?

Plot

To whom might you recommend this book? Is there a particular group or population that you believe would enjoy this book?

Does the book have any value beyond entertainment?

How has the book influenced your viewpoint?

What one thing would you tell the author to change about the plot if you were to write to him or her?

Plot

If you could choose one scene in the book to draw or illustrate, which would, you choose? What colors would you use? Why?

Can you summarize the story in:
- 25 words or fewer
- 10 words or fewer
- 5 words or fewer

If you were to visit the setting of the story, what might you see there?

Plot

What do you think is the most important event in the story? What is the least important event in the story?

List the characteristics of a good story. Which ones apply to this story?

Could you sometimes predict what was going to happen next in the book? Did it help you to better understand the story?

Identify words in the story that the author used to help you create a picture of the story in your mind.

Plot

Would you change the ending if you could? If so, what changes would you make? Why?

Why do you think the author wrote this story?

How do you think the following people would react to this story your:
- someone in your family
- a friend
- your teacher

Did you enjoy the way the story began? Explain.

Plot

Do you think the topic of this story is important?

What does the title mean? How is it important to the story?

How are the events in the story similar to the events in your own life?

Did the author of this book have an important point to make? Was this an interesting story?

Do you think there is any lesson to be learned from this story? Why or why not?

Setting

In what way does the setting of this story relate to your life or to other books you have read?

Do you think the setting for this story was real or imaginary? Why?

How would the book change if the setting was 100 years in the future or 100 years in the past?

What details does the author provide about the setting that helps build the mood for the story?

Setting

What three words would you use to describe the setting of the story?

Why is the setting of this book an appropriate place for this story to take place?

What are some alternative settings that could have been used for this book?

How might the author have collected information about the setting for this book?

Plot

Explain a problem faced by one of the characters. How was it solved?

Describe any part of the plot confused you

Which scene would make a good preview, or trailer, for a movie?

What was the turning point of the story? How did it affect the plot?

Is the plot true to life (realistic)?

Did you feel any suspense in the plot? If so, what was the final outcome?

Illustrations & Layout

Did the illustrations or page layout in this book make you want to read further? Why?

What part of the book first attracted your attention? Why?

What do the illustrations tell about the setting/time period?

What parts of the book or story might have inspired the illustrator? Why?

Do the illustrations make you think of a special place or event in your life? Explain.

Based only on the illustrations (not the words), what would you think the book is about?

Illustrations & Layout

How did the illustrations and/or diagrams help clarify the information?

How do the illustrations or page layouts differ from other books you have read? Which format is better? Why?

What information did you learn from the captions or illustrations?

What text features (diagrams, charts, tables) do you find most intriguing? Why?

Would this book be as good without the illustrations? Why or why not?

Illustrations

What media did the illustrator use? Did this help tell the story better?

Could the illustrations in the book tell the same story without the words? Why or why not?

What colors does the illustrator use to tell the story? Why might he or she have chosen these colors?

Biography

How did the author organize events in this individual's life? What event do you believe was the most significant in the individual's life?

Compare/contrast your family's culture with the culture of the main character.

In most biographies, the person has to overcome some difficulty. Describe an obstacle the person overcame.

What did you learn about yourself while reading this biography?

How would you describe the "star" of this biography? What traits did he or she possess that you relate to?

Biography

Why would an author write a biography about this individual?

What additional questions do you have about this person and his/her experience that this book did not answer?

How is this person's life different from your own? How is it similar?

What does the person about whom the biography is written value? Do you value similar things? Why or why not?

Biography

What obstacles did this person face? How did these obstacles influence his/her life?

Who do you think influenced this individual's early years?

What ethical issues did the individual face?

What character traits did you admire most in this person? Why?

How much did this person's have a teachers influence on him or her? If you had been the teacher, how would you want to influence this individual?

Theme: Personal Beliefs

Every person should have a set of personal beliefs in life. At some time in life, you may have to stand up for what you believe is right. Sometimes we do not really know or understand our beliefs until we are confronted with a hard choice or a bad event.

Explain how the idea of personal beliefs is a theme in this book.

Do any of the main characters appear to have a strong set of personal beliefs? Explain.

For the character in this story, is there any belief he/she would sacrifice for?

Theme: General Questions

Is the author trying to help you better understand some aspect of life?

Can you identify the author's message in writing this book?

Explain how a theme in this book relates to your own life.

What lessons do the characters in the story learn from their experiences?

Describe an event in this book that helped you understand the "big idea" or theme in the story.

Does the theme change the main character?

Biography

If you were going to write a biography, who would you write about? Why?

What details would you include in your biography and why?

What characteristics of the person would you like to develop yourself? Why?

What do you think school was like for the person about whom this biography was written? Explain.

Theme: Personal Beliefs

One important theme relates to good and evil. Early events in our history and culture suggest the existence of some good and/or evil in most people.

How does the battle between good and evil exist in this book?

Does good triumph over evil in this book? How?

Do you think good usually triumphs over evil? Why?

Can you think of an event in your life or in the world in which evil seemed to triumph over good?

Theme: Death

What big idea may be worth dying for? Examples could include freedom or the life of another person you love. Death may sometimes keep a character from understanding life. Some people think death is not the end, but rather the beginning. Death certainly does not end a person's legacy or contribution to the lives of others.

How did the theme of death emerge in this book?

Do any of the main characters die? If so, what big ideas do you learn about death from the events in this book?

Theme: Interaction with Nature

Different people relate to nature in different ways. Some people, such as Native American Indians, relate differently to nature than others. Americans may relate differently to nature today than they did in the past.

Does the theme of people relating to nature appear in the book you are reading?

How do the characters in this book relate to nature?

Theme: Change or Growth in Life

People need internal (within themselves) strength to deal with sad or difficult times. Developing inner strength may take a lifetime of work. Many characters find it difficult to develop inner strength.

Does a character in this book goes through a change or growth in life? How?

Do you think that any character in this book is stronger on the inside than on the outside? Who and why?

Are there any characters that are weaker on the inside than the outside? Who and why?

Theme: Change or Growth in Life

Challenges or difficulties can make people stronger. People who don't feel like they belong or fit in may face problems. When some people face challenges, they can become stronger and more resourceful.

The only constant in life is change. Do you know what that means as a theme in a book? Is that a theme in this book?

Does the theme of this book relate to the theme of a person's place in society?

Do any characters in this book feel like they don't belong? Why?

Do any characters change during the book? How?

Theme: Power

Power can relate to personal/individual power, institutional power (in work or government), or spiritual power to believe in forces that are bigger than ourselves.

Do authors have power? What is the power of the pen?

Do you think that authors have responsibility to use their power to make positive changes? Why?

Does a person with personal or individual power have the right to use it for evil? Explain.

Does any character in this book use his/her power for good? Explain.

Theme: Loneliness and Isolation

Isolation and loneliness can hurt people. Isolated and lonely people may also hurt others. All people have a need to feel cared for and loved by someone. Scott O'Dell once said, "History has a very valid connection with what we are now. Many of my books are set in the past, but the problems of isolation, moral decisions, greed, need for love and affection are problems of today as well...."

Is loneliness and isolation a theme of this book?

Do any of the characters in this book feel isolated or alone? Why? How could you help them?

Theme: Relationships

When people work with others, they need to have good communication and feel respect for others. More can be accomplished when people work together than when they work alone.

How do you think personal relationships are portrayed in this book?

Do any of the characters work together to solve a problem? If so, what big ideas do you learn from the events of this book?

Is there any event in the book that shows how some people hurt relationships? If so, what lessons can you learn from that event?

Theme: Relationships

Friendships and loving relationships can make life better. Friends share and give to each other. Some people are kind and giving to others. Some people are unkind and cruel to each other. Relationships are often a theme in literature.

Is the theme of relationships portrayed in this story?

Are there any events in this book that teach you about cruelty? If so, what lessons do you learn from those events?

Do any of the main characters teach you something about kindness or friendship? Explain.

Just the Facts

Fairy tales are stories told to entertain and instruct about good and evil. They often include supernatural beings, magic and royalty. They usually take place long ago and far away.

A fable is a fictitious story or tale, intended to teach about a truth, human emotion or behavior. Fables usually have a lesson or moral to be learned. Animals are often used in place of people in fables.

A mystery is a fictional story in which a detective solves a crime or mysterious event. The detective uses clues in the story to solve the mystery.

Just the Facts

The time and location of the story is called **setting**. There are several aspects to the setting of each story the place/geographic location, the time/date, and the mood/atmosphere.

An antagonist is a character or sometimes a group of characters that actively oppose the main character or **protagonist** of a story. Usually the antagonist represents a force that the main character must over come.

Plot is the plan of action for a play, novel, poem, short story, or any other fiction book.

Theme: Inhumanity

Some people are cruel and treat others very badly. Understanding others may help to reduce cruelty and inhumanity to others.

What does it mean to really understand others?

Do inhumanity and cruelty exist in the world today? What could each of us do to reach out to prevent it?

Is inhumanity and cruelty to others a theme in this book?

Does anyone help the character who is treated unkindly? How?

Just the Facts

Folklore is a collection of stories from a particular culture and time, and often feature exaggeration. A myth is a story about mythical or supernatural beings or events. A legend is a story handed down from earlier times, often believed to be historical.

Fantasy is fiction that asks the reader to suspend reality and believe that elements of magic, wizardry, and supernatural events are possible. It often takes place in another world or time. Science fiction is a story that takes place in the future, where people use scientific and technological developments in amazing ways.

Just the Facts

Self-help books give advice to help people solve problems or accomplish things in their life.

Philosophy is the love of knowledge. Philosophers think about life and develop ideas or beliefs about life, knowledge or behavior.

Non-fiction books are often based on true stories, history, facts, or ideas and are used to share information.

Types of non-fiction books:
- Poetry
- Plays/Narrative based on real life
- Biography
- Photo documentaries
- How-to Books
- Experiment & Activity Books
- Field Guides & Identification Books

Just the Facts

A theme can be defined as the major message the author wants readers to have about an important issue or idea.

Most books have a theme and in each theme are some important ideas are called "big ideas".

Types of themes in books:
- Power
- Change or Growth in Life
- Interaction with Nature
- Death
- Personal Beliefs
- Relationships
- Loneliness and Isolation
- Inhumanity

Experiments

How could you apply the procedures of this experiment to a different subject for research?

How else could you modify the experiment to extend your learning?

What concepts in science does this experiment teach?

Do you think that you would get the same results each time if you repeated the experiment 25 times? Why or why not?

Experiments

What would happen if you deleted a step or changed the order of the steps in the experiment?

Summarize this experiment for a friend in a way that would make him/her want to do it.

What variables could you manipulate to add to your knowledge of the topic?

Just the Facts

A **character** is an imaginary person represented in a novel, poem, short story, or any other fiction book.

A **simile** is a comparison of two unlike things, typically marked by use of "like", "as" or "than". Examples include "the snow was as thick as a blanket", or "she was as sly as a fox".

A **metaphor** uses an implied comparison or analogy to describe something. In the simplest case, a metaphor takes the form: "The [first subject] is a [second subject]." We use metaphors regularly in daily life: "She's such a peach" would be an example.

Fairy Tales

Is this fairy tale similar to other fairy tales you have read? How are they similar?

A fractured fairy tale takes a traditional fairy tale and changes it in some way. For example, the main character may be changed from male to female, or the setting may be updated to modern times. If you were going to "fracture" this fairy tale, how would you do it? Why?

Have you read other versions of this fairy tale? Do any of them come from other cultures? How did they differ from this one?

Fairy Tales

How would this fairy tale be different if it was told from another character's perspective?

What lesson do you think the author is teaching with this tale? How do you know?

If this fairy tale was made into a movie, to whom would it appeal most? Why?

Fairy tales are usually about good verses evil. What two forces are contrasted in this story?

Fairy Tales

What other fairy tales does this story remind you of?

What is the problem in this fairy tale and how do you think it will be solved?

Are there characters in this fairy tale that remind you of characters in other stories? Who and what traits make them similar?

If you could play one of the characters in the movie version of this fairy tale, who would you be? Why?

Fairy Tales

Fairy tales often feature the numbers 3 and 7 (the three billy goats, the seven dwarfs, the wolf who tries to blow down the pigs' houses 3 times). Do these numbers have any significance in this tale? If so, how do they influence the story?

Did any character have a magical power? What was the power? How would the story change if a different character had the power?

Does this fairy tale have any characters that are from royalty (for example, a king or princess)? How are they different from other characters?

Fables

Think about the characters in this fable. What are the best and worst traits the main characters possess? Which trait wins in the end?

What is the moral or lesson to be learned from this fable?

What can you learn about human feelings or behavior from the characters in this fable?

How does the setting influence or contribute to the conflict or resolution of this fable? How would the story change if the fable was set in a different place or time?

Folklore, Myths, & Legends

Picture the main character from this story. How did the author help you create a visual image in your mind?

What traits of this character make him/her have super abilities or powers?

Is this story believable? What has been exaggerated?

In what way would the story be different without the exaggeration?

If you could meet the main character what questions would you ask?

What would it be like to live in the place or during the time of this story?

Fantasy/Science Fiction

Do you think this kind of story could ever happen in real life? Why or why not?

Imagine if we had the creatures/gadgets/modes of transportation in our society that are in the book. How would your life be different?

If you could add a creature/gadgets/mode of transportation/etc. to this story, what would it be? What would change in the story?

Do you have any ideas for an invention that would make this story better? Describe your idea and how it would change the story?

Self-Help

What kind of helpful "self-help" strategies does this book provide?

What kind of evidence does the author provide to suggest that his/her strategies are effective for others?

After reading this book, what other books would you like to read?

Did this book help you? Why or why not?

Self-Help

Why did you select this book to read? What questions did you have when you started to read the book? Were your questions answered?

If you were going to write a self-help book for other kids, what would it be about?

Can you think of a fictional character that might benefit from reading this book? In what way would he/she benefit?

Did this book help you see things from a different perspective? Was it helpful?

Mysteries

How do you know that this book is a mystery (besides the label on the book)?

What clues has the author given so far to help you solve the mystery at this point in the story?

Have you decided that any characters are "innocent"? Why do you think so? Provide evidence from the story.

Do you think the author will reveal "who did it" by the end of the story or will you have to be the one to decide? What information do you need in order to solve the mystery?

Mysteries

A "red herring" is a suspect (or object) that the author adds to take some of the suspicion away from the person who really committed the crime. Describe any red herrings in the story?

Have you decided that any characters are guilty? Why do you think so? Provide evidence from the story?

If you were investigating this mystery, what steps would you take to uncover the truth?

Would you ever read the ending of a mystery first? Why or why not?

Mysteries

Think about the protagonist in the story. What are his/her good and bad traits? How do these traits help or hurt the protagonist when solving the mystery?

How would reading this story be different if you knew the solution before you started reading?

Compare yourself to the character investigating the mystery. What traits do you have in common? What traits are different?

After you finish reading this book, think about the conclusion. Was the ending as you expected?

Philosophy

Have you changed any of your ideas based on reading this book?

Does the author have a main point in this book? What is it?

Did the author try to persuade you to agree with his/her beliefs? If so, how?

What kind of support does the author give for his/her arguments?

How is the information the same or different from your own beliefs?

Humor

If you had a conversation with a character from the book what character would it be? What would you talk about? What would you ask him/her?

What makes this comedy different from a joke book? What benefits or strengths does this book have over a joke book?

Is this book similar to other books you have read? How?

How would you respond if you witnessed one of the humorous scenes from this book?

How does the author use humor to define a character in the book? Why is this character funny?

Humor

What makes a story humorous or a comedy?

What would have made this story even funnier? Why?

Which character do you think has the best sense of humor? Why?

Is there one character who has "no" sense of humor at all? If so, how does that character interact with the other characters?

Does the use of humor make this story more enjoyable? Why or why not?

Poetry

From whose perspective is the poem written? Who might be narrating the poem?

What moves you in the poem? The language? The images?

Select a phrase from the poem that caught your attention while you were reading. Do you think the author did this on purpose? Why or why not?

What do you know about the narrator's or character's feeling based on this poem?

What visual images come to mind when you read this poem?

Poetry

How would this poem change if the narrator was different?

If you turned this poem into a song, what kind of music would you use? Why?

What kind of illustration do you think would be appropriate for this poem?

What two emotions did you feel while reading any poem in this book? Did your emotions change as you read other poems?

How would the impact of this poem change if it had been written as prose?

Poetry

How does the poet's choice of words influence the visual images in your mind while you read?

How does the poet use rhythm to convey meaning in this poem?

How would this poem be different if it were written in a different poetic style? For example, as a limerick instead of haiku?

What does any poem that you choose to read aloud sound like?

Does the poem remind you of a book you have read?

Non-Fiction

Would this book be a good choice to include in a time capsule? Why or why not?

Bias happens when the author presents only one point of view on a topic that may have two or more important viewpoints. Do you think bias exists in this book? Why or why not?

How did the Table of Contents and Index help you to use this book? What improvements could you make?

What events in history did this book help you understand?

Non-Fiction

Can you identify one cause/effect relationship from events in the book?

Describe an interesting relationship in this book.

How effectively did the author present different perspectives on an issue?

How do the ideas in this book relate to your life?

What would have improved this book? Why?

Non-Fiction

How could an idea in this book improve or change the world?

Describe some professions that relate to this topic. What kinds of work do these people do?

How is this book organized? – Date, time of year, place, alphabetically, step by step. Why do you think the author organized the material this way?

How might this book change if it had been written by an author of the opposite gender, a different age, or a different cultural heritage?

Non-Fiction

If you had to make an advertisement about the topic of this non-fiction book, what would you do?

What sections of the book would you want to read first? Why?

What questions would you want to ask the author after reading the book? Why are the questions important?

What would you tell the author about a student's understanding of this topic?

How do you read a non-fiction book differently from a fiction book?

Non-Fiction

Why might a non-fiction book have more than one author? Why is collaboration important in this type of writing?

What part of this book could the author have left out without changing your understanding of the topic?

Compare what you learned in this book with what you already knew or thought you knew about the topic.

What is one big question you still have after reading the book?

Non-Fiction

How do you think the author learned the information presented in this book?

What is the most important idea the author is conveying about the topic?

What are three details the author used to make readers more interested in this topic?

Why do you think the author chose to write about this topic? Do you think the topic is important?

After reading this book, do you want to delve into this topic more deeply? What other books might you find? Where?

Non-Fiction

Is everything in the book based on fact? Does the author provide opinions? How can you tell the difference between fact and opinions?

How did the pictures and the words in the book help you create an image of the setting?

How would you find another book on the same topic? Would you want to read it? Why or why not?

Non-Fiction

Would you have wanted to live during the time that is the setting of the book? Why or why not?

When the author writes, what elements of his/her writing help you understand the importance facts of idea in the books?

Have you read a book on this topic before? If so, how is this book different? How is it similar?

Is the author an expert on the subject? How do you know?

Non-Fiction

Does the author of this book try to persuade you to believe anything? How?

Can you imagine how people dressed during this time or in this place? How would you describe the differences between the clothes in the book and what you wear?

Do you think people read non-fiction books to answer questions that they have? What steps might they take to find answers?

How-To Books

What sections of this book did you want to read first? Why? What would the other sections provide?

What recommendations would you give the author for improving this book?

What would your greatest challenge be in doing what the author recommends?

Do you need any special resources or tools to follow the directions in the book?

Non-Fiction & Fiction

If you were to write a follow up to this book, what part of this book would you like to research in more depth?

Who is the most memorable person in the book?

Describe the author's writing style. What is his/her narrative style, for example?

What questions do you now have about the time period in which the events occurred?

What would the world be like if the events in this book had not happened?

Non-Fiction

Are there places in this book you have visited before? How might visiting the places in the book improve your understanding of the events in the book?

What does this book make you think about? Do questions come to mind? Give an example of some of your thoughts or questions.

What about the setting of this book is different from the world we live in now?

Understanding Audience

Would you recommend this book to a favorite fictional character? Which one? Why?

What was the author's purpose in writing this book? Was the author successful? Why or why not?

Who is the intended audience of the book? How do you know?

Would you recommend this book to a friend? Why or why not?

Understanding Audience

What other topics or ideas might people who like this book be interested in?

Describe the type of person who might be most interested in this topic.

Do you think people who read this book will be sympathetic to the main character? Why or why not?

Inventions & How-to Books

How would this modern invention have affected another era in history?

How would your life today be different if the invention had not been created at that time?

In this how-to book, what steps might you change to improve the process?

What would it have been like to experience the first successful trial of this invention?

How did this book help you learn a skill you are interested in pursuing?

Reading Attitudes

Do you ever reread a book? If so, why do you read it again?

Imagine that reading was never invented. Would this be a good thing or a bad thing? Why?

Do you like to get books as presents? Why or why not? Have your feelings about this changed at all since the beginning of the school year?

History & Current Events

How is the issue/problem/topic relevant to your world today?

Compare your family's culture with the one you read about.

If you were to rewrite the ending of this book, could you change history?

How might you feel about the events in this book if you were living in this time period?

What person/group of people in this book faced the most challenges? Why?

What would happen if the events in this book had happened 200 years later? How might the events have changed?

Exploration Books

Have you read any fiction books that deal with this topic in the book? After reading this book, do you think the fiction book treated the content accurately?

Look at the format of the book. What other topics could be covered using this format? What non-fiction topics would **not** be appropriately covered in this format?

Suggest a plot for a piece of fiction in which this information plays a pivotal role.

Are there any opinions presented in this book that look like facts that you believe are really opinions? How can you tell what is really accurate?

Reading Attitudes

Complete this sentence: To me, reading is...

If you could choose anything to read about, what would you choose and why?

Do you and your friends talk about books or reading? Why or why not?

Have you ever seen a movie made from a book you read? If so, which did you enjoy more, the book or the movie? Why?

What helps you understand books better?

Reading Attitudes

Do you have a favorite author? If so, who is the author and why do you like the books he/she writes? If not, why do you think you have not found an author you like?

Do you have favorite genre? Which one and why? If not, what would help you like books more?

What do you know about yourself as a reader? How has this changed since last month? Last year?

Where and when do you like to read best? How does knowing this help you choose books to read?

What helps you get interested in a book? How does this help you choose books?

Reading Attitudes

Complete this sentence: Reading helps me...

What is the most difficult thing for you to do while reading? Can the teacher or anyone else help you with this? How?

What do you like most about reading? What do you like least?

Is reading important to you? Why or why not?

What new strategies are you using that have helped you become a better reader? How have they helped?

Describe how you feel when reading.

Make your own bookmark!
(Then leave it in the book for your classmates.)

Book Title: _____

Author: _____

Easy Question:

_____

_____

Challenging Question:

_____

_____

Thought Provoking Question:

_____

_____

Make your own bookmark!
(Then leave it in the book for your classmates.)

Book Title: _____

Author: _____

Easy Question:

_____

_____

Challenging Question:

_____

_____

Thought Provoking Question:

_____

_____

TIME TO READ

APPENDIX B

READING
INTEREST-A-LYZER

READING INTEREST-A-LYZER©

Based on the Interest-A-Lyzer by Joseph S. Renzulli

Name _____ Grade _____ Age _____

1.) Are you currently reading a book for pleasure?   ❑ YES   ❑ NO

2.) Do you ever read a book for pleasure?   ❑ YES   ❑ NO

3.) When I read for pleasure, I pick the following (Check all that apply):

❑ Novels/chapter books	❑ History books	❑ Picture books
❑ Newspapers	❑ Sports books	❑ Mystery books
❑ Poetry books	❑ Fantasy books	❑ Fiction books
❑ Cartoons/comic books	❑ Science books	❑ Biographies
❑ Humorous books	❑ Scary books	❑ Non-fiction books
❑ Magazines	❑ Poetry books	Other

_____

4.) I am more likely to read a book for pleasure that:

❑ a teacher suggests	❑ my friend suggests
❑ a librarian suggests	❑ has won an award
❑ is by an author whose books I have read	❑ I just happened to see (hear about) in_____

5.) Three favorite books that I would take on a month-long trip are:

1. _____
2. _____
3. _____

6.) In the past week, I have read for at least half an hour (30 minutes):
❑❑ No days   ❑ 1-2 days   ❑ 3-4 days   ❑ 6-7 days

7.) In the past month, I have read _____ book(s) for pleasure:

❑ No books   ❑ 1 book   ❑ 2 books   ❑ 3 books   ❑ More than 3 books

8.) My favorite time to read for pleasure is:

❑ Never
❑ During school
❑ Lunchtime
❑ In the evening
❑ Whenever I can

❑ In the morning before school
❑ During the midmorning
❑ After school
❑ Before falling asleep
❑ _____

9.) When I read I like to: ❑ read one book ❑ read more than one book at a time

10.) I like to receive books as presents. ❑ YES ❑ NO

11.) I have a <u>public</u> library card. ❑ YES ❑ NO

12.) I borrow books from the <u>public</u> library:

❑ Once a week
❑ Every few months
❑ Never

❑ Twice a week
❑ A few times a year

❑ A couple of times a month
❑ Hardly ever

13.) I borrow books from the <u>school</u> library:

❑ Once a week
❑ Every few months
❑ Never

❑ Twice a week
❑ A few times a year

❑ A couple of times a month
❑ Hardly ever

14.) The number of books I have at home:

❑ None
❑ 20-29

❑ 0-9
❑ 30-50

❑ 10-19
❑ More than 50

15.) If I could meet any literary character (for example, Hermione from *Harry Potter* or the dog from *Because of Winn-Dixie*), I want to meet:

● _____
● _____

16.) The last three books that I have read are:

1. _____
2. _____
3. _____

17.) I would like to read a book about:

● _____

Appendix C

Award-Winning Books

THE CALDECOTT MEDAL

The Caldecott Medal was named in honor of nineteenth-century English illustrator Randolph Caldecott. It is awarded annually by the Association for Library Service to Children, a division of the American Library Association, to the artist of the most distinguished American picture book for children. For more information about The Caldecott Medal see http://www.ala.org/alsc/caldecott.html.

2007

Medal Winner:

Flotsam by David Wiesner

Honor Books:

Gone Wild: An Endangered Animal Alphabet illustrated and written by David McLimans

Moses: When Harriet Tubman Led Her People to Freedom illustrated by Kadir Nelson and written by Carole Boston Weatherford

2006

Medal Winner:

The Hello, Goodbye Window illustrated by Chris Raschka and written by Norton Juster

Honor Books:

Rosa illustrated by Bryan Collier and written by Nikki Giovanni

Zen Shorts illustrated and written by Jon J. Muth

Hot Air: The (Mostly) True Story of the First Hot-Air Balloon Ride illustrated and written by Marjorie Priceman

Song of the Water Boatman and the Other Pond Poems illustrated by Beckie Prange and written by Joyce Sidman

2005

Medal Winner:

Kitten's First Full Moon by Kevin Henkes

Honor Books:

The Red Book by Barbara Lehman

Coming on Home Soon illustrated by E. B. Lewis and written by Jacqueline Woodson

Knuffle Bunny: A Cautionary Tale illustrated and written by Mo Willems by Mo Willems

2004

Medal Winner:

The Man Who Walked Between the Towers by Mordicai Gerstein

Honor Books:

Ella Sarah Gets Dressed by Margaret Chodos-Irvine

What Do You Do with a Tail Like This? illustrated and written by Steve Jenkins and Robin Page

Don't Let the Pigeon Drive the Bus by Mo Willems

2003

Medal Winner:

My Friend Rabbit by Eric Rohmann

Honor Books:

The Spider and the Fly illustrated by Tony DiTerlizzi and written by Mary Howitt

Hondo & Fabian by Peter McCarty

Noah's Ark by Jerry Pinkney

2002

Medal Winner:

The Three Pigs by David Wiesner

Honor Books:

The Dinosaurs of Waterhouse Hawkins, illustrated by Brian Selznick and written by Barbara Kerley

Martin's Big Words: The Life of Dr. Martin Luther King, Jr., illustrated by Bryan Collier, written by Doreen Rappaport

The Stray Dog by Marc Simont

2001

Medal Winner:

So You Want to be President? illustrated by David Small and written by Judith St. George

Honor Books:

Casey at the Bat: A Ballad of the Republic Sung in the Year 1888, illustrated by Christopher Bing and written by Ernest Lawrence Thayer

Click, Clack, Moo: Cows that Type, illustrated by Betsy Lewin and written by Doreen Cronin

Olivia by Ian Falconer

2000

Medal Winner:

Joseph Had a Little Overcoat by Simms Taback

Honor Books:

A Child's Calendar, illustrated by Trina Schart Hyman and written by John Updike

Sector 7 by David Wiesner

When Sophie Gets Angry-Really, Really Angry by Molly Bang

The Ugly Duckling, illustrated by Jerry Pinkney and written by Hans Christian Andersen, adapted by Jerry Pinkney

1999

Medal Winner:

Snowflake Bentley, illustrated by Mary Azarian, written by Jacqueline Briggs Martin

Honor Books:

Duke Ellington: The Piano Prince and the Orchestra, illustrated by Brian Pinkney, written by Andrea Davis Pinkney

No, David! by David Shannon

Snow by Uri Shulevitz

Tibet Through the Red Box by Peter Sis

THE NEWBERY MEDAL

The Newbery Medal was named for eighteenth-century British bookseller John Newbery. It is awarded annually by the Association for Library Service to Children, a division of the American Library Association, to the author of the most distinguished contribution to American literature for children. For more information about The Newberry Medal see http://www.ala.org/alsc/newbpast.html.

2007

Medal Winner:

The Higher Power of Lucky by Susan Patron

Honor Books:

Penny from Heaven by Jennifer L. Holm

Hattie Big Sky by Kirby Larson

Rules by Cynthia Lord

2006

Medal Winner:

Criss Cross by Lynne Rae Perkins

Honor Books:

Whittington by Alan Armstrong, illustrated by S. D. Schindler

Hitler Youth: Growing Up in Hitler's Shadow by Susan Campbell Bartoletti

Princess Academy by Shannon Hale

Show Way by Jacqueline Woodson

2005

Medal Winner:

Kira-Kira by Cynthia Kadohata

Honor Books:

Al Capone Does My Shirts by Gennifer Choldenko

The Voice that Challenged a Nation: Marian Anderson and the Struggle for Equal Rights by Russell Freedman

Lizzie Bright and the Buckminster Boy by Gary D. Schmidt

2004

Medal Winner:

The Tale of Despereaux: Being the Story of a Mouse, a Princess, Some Soup, and a Spool of Thread by Kate DiCamillo, illustrated by Timothy Basil Ering

Honor Books:

Olive's Ocean by Kevin Henkes

An American Plague: The True and Terrifying Story of the Yellow Fever Epidemic of 1793 by Jim Murphy

2003

Medal Winner:

Crispin: The Cross of Lead by Avi

Honor Books:

The House of the Scorpion by Nancy Farmer

Pictures of Hollis Woods by Patricia Reilly Giff

Hoot by Carl Hiaasen

A Corner of The Universe by Ann M. Martin

Surviving the Applewhites by Stephanie S. Tolan

2002

Medal Winner:

A Single Shard by Linda Sue Park

Honor Books:

> *Everything on a Waffle* by Polly Horvath
>
> *Carver: A Life In Poems* by Marilyn Nelson

2001

Medal Winner:

> *A Year Down Yonder* by Richard Peck

Honor Books:

> *Hope Was Here* by Joan Bauer
>
> *Because of Winn-Dixie* by Kate DiCamillo
>
> *Joey Pigza Loses Control* by Jack Gantos
>
> *The Wanderer* by Sharon Creech

2000

Medal Winner:

> *Bud, Not Buddy* by Christopher Paul Curtis

Honor Books:

> *Getting Near to Baby* by Audrey Couloumbis
>
> *Our Only May Amelia* by Jennifer L. Holm
>
> *26 Fairmount Avenue* by Tomie dePaola

1999

Medal Winner:

> *Holes* by Louis Sachar

Honor Book:

> *A Long Way from Chicago* by Richard Peck

1998

Medal Winner:

> *Out of the Dust* by Karen Hesse

Honor Books:

    Ella Enchanted by Gail Carson Levine

    Lily's Crossing by Patricia Reilly Giff

    Wringer by Jerry Spinelli

THE CORETTA SCOTT KING AWARD

The Coretta Scott King Award is presented annually by the Coretta Scott King Task Force of the American LibraryAssociation's Social Responsibilities Round Table. Recipients are authors and illustrators of African descent whose distinguished books promote an understanding and appreciation of the American Dream." The Award commemorates the life and work of Dr. Martin Luther King Jr., and honors his widow, Coretta Scott King, for her courage and determination in continuing the work for peace and world brotherhood. For more information about the Coretta Scott King Award see http://www.ala.org/srrt/csking/winners.html.

2007

Award Winners:

    Author: *Copper Sun* by Sharon Draper

    Illustrator: *Moses: When Harriet Tubman Led Her People to Freedom* illustrated by Kadir Nelson, written by Carole Boston Weatherford

Honor Books:

    Author: *The Road to Paris* by Nikki Grimes

    Illustrator: *Jazz* illustrated by Christopher Myers, written by Walter Dean Myers

    Illustrator: *Poetry for Young People: Langston Hughes* illustrated by Benny Andrews, edited by David Roessel and Arnold Rampersad

2006

Award Winners:

    Author: *Day of Tears: A Novel in Dialogue* by Julius Lester

    Illustrator: *Rosa illustrated* by Bryan Collier, written by Nikki Giovanni

Honor Books:

    Author: *Maritcha: A Nineteenth-Century American Girl* by Tonya Bolden

Author: *Dark Sons* by Nikki Grimes

Author: *A Wreath for Emmett Till* by Marilyn Nelson, illustrated by Philippe Lardy

Illustrator: *Brothers in Hope: The Story of the Lost Boys of Sudan* by R. Gregory Christie

2005

Award Winners:

Author: *Remember: The Journey to School Integration* by Toni Morrison

Illustrator: *Ellington Was Not a Street* illustrated by Kadir A. Nelson, written by Ntozake Shange

Honor Books:

Author: *The Legend of Buddy Bush* by Shelia P. Moses

Author: *Who Am I without Him?: Short Stories about Girls and the Boys in Their Lives* by Sharon G. Flake

Author: *Fortune's Bones: The Manumission Requiem* by Marilyn Nelson

Illustrator: *God Bless the Child* illustrated by Jerry Pinkney written by Billie Holiday and Arthur Herzog Jr.

Illustrator: *The People Could Fly: The Picture Book* illustrated by Leo and Diane Dillon, written by Virginia Hamilton

2004

Award Winners:

Author: *The First Part Last* by Angela Johnson

Illustrator: *Beautiful Blackbird* by Ashley Bryan

Honor Books:

Author: *Days of Jubilee: The End of Slavery in the United States* by Patricia C. and Fredrick L. McKissack

2003

Award Winners:

Author: *Bronx Masquerade* by Nikki Grimes

Illustrator: *Talkin' About Bessie: The Story of Aviator Elizabeth Coleman* illustrated by E.B. Lewis, text by Nikki Grimes

Honor Books:

Author: *The Red Rose Box* by Brenda Woods

Illustrator: *Rap A Tap Tap: Here's Bojangles-Think of That* illustrated by Leo and Diane Dillion

Illustrator: *Visiting Langston* illustrated by Bryan Collier

2002

Award Winners:

Author: *The Land* by Mildred Taylor

Illustrator: *Goin' Someplace Special*, illustrated by Jerry Pinkney; text by Patricia McKissack

Honor Books:

Author: *Money-Hungry* by Sharon G. Flake

Author: *Carver: A Life in Poems* by Marilyn Nelson

Illustrator: *Martin's Big Words*, illustrated by Bryan Collier

2001

Award Winners:

Author: *Miracle's Boys* by Jacqueline Woodson

Illustrator: *Uptown* by Bryan Collier

Honor Books:

Author: *Let It Shine! Stories of Black Women Freedom Fighters* by Andrea Davis Pinkney, illustrated by Stephen Alcorn

Illustrator: *Freedom River* by Bryan Collier

Illustrator: *Only Passing Through: The Story of Sojourner Truth* illustrated by R. Gregory Christie; text by Anne Rockwell

Illustrator: *Virgie Goes to School with Us Boys* illustrated by E.B. Lewis

2000

Award Winners:

Author: *Bud, Not Buddy* by Christopher Paul Curtis

Illustrator: *In the Time of the Drums*, illustrated by Brian Pinkney; text by Kim L. Siegelson

Honor Books:

Author: *Francie* by Karen English

Author: *Black Hands, White Sails: The Story of African American Whalers* by Patricia C. and Frederick L. McKissack

Author: *Monster* by Walter Dean Myers

Illustrator: *My Rows and Piles of Coins*, illustrated by E. B. Lewis

Illustrator: *Black Cat* by Christopher Myers

1999

Award Winners:

Author: *Heaven* by Angela Johnson (Simon & Schuster)

Illustrator: *i see the rhythm*, illustrated by Michele Wood

Honor Books:

Author: *Jazmin's Notebook* by Nikki Grimes

Author: *Breaking Ground, Breaking Silence: The Story of New York's African Burial Ground* by Joyce Hansen and Gary McGowan

Author: *The Other Side: Shorter Poems* by Angela Johnson

Illustrator: *I Have Heard of a Land*, illustrated by Floyd Cooper

Illustrator: *The Bat Boy and His Violin*, illustrated by E.B. Lewis

THE PURA BELPRÉ AWARD

The Pura Belpré Award is presented to a Latino/Latina writer and illustrator whose work best portrays, affirms, and celebrates the Latino cultural experience in an outstanding work of literature for children and youth. The award is named after Pura Belpré, the first Latina librarian from the New York Public Library. The award is presented biennially. For more information about the Pura Belpré Award see http://www.ala.org/alsc/belpre.html.

2006

Award Winners:

Author: *The Tequila Worm* by Viola Canales

Illustrator: *Doña Flor: A Tall Table about a Giant Woman with a Great Big Heart* illustrated by Raul Colón, written by Pat Mora

Honor Books:

Author: *César: ¡Sí, Se Puede! Yes, We Can!* by Carmen T. Bernier-Grand, illustrated by David Diaz

Author: *Doña Flor: A Tall Table about a Giant Woman with a Great Big Heart* by Pat Mora, illustrated by Raul Colón

Author: *Becoming Naomi León* by Pam Muñoz Ryan

Illustrator: *Arrorró, Mi Niño: Latino Lullabies and Gentle Games* selected and illustrated by Lulu Delacre.

Illustrator: *César: ¡Sí, Se Puede! Yes, We Can!* illustrated by David Diaz, written by Carmen T. Bernier-Grand

Illustrator: *My Name is Celia/Me Llamo Celia* illustrated by Rafael López, written by Monica Brown

2004

Award Winners:

Author: *Before We Were Free* by Julia Alvarez

Illustrator: *Just a Minute: A Trickster Tale* and Counting Book by Yuyi Morales

Honor Books:

Author: *Cuba 15* by Nancy Osa

Author: *My Diary from Here to There/Mi Diario de Aqui Hasta Allá* by Amada Irma Perez

Illustrator: *First Day in Grapes*, illustrated by Robert Casilla; text by L. King Perez

Illustrator: *The Pot That Juan Built*, illustrated by David Diaz; text by Nancy Andrews-Goebel.

Illustrator: *Harvesting Hope: The Story of Cesar Chavez*, illustrated by Yuyi Morales; text by Kathleen Krull.

2002

Award Winners:

Author: Esperanza Rising by Pam Munoz Ryan

Illustrator: *Chato* and the Party Animals, illustrated by Susan Guevara; text by Gary Soto

Honor Books:

Author: *Breaking Through* by Francisco Jimenez

Author: *Iguanas in the Snow*, illustrated by Maya Christina Gonzalez; text by Francisco X. Alarcón

Illustrator: *Juan Bobo Goes to Work*, illustrated by Joe Cepeda; retold by Marisa Montes

2000

Award Winners:

Author: *Under the Royal Palms: A Childhood in Cuba* by Alma Flor Ada

Illustrator: *Magic Windows*, illustrated by Carmen Lomas Garza

Honor Books:

Author: *From the Bellybutton of the Moon and Other Summer Poems/ Del Ombligo de la Luna y Otro Poemas de Verano* by Francisco X. Alarcón, illustrated by Maya Christina Gonzalez

Author: *Laughing out Loud, I Fly: Poems in English and Spanish* by Juan Felipe Herrera, illustrated by Karen Barbour

Illustrator: *Barrio: Jose's Neighborhood* by George Ancona

Illustrator: *The Secret Stars*, illustrated by Felipe Dávalos; text by Joseph Slate.

Illustrator: *Mama & Papa Have a Store* by Amelia Lau Carling

1998

Award Winners:

Author: *Parrot in the Oven: mi vida* by Victor Martinez

Illustrator: *Snapshots from the Wedding*, illustrated by Stephanie Garcia; text by Gary Soto

Honor Books:

Author: *Laughing Tomatoes and Other Spring Poems / Jitomates Risueños y otros poemas de primavera* by Francisco Alarcón, illustrated by Maya Christina Gonzalez

Author: *Spirits of the High Mesa* by Floyd Martinez

Illustrator: *In My Family/ En mi familia* by Carmen Lomas Garza

Illustrator: *The Golden Flower: a Taino Myth from Puerto Rico,* illustrated by Enrique O. Sánchez; text by Nina Jaffe

Illustrator: *Gathering the Sun: An Alphabet in Spanish and English,* illustrated by Simon Silva; text by Alma Flor Ada; English translation by Rosa Zubizarreta

1996

Award Winners:

Author: *An Island Like You: Stories of the Barrio* by Judith Ortiz Cofer

Illustrator: *Chato's Kitchen,* illustrated by Susan Guevara; text by Gary Soto

Honor Books:

Author: *The Bossy Gallito / El Gallo de Bodas: A Traditional Cuban Folktale* illustrated by González, Lucia

Author: *Baseball in April, and Other Stories* by Gary Soto

Illustrator: *Pablo Remembers: The Fiesta of the Day of the Dead/ Pablo Recuerda: La Fiesta de Dia de los Muertos* by George Ancona

Illustrator: *The Bossy Gallito / El Gallo de Bodas: A Traditional Cuban Folktale* retold by Lucia González

Illustrator: *Family Pictures / Cuadros de Familia* by Carmen Lomas Garza; Spanish language text by Rosalma Zubizaretta

NONFICTION AWARD WINNERS

ROBERT F. SIBERT INFORMATIONAL BOOK MEDAL

This award was established by the Association for Library Service to Children in 2001. Awarded annually, it recognizes authors and illustrators of informational books.

2007

Medal Winner:

Team Moon: How 400,000 People Landed Apollo 11 on the Moon by Catherine Thimmesh

Honor Books:

Freedom Riders: John Lewis and Jim Zwerg on the Front Lines of the Civil Rights Movement by Ann Bausum

Quest for the Tree Kangaroo: An Expedition to the Cloud Forest of New Guinea written by Sy Montgomery, photographs by Nic Bishop

To Dance: A Ballerina's Graphic Novel written by Siena Cherson Siegel, artwork by Mark Siegel

2006

Medal Winner:

Secrets of a Civil War Submarine: Solving the Mysteries of the H.L. Hunley by Sally M. Walker

Honor Book:

Hitler Youth: Growing Up in Hitler's Shadow by Susan Campbell Bartoletti

2005

Medal Winner:

The Voice that Challenged a Nation: Marian Anderson and the Struggle for Equal Rights by Russell Freedman

Honor Books:

Walt Whitman: Words for America written by Barbara Kerley, illustrated by Brian Selznick

The Tarantula Scientist written by Sy Montgomery, photographs by Nic Bishop

Sequoyah: The Cherokee Man Who Gave His People Writing written by James Rumford, translated into Cherokee by Anna Sixkiller Huckaby

2004

Medal Winner:

An American Plague: The True and Terrifying Story of the Yellow Fever Epidemic of 1793 by Jim Murphy

Honor Book:

I Face the Wind written by Vicki Cobb, illustrated by Julia Gorton (HarperCollins)

2003

Medal Winner:

The Life and Death of Adolf Hitler by James Cross Giblin

Honor Books:

Six Days in October: The Stock Market Crash of 1929 by Karen Blumenthal

Hole in My Life by Jack Gantos

Action Jackson written by Jan Greenberg and Sandra Jordan, illustrated by Robert Andrew Parker

When Marian Sang written by Pam Munoz Ryan, illustrated by Brian Selznick

2002

Medal Winner:

Black Potatoes: The Story of the Great Irish Famine, 1845-1850 by Susan Campbell Bartoletti

Honor Books:

Surviving Hitler: A Boy in the Nazi Death Camps by Andrea Warren

Vincent van Gogh by Jan Greenberg and Sandra Jordan

Brooklyn Bridge by Lynn Curlee

2001

Medal Winner:

Sir Walter Ralegh and the Quest for El Dorado by Marc Aronson

Honor Books:

The Longitude Prize by Joan Dash; illustrated by Dusan Petricic

Blizzard! The Storm That Changed America by Jim Murphy

My Season with Penguins: An Antarctic Journal by Sophie Webb.

Pedro and Me: Friendship, Loss, and What I Learned by Judd Winick

Appendix D

Sun & Cloud Templates

Appendix E

Reading Growth Graph

Watch Your Reading Grow!

Use the chart below to graph the number of minute that you have read each day during SIR.

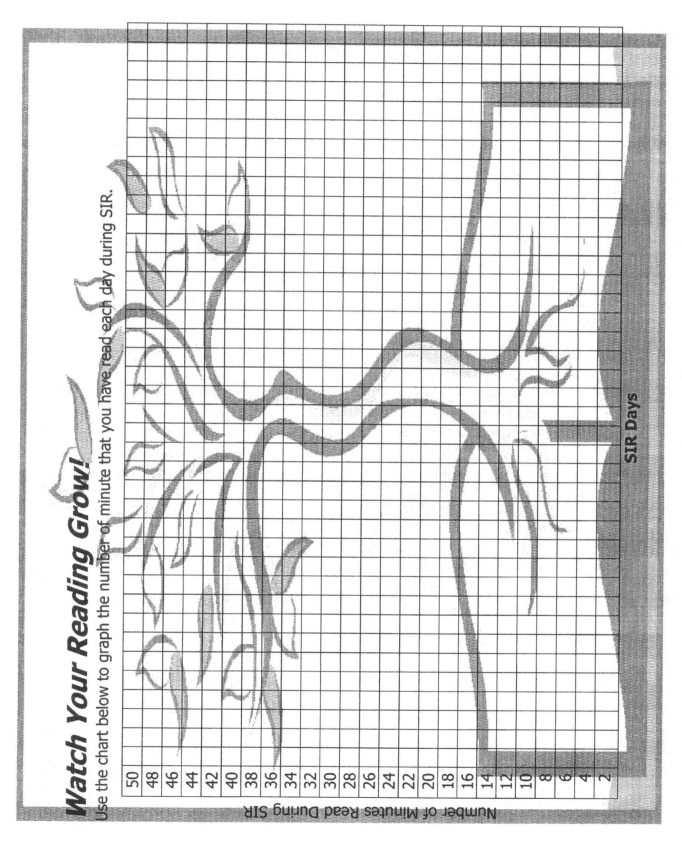

| 50 |
| 48 |
| 46 |
| 44 |
| 42 |
| 40 |
| 38 |
| 36 |
| 34 |
| 32 |
| 30 |
| 28 |
| 26 |
| 24 |
| 22 |
| 20 |
| 18 |
| 16 |
| 14 |
| 12 |
| 10 |
| 8 |
| 6 |
| 4 |
| 2 |

Number of Minutes Read During SIR

SIR Days

Appendix F

Creativity Lesson

Introducing Creative Thinking (All Grades) Lesson #1: Encouraging Creative Thinking

As a precursor to this lesson, you may want to consider sharing a read-aloud with the class focusing on a creative idea, character, or a difficult situation requiring an unusual solution, like *Archibald Frisby* by Michael Chesworth or *It Looks Like Spilt Milk* by Charles Shaw.

To prepare students for using creativity exercises on their own, the basic strategy for this lesson consists of freeing the classroom atmosphere from the usual constraints often associated with convergent production. It is important for students to learn to appreciate questions and activities for which there are no right answers. You can introduce this concept by contrasting a convergent type of question with a divergent one. Before distributing the first activity sheet, you may say something like the following:

> Today we are going to begin practicing a new kind of thinking. This kind of thinking will help us learn how to explore many different kinds of solutions to a given problem. Some problems and questions have only one right answer, but there are also many problems and questions that have hundreds of possible answers.

> Suppose I asked you, In what year did Columbus discover America? (Wait for an answer and write it on the board.)

> Are there any other possible answers to this question? (General conclusion should be negative.)

Now suppose I were to ask you, "What are all of the possible ways that you might have come to school this morning?" (Call on youngsters and list responses on the board.)

Students will probably give some fairly common responses (walk, bus, car, bicycle). At this point, you might say:

Remember, I said all of the possible ways that you might have come. Use your imagination. Let your mind wander, even if you think the method for coming to school is silly. How about by donkey or pogo stick? (Add these to the list on the board.)

By suggesting the donkey and the pogo stick, you have accomplished three very important objectives.

1. You have conveyed the idea that answers need not be feasible, practical, or realistic.

2. You have let youngsters know that you will accept these kinds of answers.

3. You have let the youngsters know that you are capable of some way-out ideas.

You can emphasize this last point by grabbing a yardstick (conveniently placed nearby beforehand) and improvising with a few hops to demonstrate a pogo stick. Students will no doubt become a little noisy, but it is very important to tolerate this reaction. If you hush them, the whole atmosphere of freedom will be lost, and they will subjectively think that this new kind of thinking is the same old game—the teacher questions and students answer.

After your examples, students may give a wide variety of answers. Let them call out their answers (rather than raising hands) as you write them on the board. Prompt students if necessary:

Any other animals that you might come to school on? How about an airplane or a rocket? Or being dropped from a plane with a parachute?

A second crucial factor at this point is the generous use of praise on your part. Enthusiastic comments such as good, great, and fantastic will help youngsters open up. Do not call on students who are not taking part. It takes some youngsters longer than others to trust the teacher and his or her classmates in this type of situation. The main idea is to let students know that you like what is going on and that you are having fun. When the flow of responses begins to slow down, say:

Let's go one step farther. Suppose you could change your size or shape. Can you think of some other ways that you might possibly come to school?

If no one responds, you might ask:

Could you make yourself very tiny and come in your brother's lunch box? Or could you change to a drop of water and come in through the drinking fountain?

Continue to fill the board as long as the youngsters are generating responses. When you finally call a halt, say:

I guess there really are many questions and problems that have several possible answers. Do you think this kind of thinking is fun?

From time to time, we are going to be working on some activities like the one we just did. The main purpose of these activities will be to practice answering questions and solving problems that have many possible answers. We will be using our imaginations to come up with some clever new ideas.

At this point, distribute the first activity sheet, "Way-out Words" and read the directions with the students. If you have any doubts about youngsters' understanding the directions, ask if there are any questions. Then ask the students to complete the first exercise.

After they have finished, allow some students to discuss their responses. Ask, "How many had that idea?" and after a few students have shared their entire lists, ask if anyone has any responses that have not yet been mentioned. Praise unusual responses from individuals, and praise the entire group for catching on.

Source:

Renzulli, J. S., & Callahan, C. M. (2000). *New Directions in Creativity: Mark 3.* Mansfield Center, CT: Creative Learning Press.

Name _____ Date _____

3 Way-out Words (a)

Words can sometimes be written in ways that make them look like their meanings. See if you can write each of the following words so that it will look like its meaning. An example of how the first word might be written is shown below.

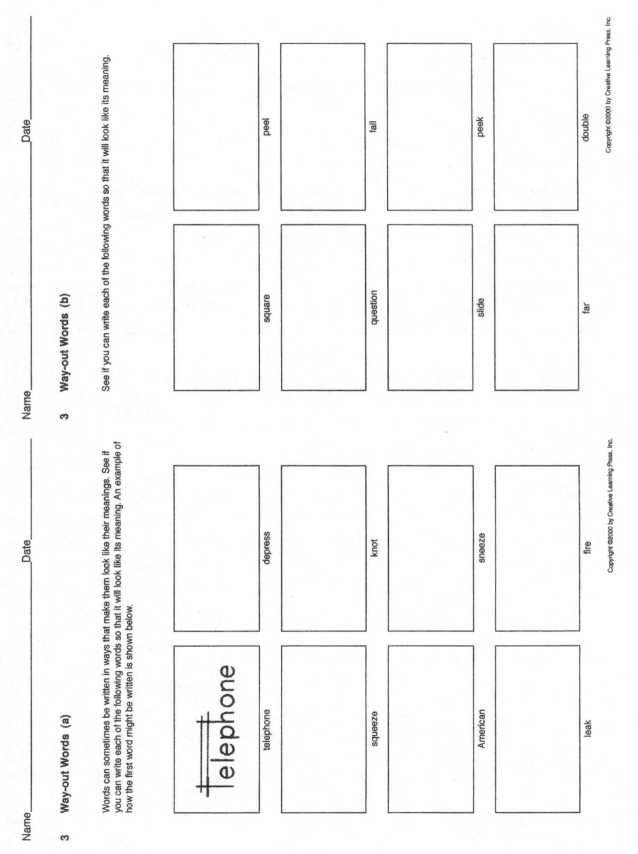

telephone	depress
squeeze	knot
American	sneeze
leak	fire

Name _____ Date _____

3 Way-out Words (b)

See if you can write each of the following words so that it will look like its meaning.

square	peel
question	fall
slide	peek
far	double

Appendix G

SEM-Xplorations Example

Bridges 101

Have you ever watched a bridge collapse right before your eyes? Most likely you haven't had this experience because bridge engineers have learned from the horrible November 1940 collapse of the Tacoma Narrows Bridge in Washington. The Tacoma Narrows Bridge was designed as a suspension bridge, like the Golden Gate Bridge (http://www.goldengate.org/) in California, and was open to traffic for only a few months. It quickly became known for the way strong winds twisted the light roadway. In its design stage, engineers, people who build and design things that make people's lives easier, did not think that wind would have had an effect on the bridge so they continued designing the bridge as planned. But soon after the bridge was built, a problem became evident. On November 7, 1940 the winds were blowing stronger than normal. This caused the roadway to bounce up and down in abnormal ways, more than it had ever before. Before long, a support bracket that was providing strength to the bridge slipped. Soon after, one suspension cable snapped and the collapse of the bridge began. Amazingly, this footage was caught on tape! Take a look at the two links below.

Tacoma Narrows Bridge Disaster, November 1940
http://www.enm.bris.ac.uk/research/nonlinear/tacoma/tacoma.html

Watch this eight second video clip to see the "twisted" effects of wind moments before the Tacoma Narrows Bridge fell apart. Scroll to the bottom of the page and click on "video clip."

Tacoma Narrows Bridge Disaster
http://www.wcsscience.com/tacoma/bridge.html
See large snapshots of the Tacoma Narrows Bridge as it tumbled down and read the details of what happened on that fateful day.

The video and photographic footage of the bridge demonstrates an important lesson to engineers and architects who build and design bridges. They need to test the effects of nature on the bridge before building the structure.

This project will give you an opportunity to study some special bridges from around the world and learn about the different ways engineers design bridges. It will give you a chance to see how natural forces affect bridges, while also learning about different styles of bridges. In the end, you'll have a chance to design and plan your own bridge while taking important factors into consideration! Right now you should take a few blank sheets of paper to use for brainstorming. As you progress through the websites and activities, write down bridges that fascinate you and record any information that would be helpful for you when designing your own bridge.

The history of bridges is tied directly to the development of various forms of transportation—many of which were invented during the 1800s and 1900s. The inventions are important to people because they have improved human's lives. Transportation makes traveling quicker than the alternative of traveling by foot, plus it also allows for a greater number of objects to be transported at one time.

In the early 1800s trains were invented. They were an important advance in transportation because they allowed people and objects to travel large distances in less time than that required by covered wagons—the previous way of traveling. Train travel quickly became very popular, creating a need for more railway lines. As the railroads expanded, it was only natural that they soon came to rivers and other waterways that prevented further rail construction. Obviously, the railroads needed bridges to allow for unlimited travel. And this is how train bridges came to be. Today, many train bridges are still in existence and use around the world.

After trains, bicycles were invented in the mid to late 1800's furthering people's choices in travel. Then came automobiles and airplanes in the early 1900's. Throughout the 1900's, these two forms of transportation, originally used by only the wealthiest people, dropped in price and became more popular and more universally used. Just as with trains, the increase in popularity of cars and bikes created a need for more roadways and more bridges. Bridge designers began experimenting with bridge designs because of the need for bridges to span greater distances. Today, engineers are still building bridges to allow people to drive to their desired destinations. For example, the Confederation Bridge (http://www.confederationbridge.com/bridge/morepics.aspx?pageid=71&lang=en) which was opened in May 1997, spans the 8 miles between Prince Edward Island, Canada, and New Brunswick, Canada. Now people can drive to the island for the first time. As you can see, this desire to push the limits of bridges is still seen throughout the world today as engineers compete to build the largest and highest bridges in history.

Bridge designing might sound fun and easy, but many important lessons need to be learned before people begin. Did you know that there are four main types of bridges? These bridges are a suspension bridge (http://www.hsba.go.jp/bridge/e-akasi.htm), a beam bridge (http://www.pbs.org/wgbh/nova/bridge/meetbeam.html), an arch bridge (http://www.pbs.org/wgbh/buildingbig/wonder/structure/iron.html), and a cable-stayed bridge (http://www.pbs.org/wgbh/buildingbig/wonder/structure/sunshineskyway1_bridge.html). (Keep reading and you will learn about each of these bridges.) In addition to choosing which main type of bridge to build, engineers need to consider several factors when creating their designs, including: the distance to be bridged, how the bridge will fit into its natural surroundings, and the forces that can affect the bridge, like the wind in the Tacoma Narrows Bridge disaster. After bridge engineers design the bridge they must present their plan, or proposal, to a group of people who will decide if they like the proposal. If they like it, then the project will be built. If they don't like the proposal, the group might ask for a new bridge design or choose a different bridge designer's ideas. Below are two websites that will give you a chance to learn more about decisions bridge designers must consider.

Building Big
http://www.pbs.org/wgbh/buildingbig/lab/shapes.html
Use this site to test out different forces, loads, materials and shapes of bridges to experiment with different considerations when building a bridge.

Craggy Rock Bridge Challenge
http://www.pbs.org/wgbh/buildingbig/bridge/challenge/index.html
Become a bridge designer in seconds by helping the mayor and townspeople of Craggy Rock make good decisions about the style of bridges required for different locations.

Did you enjoy exploring the challenges bridge designers face? What skills did you need to successfully complete your tasks on these websites? If you think problem solving was important, then you are correct! It is also important to become informed. When people become informed they gather important information from different sources before beginning to plan. Engineers need to be excellent problem solvers who can find a variety of ways to solve problems and make informed decisions.

As you begin to look more closely at bridges you will notice how bridges look different from one another—even if the bridges are the same type of design. This is because bridges are built for many different purposes. For centuries, bridge designers have had to think about more than transportation needs when designing bridges. For example, in China, bridges have been built as a symbol of culture. Take a look below at some of these impressive bridges—they are exciting and beautiful, as well as functional. Some people would even say that they are works of art! Remember to take notes on any bridge you find interesting.

Chinese Wooden Bridge in Minorities Park
http://chinadan.com/03china-bridge/01-04h.html
This website may take a minute to download, but the wait will be worth it when you see this ornate Chinese bridge. Have you ever seen a bridge like this in the United States? Probably not! How is it different from bridges you have seen? How is it similar?

Marco Polo Bridge, China
http://www.chinapage.org/history/lugouqiao/lugouqiao.html
This bridge was first built in 1192 and features a stone segmented design. More than eight-hundred years ago, the bridge was listed as one of the "Eight Scenic Spots of Yanjing (Beijing)." Is it still beautiful and interesting today? Why or why not?

Santiago Calatrava, Bridge Designer
http://www.calatrava.com/
Take a look at this master architect and engineer's modern bridge designs. Click on "bridge" and "chronology" to see pictures of the bridges and read about each one.

Bridges can serve a variety of purposes in addition to aiding highway transportation. Take a

look below to see the different functions of bridges. Did you know you can walk on top of a

bridge in Australia and a composer plays the cables of bridges to create music?

You might be amazed at what you learn about the functions of bridges, so keep reading!

Sydney Harbour Bridge
http://www.bridgeclimb.com/
Search this site to see people climb to the highest point on this bridge in Australia. Make sure to check out the image gallery (http://www.bridgeclimb.com/experience_frs.htm) and the online video (http://www.bridgeclimb.com/experience_frs.htm) to get a taste of the experience.

Royal Gorge Bridge
http://www.royalgorgebridge.com/
Ride the Royal Rush Skycoaster (http://royalgorgebridge.com/html/parkinformation/skycoaster-ride.html) in Colorado and feel the exhilaration of falling 1,200 feet off the side of the suspension style Royal Gorge Bridge. For a thrill, click on the Royal Rush Skycoaster commercial link on the Royal Rush page. Does this experience look like something you would enjoy?

Singing Bridges
http://www.singingbridges.net/about/index.html
Read about the bridge musician, Jodi Rose as she plays the cables of suspension bridges and cable-stayed bridges around the world.

Matsuo Bridge
http://www.matsuo-bridge.co.jp/english/bridges/catalog/kansai-intl.shtm
Take a look at an island that was created to be an airport in Japan. Notice the long span bridge that allows cars on top and a railway on the truss.

Covered Bridges
http://architecture.about.com/gi/dynamic/offsite.htm?zi=1/XJ&sdn=architecture&zu=http%3A%2F%2Fwilliam-king.www.drexel.edu%2Ftop%2Fbridge%2FCBbyC.html
Visit over 70 covered bridges located across the Northeast United States to learn about this early style of New England bridge design.

Rainbow Bridge
http://www.nps.gov/rabr/home.htm
The world's largest natural bridge is located in the state of Utah where thousands of people visit it each year. Click on this site to learn more about this special natural monument.

Which style of bridge was most interesting to you? Did you make notes? If you were to become a bridge designer, what type of bridge would you create? But wait—don't make your decision yet! There are still a few more bridges to consider before beginning your project.

Recently, a shift has taken place in American bridge design. Since 1975, only a handful of cable-stayed bridges have been built in America. But more recently, these bridges have become more popular. For example, there is a new cable-stayed bridge in Boston, Massachusetts named the Leonard P. Zakim Bunker Hill Bridge (http://www.leonardpzakimbunkerhillbridge.org/). There are also cable-stayed bridges being built in Toledo, Ohio, (http://www.lookuptoledo.org/servlet/com.hntb.toledo.servlets.NewsManagement?option=3), Charleston, South Carolina, (http://www.cooperriverbridge.org/) and Greenville, Mississippi (http://www.greenvillebridge.com/). There is a fifth cable-stayed bridge connecting Illinois and Missouri. Take a look at the digital video clip of this bridge below.

New Mississippi River Bridge
http://www.newriverbridge.org/
See the computer animated digital video clip of the anticipated bridge in St. Louis, Missouri opening in 2010. Click on the link and open "See the New Bridge" link.

Considering the information you have learned, what type of bridge will you create? Do you want to build a bridge for trains, bikes, cars or airplanes? Where will your bridge be located? What style bridge is best for the location? It might be easiest for you to think about an area you have

Review the information you recorded while working through this project and decide which types of bridges are most interesting to you. You might want to circle or star the information you will use as the base to your bridge sketch. Consider the activities from Craggy Rock to be sure you are choosing the most appropriate bridge for the space.

Take a blank piece of paper and decide on the bridge you plan to design. This bridge should be your own original design, but you might consider combining a few styles together. Write in the bottom corner of the page the following information: where the bridge will be built, what type of transportation will use the bridge, and the style of the bridge (suspension, beam, cable-stayed, or arch).

You can begin drawing your bridge on scrap paper until you feel comfortable to make a published copy. Bridges are hard to draw, but with practice you can really improve your style. Keep working until you feel you have done the best you can.

In real life you would have to present your proposal to a group of people who would decide if they like your ideas. Recreate this situation by contacting a local engineering firm to see if they would be interested in seeing your project. They would be able to give you good advice on how to improve your design. You might also want to display your design at your local library.

Congratulations on your perseverance and good work. You might want to attempt a more difficult level of bridge activities. There is a project called "Build a Bridge and Get Over It" geared towards middle school students.

Bridges!: Amazing Structures to Design, Build and Test, by Carol A. Johmann and Elizabeth
 J. Rieth (Sagebrush, 1999). ISBN: 1-885593-30-9.
  This book is filled with historical and technical information about bridges, as well as hands-
  on experiments demonstrating the ideas behind bridge design and construction. Projects
  range from construction of a popsicle-stick bridge to writing bridge poems. If you're

interested in bridges, this book may be for you!

Covered Bridges: Across North America by Joseph D. Conwill. (Motorbooks International, 2004).
ISBN: 0760318220 *Here you will find a history of covered bridges from the early 1800's to the present. Learn about bridges for toll-roads, bridges from the classic era of covered bridges and preservation projects today.*

The Haunted Bridge (Nancy Drew Mystery Series #15) by Carolyn Keene (Grosset & Dunlap;

Revised edition, 2001). ISBN: 0448095157.
Nancy Drew, the famous girl-detective is solving mysteries again—this one includes a creepy bridge, a lost jewel-case and an obnoxious golfer.

Hey Kid, Want to Buy a Bridge? by Jon Scieszka (Puffin Books, 2003).
ISBN: 0142500208
Joe, Sam and Fred have traveled into the past—and landed on top of the unfinished Brooklyn Bridge in New York, New York. Read about the boys exciting adventures in this fun book.

The Family under the Bridge by Natalie Savage Carlson. (HarperTrophy; Reissue edition, 1989).
ISBN: 0066402509.
Unfortunately, bridges sometimes must serve as temporary homes for people who have nowhere else to live. Read this book about a family who lives under a bridge in Paris, France.

 Internet

Golden Gate Bridge, Highway and Transportation District
http://www.goldengate.org/

Tacoma Narrows Bridge Disaster, November 1940
http://www.enm.bris.ac.uk/research/nonlinear/tacoma/tacoma.html

Tacoma Narrows Bridge Disaster
http://www.wcsscience.com/tacoma/bridge.html

Confederation Bridge
http://www.confederationbridge.com/bridge/morepics.aspx?pageid=71&lang=en

Building Big
http://www.pbs.org/wgbh/buildingbig/lab/shapes.html

Craggy Rock Bridge Challenge
http://www.pbs.org/wgbh/buildingbig/bridge/challenge/index.html

Chinese Wooden Bridge in Minorities Park
http://chinadan.com/03china-bridge/01-04h.html

http://www.chinapage.org/history/lugouqiao/lugouqiao.html

Santiago Calatrava, Bridge Designer
http://www.calatrava.com/

Sydney Harbour Bridge
http://www.bridgeclimb.com/

Royal Gorge Bridge
http://www.royalgorgebridge.com/

Singing Bridges
http://www.singingbridges.net/about/index.html

Matsuo Bridge
http://www.matsuo-bridge.co.jp/english/bridges/catalog/kansai-intl.shtm

Covered Bridges
http://architecture.about.com/gi/dynamic/offsite.htm?zi=1/XJ&sdn=architecture&zu=http%3A%2F%2Fwilliam-king.www.drexel.edu%2Ftop%2Fbridge%2FCBbyC.html

Rainbow Bridge
http://www.nps.gov/rabr/home.htm

APPENDIX H

TEACHER LOG TEMPLATES

THE SCHOOLWIDE ENRICHMENT MODEL READING FRAMEWORK

SAMPLE

Teacher: _Miss Shirley_   Dates: _(Week One)_

WEEKLY THEME:
To develop a positive classroom climate and introduce SIR and the reading logs.

	PHASE 1	PHASE 2	PHASE 3
MONDAY	BOOKS: _Matilda_ Introduce other books by Roald Dahl # of Minutes = 20	Students conferenced with: Circulated to observe and encourage students # of Minutes = 15	Choices offered: Entire class completed the Reading Interest-a-Lyzer # of Minutes = 15
TUESDAY	BOOKS: _The Librarian of Basra_ Discussion of care and usage of Classroom Library # of Minutes = 19	Students conferenced with: Worked with Carlos Maria, and Jack to find books; circulated to observe and guide # of Minutes = 16	Choices offered: Continue to read book Audio books Buddy Read Renzulli Learning # of Minutes = 15
WEDNESDAY	BOOKS: _It Looks Like Spilt Milk_ Discussion of metaphors & Similies # of Minutes = 18	Students conferenced with: Yesica Milton # of Minutes = 17	Choices offered: Creativity in Language Arts Whole Class Lesson followed by activity (Way Out Words # of Minutes = 15
THURSDAY	BOOKS: _Thank you, Mr. Falker_ # of Minutes = 17	Students conferenced with: Pedro Julissa # of Minutes = 18	Choices offered: Audio books Buddy Read Renzulli Learning Creativity in Language Arts Activity # of Minutes = 15
FRIDAY	BOOKS: _Frindle_ Introduce other books by Andrew Clements # of Minutes = 15	Students conferenced with: Ami Tania Arman # of Minutes = 20	Choices offered: Audio books Buddy Read Renzulli Learning # of Minutes = 15

SAMPLE

Weekly Reflection:

I was surprised at how quickly my students got used to the idea of reading silently for an extended period of time. I expected that getting them settled would require much effort! When they started to lose interest on Thursday, I put a sticky note by the target stop time on the clock. It really helped to focus the most inattentive students.

What went well this week:

I am able to connect with students personally and the bookmark questions are enabling me to ask conference questions even when I do not know the plot of the book.

What I will improve on next week:

As I conference with individual students, I would like to bring their awareness to the "text-to-self" connections they are making to improve their metagconitive skills.

Personal Goal For Next Week:	**Goal for Students for Next Week:**
Keeping conferences to five minutes.	Get all students to understand a text-to-self connection and have my advanced readers understand the concept within the context of the conference.

SAMPLE

Teacher: _Miss Shirley_   Dates: _(Week Six)_

WEEKLY THEME:
To increase student exposure to and comfort with the usage of non-fiction materials

	PHASE 1	PHASE 2	PHASE 3
MONDAY	BOOKS: _The Rajah's Rice_ Guest Reader: _Principal Johnson_ # of Minutes = 10	Students conferenced with: _Arman_ _Carmen_ _Austin_ _Jose_ _Pedro_ # of Minutes = 30	Choices offered: _Continue to read book_ _Audio books_ _Buddy Read_ _Renzulli Learning_ # of Minutes = 10
TUESDAY	BOOKS: # of Minutes =	Students conferenced with: _**Field Trip to the Avonlea Public Library**_ _- The librarian will provide a tour that focuses on non-fiction resources. Students may also get library cards._ # of Minutes =	Choices offered: # of Minutes =
WEDNESDAY	BOOKS: _Good Queen Bess: The Story of Elizabeth I of England_ # of Minutes = 7	Students conferenced with: _Maria_ _Juan_ _Yesica_ _Tamika_ _Tyronne_ _Ami_ # of Minutes = 33	Choices offered: _Audio books_ _Buddy Read_ _Renzulli Learning_ _Readers' Theater_ _Interest Centers_ # of Minutes = 10
THURSDAY	BOOKS: _Elephant Book: For the Elefriends Campaign_ # of Minutes = 10	Students conferenced with: _Carlos_ _Milton_ _Cheyann_ _Emmanuel_ _Marcus_ _Tania_ # of Minutes = 34	Choices offered: _Interest Centers_ _Reader's Theatre_ _Renzulli Learning_ _Buddy Read_ # of Minutes = 11
FRIDAY	BOOKS: _The Cod's Tale_ # of Minutes = 5	Students conferenced with: _Julissa_ _Mikayla_ _Bobby_ _Carlita_ _Vanessa_ _Jung_ # of Minutes = 35	Choices offered: _Interest Centers_ _Reader's Theatre_ _Renzulli Learning_ _Independent Projects_ # of Minutes = 10

SAMPLE

Weekly Reflection:
Wow, what a busy and productive week! The kids seem re-energized by the principal's visit and the short trip to the library. Meeting the goal of exposing the students to non-fiction materials required a bit of work to collect interesting and challenging books, but I am pleased with the results. I think we'll continue the focus on non-fiction into next week.

What went well this week:
Providing students choices in Phase III. They really respond well to having interest-based choices.

What I will improve on next week:
I want to be able to move more fluently between different Phase III options so that all students have some support from me.

Personal Goal For Next Week:	**Goal for Students for Next Week:**

I want to provide more freedom during Phase III and maintain a relaxed state of mind while students work independently.	*Have all students be able to identify 3 to 5 questions for the current non-fiction book they are reading.*
	
	   3 for below grade level readers
	   4 for on grade level readers
	   5 for advanced readers

SAMPLE

Teacher: _Miss Shirley_   Dates: _(Week Twelve)_

WEEKLY THEME:
To provide more time for independent investigations.

	PHASE 1	PHASE 2	PHASE 3

MONDAY	BOOKS:
	Babe: The Gallant Pig
	   Introduce other Dick
	    King-Smith books
	
	# of Minutes = 10
		Students conferenced with:
		Julissa Carmen
		Arman Tyronne
		Austin
		Tamika
		Pedro
		# of Minutes = 40
			Choices offered:
			
			# of Minutes =

TUESDAY	BOOKS: _1 story from More Stories to Solve_ # of Minutes = 5	Students conferenced with: Carlita Juan Vanessa Maria Tania Emmanuel Mikayla # of Minutes = 45	Choices offered: # of Minutes =
WEDNESDAY	BOOKS: _The Great Brain_ (student recommendation) # of Minutes = 5	Students conferenced with: Carlos Julissa Jose Austin Yesica Milton Jung Ami # of Minutes = 45	Choices offered: # of Minutes =
THURSDAY	BOOKS: _Chasing Vermeer_ # of Minutes = 10	Students conferenced with: Austin Pedro Tyronne Carmen Tamika Carlita # of Minutes = 40	Choices offered: # of Minutes = 0
FRIDAY	BOOKS: # of Minutes = 0	Students conferenced with: # of Minutes = 0	Choices offered: _Interest Centers_ _Renzulli Learning_ _Independent Projects_ _Buddy Read_ _Independent Reading_ # of Minutes = 50

SAMPLE

Weekly Reflection:

Everyone (including me) loved the putting aside an entire day for Phase 3. I have been so impressed with Arman's research on important figures in African American History. After reading Lives: Poems About Famous Americans, he is planning to write a book of poetry using the information that he has uncovered.

What went well this week:

My advanced readers are finally reading books that are challenging for them. This has been a process because they always wanted to read books that were too easy for them. This is a huge success!

What I will improve on next week:

I want to continue to increase the complexity of student conferences by asking more open-ended questions and increasing student awareness of the strategies they utilize as readers.

Personal Goal For Next Week:	**Goal for Students for Next Week:**
I'm meeting with our librarian and the high school media specialist next week to try to find additional challenging interest-based books for my advanced readers.	*Have all students identify the reading strategies they used as part of their conference—at least 2 strategies per student conference.*

The Schoolwide Enrichment Model Reading Framework

Teacher: _____   Dates: _____

WEEKLY THEME:

	PHASE 1	PHASE 2	PHASE 3
MONDAY	BOOKS: # of Minutes =	Students conferenced with: # of Minutes =	Choices offered: # of Minutes =
TUESDAY	BOOKS: # of Minutes =	Students conferenced with: # of Minutes =	Choices offered: # of Minutes =
WEDNESDAY	BOOKS: # of Minutes =	Students conferenced with: # of Minutes =	Choices offered: # of Minutes =
THURSDAY	BOOKS: # of Minutes =	Students conferenced with: # of Minutes =	Choices offered: # of Minutes =
FRIDAY	BOOKS: # of Minutes =	Students conferenced with: # of Minutes =	Choices offered: # of Minutes =

Weekly Reflection:

What went well this week:

What I will improve on next week:

Personal Goal For Next Week:	Goal for Students for Next Week

Appendix I

Student Log Templates

Dates: __September 18__ through __September 22__

	Book Title		
MONDAY	Surviving the Applewhites	Pages Read	166 - 186
	By Stephanie Tolan	Minutes Read	35
		Conf. Y/N	Y
TUESDAY	Surviving the Applewhites	Pages Read	187 - 216
	By Stephanie Tolan	Minutes Read	35
		Conf. Y/N	N
WEDNESDAY	City by David Macauly	Pages Read	1- 58
		Minutes Read	40
		Conf. Y/N	N
THURSDAY	City by David Macauly	Pages Read	58 - 112
		Minutes Read	40
		Conf. Y/N	N
FRIDAY	Inkspell by Cornelia Funke	Pages Read	1-15
		Minutes Read	20
		Conf. Y/N	Y

This week's writing prompt:

If you could change the behavior of any character, which one would you change? Why?

Reflection Section

At first when I started writing this, I thought that I would say that Jack in Surviving the Applewhites was the character whose behavior I would change. Now, however, I think that his behavior was tied to the plot too much. After all, if he had never been as naughty as he was, like lighting the fires and skipping school and stuff, then no one would have tried to help him.

Instead, I wish that the father would have paid more attention to Jake because it really seemed like he needed a dad during lots of this story. He is the character that I would change to make him pay more attention to Jake. I think that if the author had done this, Jake would have had a better attidude for more of the story.

Conference Information

Date:	Book: *Surviving the Applewhites*	
	Did the student read aloud? (Y)/ N	Is this book a good match (Y)/ N
	Conference Focus: *Plot & character development*	Focus for Next Time: *Using inferences to describe aspects of the book*
Length: 6 min.	Notes: *Alex will use post-it notes to mark parts of the book where he has questions about the plot.*	

Dates: _____ through _____

Book Title			
MONDAY		Pages Read	
		Minutes Read	
		Conf. Y/N	
TUESDAY		Pages Read	
		Minutes Read	
		Conf. Y/N	
WEDNESD		Pages Read	
		Minutes Read	
		Conf. Y/N	
THURSDAY		Pages Read	
		Minutes Read	
		Conf. Y/N	
FRIDAY		Pages Read	
		Minutes Read	
		Conf. Y/N	

This week's writing prompt: